CLIO'S BASTARDS

or,

*the wrecking of history
and the perversion of our
historical consciousness*

CURTIS R. MCMANUS

 FriesenPress

Suite 300 - 990 Fort St
Victoria, BC, V8V 3K2
Canada

www.friesenpress.com

Copyright © 2016 by Curtis R. McManus
First Edition — 2016

ISBN
978-1-4602-8866-5 (Hardcover)
978-1-4602-8867-2 (Paperback)
978-1-4602-8868-9 (eBook)

1. HISTORY

Distributed to the trade by The Ingram Book Company

TABLE OF CONTENTS

The Preface
xi

The Introduction
1

Chapter One
The Wars
27

Chapter Two
The Sophists
63

Chapter Three
The Cynics
89

Chapter Four
The Hippies
111

Chapter Five
The SocProgs
133

Chapter Six
The Traditionalists
171

The Conclusion
215

Bibliography
233

p.s.
242

For Clio
(...and Urania, too)

THE NOTE ON SOURCES, AND OTHER MATTERS PEDESTRIAN AND PHILOSOPHICAL[1]

The historical sociologists and sociological progressivists whose scholarship is examined in this work were not so examined out of any malice or animus on my part. I do not know them nor do they know me. The selection of their scholarship was entirely arbitrary and in some cases totally accidental. There was no methodology applied because, as American historian John Lukacs once coltishly observed, "history has no methodology." While it did require a heroic "act of self-compulsion" to wade through the odorous and fetid mind of sociology—I did it so you didn't have to—in the end and in every meaningful way, this book is concerned with only one thing: thought. Nothing more. If my handling of sociological historians seems rough or mean spirited I assure you, that was never my intention. The sight of untruths being brought to ground and set to run is rarely if ever a pretty one.

Whilst most of the sociological scholarship cited in this book is of recent vintage, there are numerous and abundant references throughout *Clio's Bastards* to works that are considered ancient, long out of date and, it would seem, *therefore* irrelevant. Indeed, one early reviewer of this manuscript sputtered in disbelief that much of my source material "predates the industrial revolution!" I would like to add to his perplexity. Some of the sources cited herein are from the 1950s. And they are cited without irony. And that, of course, is precisely my point. Wisdom is not a commodity exclusive to the "modern" age, something that appeared of a sudden after the cultural and social revolutions of the 1960s. Wisdom is ancient, sublime, and transcendent; it is not periodic, political, or ideological. And we can press that point further yet: Wisdom does not even wish to be in the same room as Politics and Ideology. Politics and Ideology create conflict, wars, and confusion. Wisdom does not do this. And in this ideological and hyper-political age of ours, then, it is correspondingly difficult to find true wisdom.

Look around today. Where are its works?[2]

All dictionary definitions quoted in the text are derived from my *Funk and Wagnall's New Practical Standard Dictionary*. The 1952 edition. This work was not chosen for any particular reason. Even my acquisition of it was accidental. It happened to be the only dictionary that lay immediately to hand as this book was in progress. That it predates the moral, spiritual, and intellectual confusion of the 1960s was merely serendipity. My mind has come to depend on this dictionary. It is a weighty two-volume door-stopper, muscular in appearance, virile in content, and thus offers a measure of precision, clarity, and focus in an age that lacks same. In the course of preparing this book, the realization slowly developed that the men and women who write dictionary entries are in fact philosophers of a sort, extracting the true meaning and essence of words and to whom, now, I offer my deepest thanks. Dictionaries are, it is plainly clear, works of philosophy as well as art.

On matters of error or omission I am happy to admit to and accept responsibility for either, for I am neither a professional historian nor a professional philosopher. I was trained, educated, and disciplined in history and philosophy; I taught them for years and have come to be a lover of them. But I profess no expert status.

I was once admonished by one of my old university professors to never use the pronoun "we" in academic writing unless I chanced to have a frog in one of my pockets at the time. Fair point. I have consistently adhered to this admonition throughout the years. Even as a teacher I resolutely refused, *in toto*, to even countenance the use of "I" in any writing of any kind.[3] The students had been pestering me to allow it because apparently, they had been encouraged to do so in their carefree and unruly high schools. It was strange. They seemed to have been possessed of an implacable desire to give me their "opinions" on history which of course necessitated the use of "I." I told them, "I do not want your opinions. I want your thought." Too, I am given to understand that the use of "I" is actually quite common in the academy these days.

But I beg for a concession in this instance.

I use the pronoun "we" and its cousin "us" (though still not "I" at least not in the text proper) throughout the book. And that may seem strange upon the first but there is a reason for it and poetic structure can help elevate that reason:

I use "we,"
because you, like me,
are a human being.

And that is what this book is about: an examination of our long, tortured, and still incomplete search for a greater knowledge, appreciation, and understanding of that condition, of being human.

Endnotes

[1] The phrasing there comes from English writer George Trevelyan's 1913 essay. *Clio a muse, and other essays literary and pedestrian* (London: Longman's, Green, and Co., 1913). Also, I must thank Canadian philosopher John Ralston Saul, whose book *Voltaire's Bastards* provided the inspiration for the title of this book.

[2] The question there is borrowed from the impossibly talented English writer Martin Amis (before whom I stand in awe and admiration; I won't even begin to get into how I feel about Plato). Amis asked that question about extremism and fanaticism in the preface to his book, *The Second Plane: September 11, Terror and Boredom* (New York: Alfred Knopf, 2008), p. x. Extremism and fanaticism are manifestations of Ideology not Wisdom. Wisdom would be ashamed to express itself in such ways. Too, I am made faintly sad here because the question I ask there was a question asked first 2,500 years ago by Diogenes the Cynic. The reasons for my sadness will become apparent in Chapter Three.

[3] The phrase *in toto* derives from the Latin and means "completely, without exception; altogether." See: *The Oxford Dictionary of Foreign Words and Phrases*, edited by Jennifer Speake (New York: Oxford University Press, 1997). I thank my old Asian history professor Man Kam Leung for this book, one of about two dozen I received as payment for helping him box up several *thousands* of the books he had acquired throughout his academic career. How bad was it? There were trails.

THE PREFACE

In 1965, Mr. John Hallowell, an American philosopher and professor at North Carolina's Duke University, wrote the following:

"We seem to be divided today between those who believe that there is a reality or measure transcending society to which ultimately all of us must conform, and those who believe that reality is something we can 'make' to conform to our desires. The older view of life called for the cultivation of character, the acquisition through habit and education of virtues conducive to a truly human existence. The newer view calls for the acquisition of technical skills, the possession of which, in time presumably, will dispense with the need for character. But when that day comes, when social conditioning in the form of Skinner's Utopia takes the place of education, when the moral problem has been translated into a problem of social engineering, man himself is likely to have disappeared."[1]

There is much going on here in this brief passage. First, Mr. Hallowell identifies not by name but by suggestion the two principal poles of perception in modern Western thought: desirable philosophy and ruinous sociology. Second, he wrote this in 1965 when philosophy was still in fighting trim but just before sociology convulsed the Western world in a cultural and social revolution whose lingering effects worsen with each passing year, further wrecking and perverting our understanding of what it means to be a human being. Third, those intellectual divisions of which he spoke, they are worse now. The philosophical way is in full retreat having been bested and displaced by reductive, mechanistic sociology.[2] And fourth, the entire passage can be read as a warning from history, a warning that *Clio's Bastards* does not ignore.

Endnotes

[1] John Hallowell, "Plato and His Critics," *The Journal of Politics*, vol. 27, no. 2, May 1965, p. 289.

[2] During a recent summer vacation in 2015, I had some free time so I sat in on a philosophy class at the University of Saskatchewan. The professor made an offhand comment during the course of the lecture suggesting that philosophy as a discipline was not in very good shape. Curious, I raised my hand and asked: "Is it really that bad?" With a grim and painful smile, E. DeLathouwer replied with words whose substance ran something like this: "your grandkids probably won't have any philosophy to study."

THE INTRODUCTION

"Rage—Goddess, sing the rage..."
Homer's opening invocation to the muse in The Iliad, p. 77.

"For the tiresome thing about ignorance is precisely this...no one who does not
believe that he lacks a thing desires what he does not believe that he lacks."
Plato, The Symposium, p. 83.

"I see world history as a picture of endless formations and transformations, of the marvel-
lous waxing and waning of organic forms. The professional historian, on the contrary,
sees it as a sort of tapeworm industriously adding on to itself one epoch after another."
Oswald Spengler, Decline of the West, pp. 21-22.

"I do not envisage that this blast of my trumpet will bring down the walls of pseudo-
science which are manned by too many stout defenders. Nevertheless, there are still some
people about who like to use their brains...and it is for them that this book is intended."
Stanislav Andreski, Social Science as Sorcery, pp. 16-17.

For the past thirty years, historians across the Western world have been on
the front lines of a much larger and, today, increasingly desperate struggle
whose precise nature and purpose remain gravely misunderstood. These struggles are variously called the "culture wars" or the "history wars," and the pro-
tracted, seemingly ceaseless nature of the conflict suggests an inability to reckon
rightly with the vital core of the issues and ideas at stake. Even the terms of
reference and frames of debate are wholly inadequate. We daily hear mention,
still, of those fossilized paradigms of "right versus left" or "conservative versus
liberal," but those increasingly empty characterizations miss the essential point
entirely thus abetting our intellectual confusion.

The struggle with which the West is contending today is not political: it is philosophical. And the content of the debate is not of recent vintage; it is ancient and stretches back to the origins of Western civilization itself.[1] It is a contest between two broad and competing visions of the world and what it means to be human being in it. On the one side, there is a body of corrosive and toxic ideas whose most articulate proponent, Karl Marx, openly advocated for the wrecking, confusing, and undermining of Western civilization. And on the other side there are a set of ideals, first formalized in the writings of the Athenian philosopher Plato, which seek after truth and are animated by the search for understanding and wisdom. In simple terms, then, the history and culture wars are a struggle between sociological theorizing and the philosophical way, and the discipline of history is merely one of the many and sundry battlegrounds upon which this much larger war is being fought.

The History Wars

History wars erupted right across the Western world in the 1990s and 2000s although to call it a "war" in Canada would be to grossly overstate the case. The only thing that raged here was not war but silence. Only two historians fought in the history wars in any meaningful public way; and Canada's philosophers seemed to have been, impossibly, even more silent than our historians, for we in Canada do not like dissent.[2] The very first English-speaking settlements in this country were comprised largely of Loyalists. They were called "Loyalists" because they were loyal to King George, and after the American Revolution against the king broke out in 1776 tens of thousands of them came to Canada, for they did not like dissent. And so it has gone ever since. The wars in the 1990s though, struck with great ferocity throughout the West—including a reluctant Canada—and were fought between what we will call, loosely, the Traditionalists and the Sociological Progressivists or SocProgs (pronounced: *sock*-prawgs), a designation that the thoughtful reader will relish for its unexpected but pleasing Bolshevik-Orwellian tint.[3]

The history wars were wide-ranging and struck at the very core of the discipline itself. The content of history was upended, its goals were altered, and the very way in which the discipline is practiced was fundamentally reordered and turned upside down. Traditional modes of inquiry were hastily and unthinkingly rejected and, just as unthinkingly, replaced with radical new sociological approaches to the study of the past. These changes, greeted with glee by most and with something approaching very real and genuine horror by the rest, mutilated and disfigured one of the oldest and proudest disciplines in the academy.[4] And this deformation occurred right across the West, in the United States, Britain, Australia, Canada and elsewhere. Depressingly, the dynamics of the history wars in each country, the issues and ideas at play, and indeed often times the very language used were in almost all instances precisely the same mostly because in all instances the cause of the war was the same. To put it simply but not to oversimplify: the sociologists came. And war followed with them.

In the broadest sense, the SocProgs went to war with the Traditionalists over who and what ought to be the subject of historical inquiry. Down to the 1960s, Traditionalists in most Western nations tended to focus on politics, war, diplomacy, and the nation. Historians charted the growth, maturation, and development of their countries and these histories were often written in celebratory, providential, almost teleological terms. That approach to history was shattered in the sixties and that shattering later morphed into the history wars of the nineties. In both ages, the SocProgs cancelled and then exiled this type of top-down approach to the past and instead placed at the centre of their history the marginalized, the disinherited, the voiceless, and the powerless.

The SocProg goal in doing so was twofold: to give a "voice" to those whom the Traditionalists had ignored or "excluded" and to "expose" the "systemic" attitudes and beliefs of "society" that had caused, enabled, and perpetuated the oppression in the first place. Thus historians were no longer exploring the past with the aim of explaining the nation to its citizens: they were writing history on behalf of Justice itself.

This political project of the SocProgs, their program of Justice, can be traced back to a couple of sources the first of which revolves around their cancellation of Truth. As the hoary cliché has it, the first victim in war is often the truth; the same holds true for the early days of the history wars. One of the first things the SocProg set did when they arrived in the late sixties—they were called the New Left back then—was to cancel the truth or at least refuse its existence. Happily, this cancellation was not a terribly difficult enterprise to effect, for the SocProg's inspirational political guru Karl Marx had already paved the way some one hundred years earlier. One is faintly surprised to learn here that all one need do to cancel the truth is to just say so, which is what Marx did in a fit of over-confidence in *The Communist Manifesto*: "Communism abolishes eternal truths!"[5] He then went on to "abolish" religion and morality in the same sentence. Human nature itself then followed.[6]

In abolishing eternal truth, religion, morality, and human nature, Marx was essentially binning the Western world's Greco-Christian inheritance and, with it, the accumulated wisdom of something like 2,400 years. A not insubstantial portion of that wisdom is embodied in the Seven Virtues (faith, hope, charity, wisdom, moderation, courage, and justice) and the Seven Sins (greed, lust, pride, gluttony, anger, sloth, and envy[7]) which are essentially broad statements of vision that address the realities of being human; they recognize and validate human nature and its twin capacities for transcendence and its many opposites. But since Marx abolished human nature—and since sociology still operates under that very toxic untruth ("we aren't born with instincts"[8])—then neither sin nor virtue, neither religion nor morality matter; they do not reflect anything real or timeless, anything eternal. And it was thus that the foundation was laid for Marx's larger mission to "act in contradiction to all past historical experience!"[9]

Now of course one cannot simply "abolish" truth without having at least some justification for it or at the very least a replacement. Truth is sensitive on that point. She insists on being given reasons for her dismissal; at the very least, she desires to view her replacement. And here we ascend to the dizzying philosophical heights of the 1960s. One of the principal substitutions for truth was something called "deconstruction," a philosophy developed in the sixties by Marxian acolyte Jacques Derrida. English scholar Christopher Butler explains that this "philosophy" posits the rather strange proposition that "we are caught within a linguistic system that does not relate to an external reality" and thus neither our words nor our ideas can capture anything real or anything true.[10] The word philosophy there is nestled in quotation marks because it is a philosophy that apparently cannot be defined. Butler: "To attempt to define deconstruction is to defy another of its main principles, which is to deny that final or true definitions are possible."[11] And so we see here—whilst Truth smiles at us, gently though and with patience for she is a forgiving mistress—the kind of trouble we get into when we "abolish" truth.[12] We end up with a philosophy whose central thesis prevents it from managing the modest task of even defining itself. We end up with destabilizing, self-cannibalizing thought. We end up with the sixties. But at least it was clothing of a sort and it hid the nakedness of Marx's position.[13]

Truth, then, was annulled in the sixties, though perhaps "annul" is the wrong word. Truth was repudiated. Repudiate: "*To refuse to acknowledge; to refuse to have dealings with; cast off; reject.*" And the Western soul today shivers confusedly in the shadow of that repudiation, for these ideas have become firmly lodged and deeply entrenched in us. We daily hear people solemnly declare—but quite without thinking the matter through—that there are no truths, truths are relative, whose truth, what truth, there is not one truth but many truths, and the always sturdy and reliable "well, that's just your opinion." In reflection, though, we clearly see here something to which we shall have occasion to return frequently throughout this book: it is not the presence of an idea but rather an absence, a nullity or a non-existence, a negation merely that forms one of the essential pillars of the SocProg world view.

Canadian historian and sometime-SocProg Christopher Dummit suggests that it is precisely this nullity, this negation that formed the seedbed out of which their political project grew. After the SocProgs cancelled the truth, they were left with the unappetizing prospect of nothing. There was no longer any goal. After all, if historians are not seeking the truth then what is it, exactly, that they are seeking? The answer to that question became Justice and a desire which sometimes resembled a crusade to avenge the victims of history by excoriating the fetid and corrupt bourgeois societies responsible for perpetuating that injustice and oppression. In so many words, the cancellation of truth resulted in the discipline of history becoming a tool to serve the ends of political ideologies and identity politics.[14]

The home of identity politics and all of those "race-class-gender-power-authority" theories that underpin virtually all SocProg scholarship—and the second source of their project of justice—is sociology. The sociological world-view is concerned with ripping away all of the "decent drapery of life," as Burke would have it, and exposing the corruption and criminality that apparently lay at the heart of "society." Sociologists seek out attitudes and beliefs that foster and perpetuate injustice, discrimination, and inequality; and they are actively on the hunt, today still, for hypocrisy and inconsistency.

A commonly used introductory sociology textbook explains its incoherent mission this way.[15] Sociologists turn their steely gaze toward "groups and organizations." They poke around there "behind the scenes" in order to see "what is really going on." They grab hold of those "pet images" and that "sugar-coated imagery" that the person, group, or institution who was unfortunate enough to have attracted the gaze of a sociologist in the first place "presents to the public." And then they dramatically expose it as a lie and show the world that it was "evil in disguise."[16] Now of course this project in which sociologists run amok, harassing and interfering in the lives of people, groups, and institutions does, as you may imagine, provoke hostility. Even they admit that their project "brings sociologists into conflict with people" who apparently "feel threatened" by what sociology threatens to expose to the world and who would prefer, quite reasonably, to just simply avoid engaging with sociologists at all. One sympathizes. But, Valiant Sociology persists. Such danger is all in a day's work; it's "all part of the adventure—and risk—of being a sociologist."

Sociologists engage in this project of "unmasking" because they are fervently committed to the idea of remaking the world according to their own vision of it. Our textbook modestly proclaims that sociology's overall goal is nothing less than this: "to alleviate human suffering and make society a better place to live."[17] This goal, the authors assure us, is "the majority position" amongst sociologists.[18] But we need to hold up here for just a second. Any academic discipline that adopts the goal of remaking of society ought to be treated with nothing less than the highest degree of suspicion.[19] At the very least, that. For one, the very project itself presupposes that sociology has discovered all of the answers that are needed to make society better. And so two, the sociological project forecloses on and excludes visions of the world other than its own. And furthermore three, any halfway decent historian knows that there have been many other people throughout history who also believed that they too had found a way to "make society a better place to live" (Robespierre's bloody and murderous "republic of virtue" springs to mind here as the first modern example) and these projects usually end poorly. Historians know this, which is why there has never been a history textbook yet written that claimed that its aim was to make "society" a better place because to do that one must, of necessity and by definition, make *the people* of which society consists better. And historians know that this has always been a sticky proposition. But since sociology is animated by the ideas of a man who openly proclaimed to be acting in contradiction to all past historical experience, then history has nothing to say here. And the loop stays closed.

Remaking the world so that it accords more closely with sociology's desires, though, is hardwired directly into the subject itself. The two principal founders of this subject, August Comte and Karl Marx, both explicitly favoured activism toward that end. Marx once famously claimed that "the point of philosophy is to change the world [it wasn't; nor is it]" and that was an idea that grew out of his credulous and strikingly naive understanding of history itself as a "process moving toward a final world revolution and world renovation [again, it wasn't; nor is it]."[20] Let's never mind for right now, though, how monstrously wrong he was; let's instead marvel at and be awed by his audacity. Audacious: "*Impudence, boldness; daring.*" But also: "*presumptuous; shameless; insolent.*"

For his part, Comte, the man who gave sociology its name, conceived of it as "a doctrine of progress" that was inextricably wedded to social reform.[21] Comte, who eventually died a "pathetic" lunatic, apparently took to calling himself in his later years a "High Priest of Humanity."[22] Surely it must be distressing—it *must* be—that the sociological project develops out of, and today still bears the marks of, Comte's lunatic conceits and Marx's fevered and delusional visions of final goals and endpoints, of destinations and "renovations." But it is, apparently, not. And so the SocProg project remains: they will reshape the world on behalf of humanity to make it resemble what they think it should be.

The elevated moral purpose of the SocProgs, their righteousness, their excellence, and their project of Justice simply cannot be challenged or questioned. After all, who in their right mind is going to argue against Justice or Equality or Liberty? The answer is, of course, no one. And this reluctance to challenge the SocProg vision because of the mistaken idea that it is impossible to do so is precisely how and why their ideals have become the new orthodoxy not just in history departments and universities but also in our collective cultural consciousness as well. This latter point must again be emphasized: the problems afflicting history departments are not confined to history departments—they are afflicting Western culture as a whole. In fact, it will be argued here that pervasive and ubiquitous sociological theorizing has quietly co-opted and *replaced* traditional liberalism and has become the dominant way of seeing, explaining, and understanding the world in the twenty-first century. It is likely not even appropriate anymore to refer to something called "liberalism." We might do better to start calling it SocProgism.

The Battle

Whilst the SocProgs broke truth and deformed the discipline of history, the Traditionalists, meanwhile, were busy fumbling with their ideas, totally unable to develop a sensible response to this assault. We look back on the history wars in Canada and see that the Traditionalists published precisely this: a single 186 page polemic and a single twelve-page journal article. When thoughtfully considered as a unity (198 eight pages) we realize with a dulling sense of ennui that Canadian historians could not even manage to muster a full 200 pages of text to save their discipline.[23] Most Nancy Drew mysteries exceed 200 pages. So, yes, the Traditionalists fought but they fought feebly. They were always on the ropes and that occurred, in part, because the SocProgs maintained the offensive so well. That is still the case today. The SocProgs are so difficult to corner, so terribly hard to challenge, so *slippery* precisely because they write history on behalf of Justice. No Traditionalist made similar claims and so, unable to match the high moral purpose of the SocProgs, the best that the Traditionalists could come up with was to grump and pooh-pooh. But there needed to be more than grumping and pooh-poohing.

The ancient Chinese strategist and general Sun Tzu observed, 2,500 years ago, that there are two key elements vital to victory in battle. "If you know the enemy and know yourself," he wrote, "you need not fear the result of a hundred battles." But he cautioned: "If you know neither the enemy nor yourself, you will succumb in every battle."[24] And this is the principal reason why the Traditionalists lost the history wars. They did not understand the essential nature of the enemy they were fighting and, even stranger, they did not understand themselves very well, either. The proof of this latter point is easy to find because had they understood who and what they were and what they represented they would have been easily able to write more than 198 pages of grumping and pooh-poohing.

The Traditionalists first needed to understand and then explain just who these SocProgs were and where they came from. Then they needed to carefully and actively examine SocProg scholarship for intellectual flaws rather than merely carp about it. Then they needed to develop, articulate, and explain the virtues of traditional modes of historical inquiry and defend them. Then they needed to draw clear and distinct lines between history and sociology emphasizing that one is a generalizing "science" and that makes it fundamentally and essentially different from the other, a particularizing humanistic discipline. But most of all they needed to articulate a broader vision of history. If the SocProgs write for Justice then for heaven's sake the Traditionalists should have been able to figure out why they write history—something more than just politics and the nation—and then explain that. But they never did any of these things. And that is confusing and sad and terrible all at the same time.

The Capitulation

The history wars, though, are over now. No one is arguing against the SocProgs these days. Literally no one.[25] At least not in Canada at any rate. SocProg scorn and public shaming turned out to be highly effective. That the Americans are still churning out books on their history wars suggests that debate and dissent still matter, but Canadian historians evidently think there has been enough of that even though there was virtually none in the first place. When well-known and respected Canadian labour historian Bryan D. Palmer got a hold of American historian Ernest Breisach's 2004 book *On the Future of History*, he unfortunately *opens* his review with this churlish bit of business: "Yet another book on the challenge of post-modernism to the writing of history!"[26] That is not the best way to respond to an invitation to debate, especially when we are fully aware and fully mindful that on this particular topic, Canadian historians have published almost nothing at all (or at least the next best thing to nothing). And if it's not nothing it'll do until nothing gets here.[27]

In his review, though, Palmer revealed more than he likely intended when he implied that debate and dissent in history departments across Canada have been virtually eliminated. He writes: "If debates do not exactly rage in the profession now, differences of quite pronounced importance erupt routinely and, more significant, can be read between the lines of texts that, if engaged critically, would reveal numerous contentions." Welcome to Canada, then—a country where "numerous contentions" of "quite pronounced importance" "erupt routinely," but only "between the lines of texts." Palmer did not come right out and say it but Christopher Dummit did: debate over history in Canada is very nearly dead. He observes that history departments have become hostile to "conservatives," and that this has resulted in a culture in which the absence of debate is "increasingly striking."[28] Dummit there uses the word "increasingly" which suggests that the problem is not getting better. It's getting worse.

The Traditionalists have ceded the field to the SocProgs and today their goals, purposes, methods, and attitudes are now so deeply embedded in our history departments and collective cultural consciousness that we have ceased to question their legitimacy. We accept them as normal. Ideas that caused a revolution in the late 1960s and early 1970s—Marxian sociological ideas about race, class, gender, sexuality, power, authority, truth etc—are now taken for granted as true, accepted as right, and we in the West have surrendered and submitted to them. But surrender and submission do not always betoken acceptance and embrace. In a war there is always resistance, even if the actual fighting is over. When they weren't busy helping the Germans gas Jews, for example, even the French managed to maintain a resistance.

Happily, this notion of "resistance" figures large in SocProg history. The SocProgs frequently, lovingly, write about men and women who "resist" authority, who "resist" compulsion, who "resist" intemperate government agents and "the elites." The very concept of Authority in the SocProg universe is, by definition, Bad and thus acts against it are, by definition, Good. SocProg historians valorize the rebel, the resistance fighter, the man who challenges the powerful, the oppressors, and "the elites." It naturally follows, then, that SocProgs should appreciate this book (it is likely that they won't but one can always hope). *Clio's Bastards* is an offering that challenges the authority and intellectual orthodoxies of the SocProgs. Orthodoxy: "*Belief in established doctrine.*" The word comes to us from the Greek *orthos* meaning "right," and *dokeo* which means "think." Put together, and with yet another unexpected nod to Orwell, those words mean RightThink. *Clio's Bastards* rejects RightThink.

The Resistance

The biggest part of this resistance and the larger overarching concern of this book deals with something that was totally ignored in the history wars and to which no historian in Canada has given any thought since (or before, for that matter): namely, the cultivation and development of a good and proper historical consciousness. History—or, stated more broadly, looking at, understanding, thinking about, and explaining our world—is definitely not a passive activity, not by any decent measure. There are certain skills and tools that are absolutely necessary in any interaction with the past, in writing it, reading it, thinking about it, approaching it, talking about it. And if we are to catch up with the SocProgs, developing this consciousness, this power of perception, must be our goal.

In order to achieve these needful aims we will begin with some background and context. Chapter One examines the initial shattering of the discipline of history in the 1960s and the sour ideological and sociological ideas which underwrote same. The sixties bounced back in the 1990s and 2000s, creating still more confusion in what we today call history and culture wars. The flaccid response of Canadian historians to this onslaught is considered before an examination of the depths and degrees to which the historical profession itself submitted to the new thought. This chapter clearly shows how the SocProg march through our institutions was never even up for debate amongst Canadian historians, not really. As we will see, debate was neither sought, desired, nor even encouraged. Indeed certain presidents of the Canadian Historical Association seemed to have used the annual meetings to annually heap scorn and contumely on Traditionalists. At times, we get the very real and distressing sense that the only things missing from these re-education sessions were Red Guards and dunce caps and so one of the crucial and necessary aims of this book is to deflate SocProg pride and self-wonderment.

SocProgs are actually relics from the past (so, too, are Traditionalists, but everyone just usually assumes that to be the case anyway). The SocProg project is almost entirely rooted in the worldview of sociology and sociology itself is the principal tool and manifestation of the ideology of Karl Marx. The Marxian-SocProg project is constructed around a set of core ideas and beliefs— it's more an attitude really—that are essentially destructive and which involve to greater or lesser degrees but always more or less consistently, the rejection of: truth, reality, objectivity, standards, morality, conventions, traditions, customs, and timeless universals. It's all right there in Marx's *Manifesto*. Even sociology's fetish-pet "social construction" makes an appearance.[29] Marx's words and ideas echo across time, and when they arrive here in the twenty-first century, they have been pacified, stripped of their bombast, and enter into our introductory sociology textbook and from thence into the minds of young undergraduates and then out into the world. To restate the pressing nature of the problem: this has been going on now for more than forty years.

Marx: "But don't wrangle with us so long as you apply, to our intended abolition of bourgeois property, the standards of your bourgeois notions of freedom, culture, [and] law! Your very ideas are but the outgrowth of the conditions of your bourgeois production!"[30] One hundred fifty years later, sociology explains to us that schools are not good and essential but rather hot-house dens in which students are inculcated in "bourgeois notions of culture."[31] We can clearly detect the faint but still pulsing echo of Marx's disdain as it dribbles pathetically out onto the page of our sociology textbook: "Consider the values and work habits that are taught at school: obedience to the teacher, punctuality, and turning in neat work on time. These traits are highly desired by employers who want dependable, docile, subordinate workers."[32] The toxic hostility in those words is slight but it is plainly there and it colours everything that sociology touches. Respect, obedience, punctuality, quality; none of these things are good in and of themselves. They are "social constructs," tools of an oppressive social order. But none of what is going on here is new—in its essential properties, that is, not its accidental properties—and in order to demonstrate this idea, Chapters Two and Three will escort the reader back to ancient Greece.

Ancient Greece is the intellectual and spiritual home of Western civilization. And it was at Athens in the fifth and fourth centuries BC where SocProg beliefs and attitudes were first made manifest in the philosophies of the Sophists and the Cynics. The Sophists were a group of wandering, not to say homeless, thinkers who were the first to engage in "sociological theorizing." They identified and explored the tensions between what they termed Nature and Convention—or, that which is natural for people and that which is considered an arbitrary and restrictive "social construct." This exploration of theirs then led on to a social project which consisted of "unmasking" and "debunking" just about every traditional Athenian custom, value, and belief they could get their hands on, all with the aim of emancipating the individual from the restrictions that impeded greater personal freedom. And this is precisely what the SocProgs do; it is an indispensable tool in their intellectual kit. The radical relativizing of all things with the consequence that there are no truths, standards, beliefs, values, customs, or traditions that can be held up as universal and timeless first poisoned Athens over two millennia ago. In sum here, and essentially, the Sophists arrived and proceeded to "talk all traditional values out of existence."[33]

The Cynics in chapter three provide us with still more evidence that SocProg sophistication is nothing new. The Cynics openly attacked Athenian culture and society. They rejected Athenian morality, disregarded custom, and spat on tradition as a meaningless triviality. The chief Cynic of that time, Diogenes, was famous for rejecting all social and cultural norms saying that his principal aim in life was the essentially negative and destructive task of seeing through the sham of things in pursuit of a more perfect freedom, a freedom that philosophers have come to call "negative liberty." Negative liberty is a liberty in which the individual seeks freedom from a thing (a custom, a convention, a tradition, a moral, a religion or, more commonly these days, a gender), a liberty that seeks the removal of all restrictions that limit or inhibit the person. The Cynic Antisthenes was the first philosopher to imagine a world in which there was no government, no wealth, no private property, and no religion. And of course the reader will recognize this world of pure negative liberty as the utopia that Marx would promise 2,400 years after the Cynics. Negative liberty was the principle upon which Marxism as an idea was built; the whole thing was predicated on it. And that ideal of negative liberty wholly saturates the sociological consciousness.

The experience of the Athenians clearly show us that the SocProgs are not "new," "advanced," or "progressive" as they suggest in their many and varied self-definitions, and that of course begs the question. The deeply gifted philosopher-historian Oswald Spengler reminded us one hundred years ago of something we have apparently forgotten: "it is, and has always been, a matter of knowledge that the *expression-forms* of world history are limited in number and that eras, epochs, situations, and persons are ever repeating themselves true to type."[34] He is offering us here the unexceptional idea that, since we as humans are finite rather than infinite beings, limited not unlimited, the number of *expression-possibilities*, say, is correspondingly limited. And so those limited and finite *expression-forms* of which he spoke will manifest themselves at irregular intervals and when certain conditions prevail.

The conditions for the appearance of Sophistry and Cynicism seem to be this: there must be a comfortable, fattened, and settled society to wreck; there must be a society that is suitably confused, amused, and apathetic enough to stand by and smile at the wrecking; and of course the society must be one in which the citizens are entirely free, by law, to wreck it. And there is no social or political order more amenable or more suitable—there is no soil more *fertile*—for the development of Sophistry and Cynicism than democracy. Democracy practically invites it.

Our first destructive bout with Sophistry and Cynicism occurred when the principles of Justice, Equality, and Liberty—but especially Liberty—had reached their summit and fullest expression in ancient Athens, the world's first democracy. But after the collapse of antiquity and the end of that first experiment in democracy, those principles would not reach those same heights again until "modern" times, until the 1960s.[35] And it was during that age when the West experienced the re-appearance of the SocProg "*expression-form*" whose principal philosopher and archetype, Karl Marx, was at his very core and being both a Sophist and a Cynic. Indeed, he cribbed, borrowed, or otherwise plundered from antiquity some of his most foundational ideas including the very idea of negative liberty pioneered by the Cynics. Far from being new, advanced, or progressive, SocProgs are revelatory of the cyclical nature of Western history itself and they are characteristic features associated with democracies entering their final decadent phase.[36] (We do know that our "modern" democracies are not permanently healthy, stable, and unchanging entities, right?)

To reinforce the point: American philosopher John Hallowell suggested that the Sophistry that we are confronting in this "modern" world is "not essentially different" from the Sophistry against which Plato fought in the ancient world.[37] And there is much there in that simple observation that has a direct bearing and meaningful impact on Western history itself, as an idea. Sophistry appeared in and then saturated the moral, intellectual, and spiritual life of ancient Athens, the birthplace of the Western soul; Sophistry then disappeared for a very long time; Sophistry has now re-appeared, albeit in different clothing, and has once again saturated the spiritual and intellectual life of the

Western soul. And again, this begs the question, a question whose answer may be unappealing. Hallowell reminds us—or perhaps it may be better read as a warning—that Plato was writing at a time when Greek civilization was "in its death throes."[38] There really are lessons to be learned from history. But as Hegel famously lamented, the only thing we learn from history is that we learn nothing from history.

Speaking of which, former Hippies wallow in a wanton and unseemly glory, taking unwarranted pride in how creative and original they were.[39] Chapter Four, however, is more concerned with how *un*original and *anti*-creative they were. The decade that has been ceaselessly and wrongly valorized and mythologized as a time in which "youth" threw off oppressive custom and traditional values and beliefs and thence charted a brave new course to a better world in which the tyranny of society was completely overthrown thus freeing the individual to return to nature has all been thought, said, or done before. Sorry.

Too, the 1960s were not a spontaneous eruption of cosmic brotherly love and affection that had been suppressed by rigid 1950s morality as the caricature has it. The anarchy of that decade was simply a physical manifestation of the negative liberty that sociology was counselling in Western universities at that time. Some of the more sensible sociologists later offered oblique apologies for the chaos of that decade.

The sixties matter only for this reason: the Sophistry and Cynicism of that age have, today, become entrenched right across the Western world and struck themselves deeply into the Western soul. Now, before you dismiss that idea as mere "right wing" posturing, Peter Berger, the man who formed and shaped modern sociology—and who would renounce it at the end of his career as "a bankrupt enterprise"—made that very observation in 1992. Right around the time that sociology's demented and unruly problem child "political correctness" was muscling up for its delirious rage against thought, Berger wrote: "the late sixties have not disappeared; they have become institutionalized, both culturally and politically."[40] That remains the case today, only more so. And it was precisely this institutionalization of the Marxian philosophies of the sixties that created the conditions out of which the history and culture wars would develop in the nineties and which we are still fighting today (everywhere but Canada that is).

We, today, exist in the wake of the sixties, still. We breathe its stale air, its sour politics, and its Sophistry and Cynicism which are complemented this time around by chimeric dreams of "progress." The idea of progress, of history itself *aiming* at something, did not exist in antiquity. Neither the Greeks nor the Romans ever saw history as something that was "going" somewhere. That idea is a comparatively recent addition to Western thought. Progress actually began its life in the fifth century as a Christian concept which Marx later appropriated in the nineteenth century. Modern Sophistry and Cynicism are different from their Athenian counterparts only in that there is a goal this time, a purpose: "to make the world a better place to live."[41]

The SocProg vision of progress and their ideas for making our world better can be found in their scholarship which is where *Clio's Bastards* moves next in Chapter Five. The SocProgs undertake their project on behalf of Justice, Liberty, and Equality, and so a thorough, extensive, and detailed examination of the products of their minds is necessary. We will actively and with enthusiasm examine SocProg wares and see how their ideas hold up under scrutiny. The SocProgs, for example, claim to be acting on behalf of Justice. They seek what they call "social justice" and modestly call themselves "social justice warriors." But we must consider their vision of Justice for the Justice of a radical political ideology is not the same as the Justice of the Virtues. And that is especially true if the ideology in question originates out of a philosophy that rejects, refuses, and denies not only morality and religion but also human nature itself. Out of such a swamp we get a perversion of Justice. We get *negative* Justice. We get everything but Justice.

We will explore SocProg scholarship for other equally substantial reasons as well. Few scholars have seriously engaged, critiqued, and wrestled with SocProg scholarship which is odd because everybody knows it's bad if we define bad as uninteresting, unoriginal, unreadable, and unsatisfying. Only nobody is saying anything. This is still a war, and as Sun Tzu reminds us, "the way [in war] is to avoid what is strong and to strike at what is weak."[42] The weakest rampart in the SocProg fortress is their scholarship. Writing is thought expressed. If the writing is bad, then it necessarily follows that the thinking is bad. SocProg thinking and writing are bad because they derive almost entirely from sociological theories and Marxian ideologies and this necessarily means that their consciousness, their *thought*, is mechanized. And mechanized thought does not conduce to quality. The really disturbing implication here is that SocProgs do not think, not as such. They believe, they have conviction, they have solid political grounding and a firm ideological education, but none of this is the same as active and rigorous philosophic thought.

And, yes, before you ask, their scholarship has a fragile and confused *anti*-relationship with beauty, humour, and creativity.

And, too, the work of one SocProg in one country is virtually indistinguishable from the work of another SocProg in another country.

On another continent, even.

So then, what is to be done?[43] After unmasking the unmaskers and after seeing through the sham of the shammers (Sham: *"to delude with pretences;"* Shammer: *"one who shams"*), what then are we left with? Once we jettison the SocProg way with its visions of goals and end points achieved through destruction and negation, what possibilities open up to us? If we do not want ideology or sociology or Sophistry or Cynicism as a substitute for thought, what then remains? The answers to these questions lie, not surprisingly (indeed *revealingly*) in ancient Greece.

The Greeks were the first to develop the fundamentals of genuine, active thought and philosophic inquiry.[44] The intellectual tools they used then still form the foundation for thought and inquiry today. They are simple tools revolving as they do around quite simple and basic concepts: seeing, perceiving, knowing, and understanding. But all of those words have deep-shooting philosophic roots. Greek thought, unlike SocProg thought, is neither self-conscious nor is it pretentiously sophisticated. Greek thought is simple at the same time as it is infinitely difficult. In addition, we find something in Greek philosophy that is totally lacking in SocProg scholarship: purity. And so, if we seek to develop a grounded and humanistic historical consciousness rather than its infinitely less satisfying mechanical-theoretical counterpart, we must expend most of our energies toward developing the virtues of fidelity, understanding, and honesty.[45] Above all else and above all things, honesty matters in reading, writing, and working with history, or even in just simply trying to understand our world today. And honesty means so very much more than just not telling lies; honesty reaches out after understanding and wisdom itself.

But because developing these virtues is the work of a lifetime rather than the work of a three-month seminar course—*Honesty 101* say—perhaps it is no wonder that the SocProgs embrace theory. It is simply easier there in the catatonic SocProg mind (Catatonic: "*an immobile or unresponsive stupor*") because their theories think for them; their ideologies provide automatic answers, and their political convictions rid them of the necessity of cultivating those intellectual and spiritual virtues that are in fact necessary when working with history, when we make attempts at coming to terms with this world, when we face it down and try to understand it, when we try to discover who we are and why we do what we do as all the great historians and philosophers of the past have done.

"On to Victory!"

This book, then, is a work of both history and historiographical criticism. It is historical in that it seeks to tweak super-abundant SocProg pride by demonstrating that they are merely the most recent incarnation of a spirit and attitude that has existed for as long as the Western tradition. SocProgs are a type. They are not evolutionary, despite what they say. They do not represent the next step in mankind's moral, ethical, and intellectual development, a pervasive conceit that seems to afflict most "progressives."[46] By the way, the Greeks had a variant of the word "pride." It was hubris. Hubris means "excessive pride towards or defiance of the Gods, *leading to nemesis.*" In its turn, nemesis means "The *inescapable* agent of one's downfall."[47] In other words, the very moment when Hubris makes itself manifest Nemesis begins seeking it out.[48] And Nemesis will always find Hubris. That is a natural law of our moral world. That is a principle by which it functions. Now, this universal and timeless principle was one of those "eternal truths" which Marx claimed to have "abolished." But if she hasn't already Nemesis will quite soon locate Mister Marx, somewhere in the deep of the heavens, maybe in the firmament Plato's Forms and there, at that moment, deal him his reckoning.

This essay is also historiographical in that it examines and critiques the many and several fundamental flaws in SocProg scholarship. And unlike many SocProgs who are content with destruction and negation merely, the final chapter of this work will elaborate on a positive and constructive alternative way of seeing, an idea for a philosophic, reflective, organic historical consciousness that is not bound by theories or shabby ideologies or sham politics and which is also shorn of any and all notions of trying to "make the world a better place to live." It is a consciousness rooted in being human and that seeks understanding and wisdom of that condition. After all, shouldn't one first understand what it means to be a human being before going about trying to change the world?

The thoughtful reader need not be alarmed or made uncomfortable at the prospect of returning to ancient Greece to satisfy the larger aims of this book. Once we begin our excursions there you will be quite comfortable with it so don't worry. You will clearly and with very little trouble recognize yourself. There is a reason why Jacob Burckhardt, the great nineteenth century historian, once remarked of the Greeks that "their soul has passed over into us." There are, too, other more general but still very important reasons for revisiting the Greeks. Their experience is so vital and essential to our world that without an understanding of the Greeks there can be almost no understanding of just about everything else that came after them. And this lack of knowledge is a *huge* blind spot for the SocProgs.

The venerable sociologist Peter Berger once remarked (and it remains true today—truer, in fact, in this age of hyper-specialization) that sociologists betray what he called an almost "barbaric" lack of knowledge and understanding about the past.[49] Specifically, he was referring to the sociological penchant for studying society without any knowledge of the oldest of the disciplines in the Western world: history and philosophy. The result of this ignorance, Berger feared, would be the development of a "narrow expertise without wider horizons" complemented by "a total insensitivity to the uses of language."[50] And on that score, he was exactly right. But again—and this borders very close on being intellectually criminal—if the SocProgs do not even have a basic understanding of history and philosophy, if they do not even have a basic *knowledge* of the ancients, by what right then do they seek to "make the world a better place to live"?

We may with disturbing profit take this idea still further. It is not just the SocProgs who eschew philosophy and history, but the wider culture as well. It is sadly the case today that philosophy and history are frequently snickered at, seen as antiquated disciplines with no real practical value, no real-world use.[51] That is simply not the case, but we accept it as so. And in the place of philosophy and history, our culture now fetishizes science and skill (what the Greeks called *techne*), and this has resulted in what American philosopher Robert

Cushman called the "disastrous subordination" of wisdom to science.[52] The full implications of this development—its effects on our civilization, on *us*—are yet poorly understood and only dimly apprehended. But there will be a cost and future historians will be able to clearly see the amount we had to pay for the remaindering of those disciplines, the only two disciplines that habituate people to active philosophic thought. Marxian junk sciences like sociology do not ask us to think. Sociology, like Marx himself, desires only our submission.

The Athenian philosopher Plato remarked 2,500 years ago that "the beginning is like a God which, as long as it dwells amongst men, saves all things."[53] The discipline of history in the West does in fact need saving and people do in fact need an alternative way of seeing, understanding, and explaining the world separate and apart from ruinous and destructive sociology. The SocProg way has become so culturally dominant today that it is hard to conceive of its enormity. Our universities, our media, our schools, our institutions, our *souls* have been saturated in those SocProg ideas concerning race, gender, power, sexuality, authority, etc. We are like the character of Winston in George Orwell's *1984* trapped in the world of Big Brother's RightThink. Winston is vaguely aware throughout the novel that there was a time when life was better, richer, and fuller; a time when life was not governed by RightThink. It is likely that the majority of students and citizens in the West are not even aware that there is in fact an alternative to the SocProg worldview but there is, and we find it back at the beginning, in philosophy. Without philosophy we can get nowhere.[54]

Going back to the beginning allows us to reorient ourselves, to remove ourselves from the sticky conceits and the increasingly destructive messiness of the SocProg project to gain a purer, clearer understanding of our world. In Canada, there has never been a counter-vision offered, a clear explanation of who these SocProgs are, where they come from, the nature of their scholarship, and precisely why their ideas are so badly, deeply, *irredeemably* flawed. Likewise, very few historians have ever codified or explained what it is, exactly, that Traditionalists do and how they see and understand the idea of history. And so *Clio's Bastards* is an offering, animated by a spiritual duty to the sanctity of the discipline—nay, to thought itself—to "puncture the smelly orthodoxies now contending for our souls."[55]

Endnotes

[1] Writing of the culture wars in the United States, the wise and perceptive American jurist Robert Bork observed that "these developments have been coming for a long time and *may be inherent in western civilization.*" Italics added. He is, of course, correct, and *Clio's Bastards* is essentially a book-length validation of that single but very perceptive observation. See his *Slouching towards Gomorrah: modern liberalism and American decline* (New York: Regan Books, 1996), p. xiii.

[2] Dissent from prevailing orthodoxies in Canada is, as a general rule, frowned upon. One wag wrote after leaving the country that he had been a failure as a Canadian because "the patience, the mildness, the taste for conformity that seemed prerequisites for a tolerable life were beyond me." The writer in question was Bruce McCall. The quote can be found in Robert Bothwell's *The Penguin History of Canada* (Toronto: Penguin, 2006), p. 405. Idle question: Where *are* Canada's philosophers anyway—in the public realm I mean?

[3] From Orwell, we have the delectable "Ingsoc" as well as MiniPax, prolefeed, RecDep, TeleDep *and* FicDep. From the Bolsheviks we have Gulag, ComIntern, Zek, and my personal favorite Cheka, a shortened version of what in English is called the "All-Russian Extraordinary Commission for Combating Counter Revolution and Sabotage," which was founded by Felix Dzerzhinsky, or "FeDzer." Too, I associate progressives and sociology together for the simple reason that they, progressives, draw their nourishment and sustenance from the buffet of sociology, a buffet which is the intellectual, moral, and spiritual equivalent of a Denny's.

[4] The discipline of history is one of the few academic disciplines to have its own muse: Clio a daughter of Memory. The muse of philosophy is Urania. Sociology doesn't have a muse. It has Karl Marx.

[5] Karl Marx and Friedrich Engels, *The Communist Manifesto* (New York: Washington Square Press, 1964), p. 92. Exclamation points added for flavour, for humour, for conveying a deeper appreciation of the profoundly disordered state of his mind. In fact, most subsequent quotations of Marx will have the exclamation point added, for it is only fair: *The Communist Manifesto* is itself an exclamation point.

[6] Marx, *Manifesto*, p. 92

[7] Hard as I may try, I can *never* list all of the Sins without difficulty. I can rattle off the Virtues in seconds, but I always have to grope blindly for that sixth or seventh Sin. In the end, I usually have to ask somebody. Here, in this instance, it took about six or seven hours for my mind to finally cough up the Sin in question (gluttony).

[8] James Henslin et al, *Sociology: a down to earth approach* (Toronto: Pearson, 2010), p. xvii

[9] Marx, *Manifesto*, p. 92.

[10] Christopher Butler, *Postmodernism: a very short introduction* (London: Oxford University Press, 2002), p. 19.

[11] Butler, *Postmodernism*, p. 19.

[12] Mistress: "*a woman in authority or control, or to whom service is rendered.*"

[13] Interestingly, Derrida's philosophy was a part of that wider school of French thought which included the nihilism of Jean-Paul Sartre. Sartre developed ideas that move against truth, in part, because he and others were embarrassed and humiliated by their inaction and passive collaboration during the Nazi occupation. As Australian essayist and critic Clive James put it: "The bad conscience was so bad that it would have rather undone its own culture than face itself." In other words, in order to avoid reckoning

with the guilt and shame that came with collaboration, Paris—as evidenced by the philosophies of Sartre and Derrida—"became the world's production center for new ways of proving that the critical intelligence can operate with no fixed connection to reality." See Clive James, *Cultural Amnesia: notes in the margin of my time* (London: Picador, 2007), p. 59.

[14] Christopher Dummit, "After Inclusiveness," contained in *Contesting Clio's Craft: new directions and debates in Canadian history* Christopher Dummit and Michael Dawson eds. (London: Institute for the Study of the Americas, 2009), p. 113.

[15] All quotes here taken from Henslin, *Sociology: a down to earth approach*, p. 7.

[16] Peter Baehr, "The Undoing of Humanism: Peter L. Berger's sociology of unmasking," *Soc*, 2013, vol. 50, p. 387.

[17] Henslin, *Sociology*, p. 11.

[18] Henslin, *Sociology*, p. 12.

[19] See Paul Johnson, *Intellectuals* (New York: Perennial, 1988), for a thorough explanation as to why "intellectuals" should not be trusted to govern, lead, or shape public policy. The chapter on Marx is withering, sobering, and in the end, just plain sad.

[20] Karl Lowith, *Meaning in History* (Chicago: University of Chicago Press, 1949), p. 33. By the way, Marx's philosophy has been referred to as "philosophical incendiarism," and thus is not really philosophy at all because philosophy, by definition, rejects "incendiarism." See Arthur Koestler, *Darkness at Noon* (New York: Scribner, 1968), p. 180.

[21] Peter Berger, *Invitation to Sociology: a humanistic perspective* (Woodstock NY: The Overlook Press, 1973), p. 6.

[22] Jonathan Turner, Leonard Beeghley, Charles Powers, *The Emergence of Sociological Theory* (Belmont CA: Wadsworth, 1989), p. 37. The full idea from Turner: "It is perhaps embarrassing to sociology that its founder was, by the end of his life, a rather pathetic man calling himself the High Priest of Humanity." Historians do not call themselves High Priests of Humanity. I did, however, study under some Marxists who certainly believed that of themselves.

[23] Jack Granatstein's *Who Killed Canadian History* and Michael Bliss's "Privatizing the Mind: the sundering of Canadian history," in the *Journal for Canadian Studies* vol. 26, no. 4, 1991-1992, pp. 5-17. Christopher Dummit and Michael Dawson made an attempt in 2009 to reignite the debate with a collection of essays contained in *Contesting Clio's Craft: new directions and debates in Canadian history*. But only one essay, Dummit's, dealt squarely and directly with the wreckage of the history wars, and how this disorderly mess might be made whole once again. In effect, he is seeking a synthesis of the two sides but, by and large, does not question too loudly the value of SocProg scholarship. An additional side note here: in his 2010 review of *Contesting Clio's Craft*, UWO historian Jeffrey Vacante outlined a history of the history wars and mentioned the two works by Bliss and Granatstein as the *only* academic response to the SocProg assault. See Jeffery Vacante, review of Dummit, Chris; Dawson, Michael eds *Contesting Clio's Craft: new directions and debates in Canadian history*, H-Canada, H-Net Reviews, September 2010. And of course, nothing has been published since.

[24] Sun Tzu, *On the Art of War* translated by Lionel Giles (London: Department of Oriental Books and MSS, British Museum, no date), p. 25.

[25] Ezra Levant and his valiant little band of resistance fighters at *The Rebel.Media* are the only dissenting voices in the public domain here in Canada. Like him or hate him, Ezra and his crew deserve gratitude

from *all* Canadians for keeping alive in this country the spark of free speech and, above all, dissent. Without Ezra, there simply wouldn't be any dissent in Canada—there would only be RightThink.

[26] See Palmer's review of Breisach's book in the *Journal of American History* December 2004, pp. 1112-1113. The exclamation point is, sadly, contained in the original.

[27] The line is from the film *No Country for Old Men*, slightly modified. By the way, when Granatstein and Bliss published their single book and single article the historical establishment fell on them like a ton of bricks (or perhaps the better image is a pack of angry dogs). There were responses, mostly to Granatstein, from Greg Kealey, Linda Kealey, Joan Sangster, Ruth Pierson, Veronica Strong-Boag, Steven Maynard, Brian McKillop, Timothy Stanley and others. Please see the list contained in David Churchill's "Draft Resisters, Left Nationalism, and the Politics of anti-Imperialism," in *Canadian Historical Review*, vol. 93, no. 2, June 2012, p. 230, footnote 4. Churchill and many other Canadian historians insist on denigrating Bliss and Granatstein's contributions by dismissing them as "polemics," a patronizing designation that *may* hold in the case of Granatstein, but certainly not in the case of Michael Bliss.

[28] Christopher Dummit and Michael Dawson, "Introduction: Debating the Future of Canadian History: preliminary answers to uncommon questions," in *Contesting Clio's Craft: new directions and debates in Canadian history* (London: Institute for the Study of the America's, 2009), p. xiv. See also, Terry Glavin's brief interview with Christopher Dummit in "Harper Tories don't trust Historians- for good reason," *The Vancouver Province*, blogs.theprovince.com/2013/02/14

[29] Marx, *Manifesto*, p. 91. The phrase-cliché "pet fetish" has gentle colours suggesting, as it does, merely a really favorite thing. "Fetish-pet," though, takes on grotesqueries suggestive of that sexual freak from the cellar scene in Quentin Tarantino's *Pulp Fiction* and so "fetish-pet" here works better than "pet-fetish."

[30] Marx, *Manifesto*, p. 87.

[31] This is what sociology dementedly calls "the hidden curriculum."

[32] Henslin, *Sociology*, p. 318. To continue with the lunacy: "Or just consider the emphasis on 'proper' English. Members of the elite need people to run their business empires and they are more comfortable if their managers possess the 'refined' language and manners that they themselves are used to." There is just so much wrong here that I simply don't know where to start. There is no *thought* here. By the way, most sociology textbooks are written at something like a middle-school level of complexity. The texts are simple and easy to read, and usually come with lots of graphs and glossy photos; lots of charts and "dialogue boxes" and such.

[33] Werner Jaeger, *Paideia: the ideals of Greek culture* vol. 2 translated by Gilbert Highet (New York: Oxford, 1945), p. 28

[34] Oswald Spengler, *The Decline of the West* translated by Charles Francis Atkinson (New York: Vintage, 1962), p. 4. Italics in original. Spengler occupies a curious place in the academy. No one really teaches him much anymore but his thought is always there, looming. I actually think he frightens some people. Too, Spengler there might have been giving early voice to what we call "chaos theory" or the idea that there are regularities and patterns within complex systems (including human systems). For a simple but very clear explanation, pluck Michael Crichton's *Jurassic Park* (New York: Ballantine, 1990) off your bookshelf and on pp. 79-83 you'll see he actually does a pretty good job of explaining it in simple terms.

[35] We will cover this ground later in the book, but is helpful here to remember what English philosopher Roger Scruton once observed—that democracy in Western history is not the rule, it is the exception. Our first bout with democracy only lasted a few hundred years. Our second experience with democracy has lasted now for about 240 years.

[36] Just as America was about to begin its experiment in democratic principles and ideals that inaugurated the modern democratic age, statesman John Adams wrote the following to a friend: "Democracy never lasts long. It soon wastes, exhausts, and murders itself. There never was a democracy yet that did not commit suicide." See Richard Hofstadter, *The American Political Tradition* (New York: Vintage, 1948), p. 13.

[37] John Hallowell, "Plato and His Critics," *Journal of Politics*, vol. 27, no. 2, May 1965, p. 289.

[38] Hallowell, "Plato and His Critics," p. 274.

[39] I studied under some of these types at university and it was always an interesting experience. They would hearken back to the sixties or even the seventies (!?) and dreamily reflect on how they "de-centred power," "challenged" authority, and "attacked" our culture's literary and historical canon.

[40] Peter Berger, "Sociology: a disinvitation?" *Society* Nov/Dec 1992, p. 13.

[41] While we're here the basic idea can be sketched out: the Greek idea of history was one in which there was not a trajectory to history but rather a "cycle of history." That changed with the Christians who "broke down the foundation on which Greek philosophy and science had been built" and then turned the idea of history into "the coordinated movement of mankind toward an ultimate goal." Marx in the nineteenth century kept the idea of "progress" but of course he "abolished" the religious elements in his pursuit of that "final revolution" that he was always on about and which would lead *his* Believers to *his* Promised Land. See Hajo Holborn, "Greek and Modern Concepts of History," *Journal of the History of Ideas* vol. 10, no. 1, January 1949, pp. 6-7. You may also want to check out Koestler's *Darkness at Noon*, p. 170. The main character, Rubashov, muses about a "swing" to history: "We seem to be faced with a pendulum movement in history, swinging from absolutism to democracy, from democracy back to absolute dictatorship." Koestler was himself a Bolshevik before he gave it up later in life. Many Bolsheviks and Marxists seemed to have done that. Martin Amis's father Kingsley—he of *Lucky Jim* fame—did that.

[42] Sun Tzu, *Art of War*, p. 53.

[43] The stirring, dramatic-cum-prophetic revolutionary question "What is to be done?" was the title of one of Vladimir Lenin's pamphlets. But the Russian writer Vladimir Nabokov, loathing the Bolsheviks and their revolutionary cause, lampooned the title when he sketched a buffoonish revolutionary character who titled his pamphlet with the much more mundane and moronic question "What to do?" See Martin Amis, *Koba the Dread: laughter and the twenty million* (Toronto: Vintage, 2003), p. 37.

[44] I pointedly use the phrase "active thought" because I have, over time, become disgusted with the phrase "critical thought." It has become a cheap and promiscuous phrase mostly because sociologists use it to describe what they claim they are encouraging students to do when they look at their society. But there is simply no "critical thought" involved when one comes to a question whose answer is already provided. The sociologists might want to start saying that they foster "cynical thought" rather than "critical thought," and so because of this cheapening of the phrase, its *devaluation*, I now use phrases like "active thought" or "philosophic thought."

[45] During six years in the academy as an undergraduate and a graduate student, I honestly do not recall ever once hearing any of these words spoken.

[46] Not surprisingly, this book was rejected by the University of Toronto Press. But in his very gracious and encouraging—and oddly lengthy—rejection letter, kindly editor Mr. M. Harrison quite unconsciously acted as the conduit for precisely this progressive conceit when he wrote: "For quite a long time I shared a conservative ideal until I started to think that, *historically speaking, it was no longer a viable position.*" Personal Email to the Author 3/3/2014, 11:31 a.m. It is "no longer viable" because *entrenched* in the progressive mind is the Marxian idea that history has a goal, a destination, and desirable final end point; and that they, the progressives, represent the next step in that evolution of humanity on the march

toward that final goal. Ultimately, the progressive mindset reveals little more than a shabby understanding of history and what it means to be a human being, and in this they are merely taking their cue from Marx who suffered from a similar ignorance.

[47] These two definitions derive from the online Oxford English Dictionary.

[48] And of course this Greek concept entered into Christian thought as "Pride goeth before a fall," which is just one example of the rich intermingling of Greek and Christian thought. St. Augustine and St. Thomas Aquinas represent that intermingling in its completeness. Greco-Christian thought is a mighty river that flows 'neath our feet. Sociology is an irritating puddle.

[49] Peter Berger, *Invitation to Sociology: a humanistic perspective* (Woodstock NY: Overlook Press, 1973), p. 12. The full idea reads: "We shall readily admit that there is much that passes today under the heading of sociology that is justly called barbarian." And, prefiguring his renunciation of 1992, Berger wrote in 1963 that "the foolishness of some sociological work could be easily avoided by a measure of literacy in these two areas." See *Invitation*, p. 168.

[50] Berger, *Invitation*, p. 12. The philosophizing psychiatrist Viktor Frankl also recognized the problem of this "narrow expertise without wider horizons." Frankl writes: "What is dangerous is the attempt of a man who is an expert in, say, biology to understand and explain human beings exclusively in terms of biology. The same is true...for sociology as well. At the moment at which totality is claimed, biology becomes biologism...and sociology becomes sociologism. In other words, at that moment, science is turned into an ideology." He goes to write that today, "Reductionism has become the mask of nihilism." A chill should run up your spine if you think too long on that last sentence there. See Frankl's *The Will to Meaning* (New York: Plume, 2014), p. 8.

[51] A former student, M. Pennington, remarked to me one day after class that he had initially arrived at college thinking about majoring in sociology "because it sounded bankable." At the time we were speaking, he was contemplating a move toward history and philosophy and it is a move which I pray he undertook.

[52] Robert E. Cushman, *Therapeia, Plato's Conception of Philosophy* (Chapel Hill NC: University of North Carolina Press, 1958), p. xvi. Students are migrating by the thousands to sociology or psychology or "business." How did "business" end up at Universities?

[53] Hannah Arendt, "Tradition and the Modern Age," in *Between Past and Present: eight exercises in political thought* (London: Penguin, 1977), p. 18.

[54] The German philosopher-historian Oswald Spengler once observed that "all genuine historical work is philosophy, unless it is mere ant-industry." See *The Decline*, p. 41. Spengler is usually seen as a brooding and dour German meta-physicist—and the photographs we see of him do nothing to dispel this notion—but his work actually contains a good deal of rich, coltish humour.

[55] Found in Theodore Dalrymple's *Life at the Bottom* (New York: Ivan R. Dee, 2003), p. 244.

CHAPTER ONE

THE WARS

"When the nation's history is poorly taught in schools, ignored by the young, and proudly rejected by qualified elders, awareness of tradition consists only in wanting to destroy it.
Jacques Barzun, From Dawn to Decadence, p. 775.

"We often find those who have achieved a critical attitude to the traditional have also adopted a largely, or wholly, uncritical attitude to the untried, or even failed alternatives whose attraction is verbal rather than real."
Robert Conquest, Dragons of Expectation, pp. 6-7

"What concerns us is not what the historical facts which appear at this or that time are, per se, but what they signify, what they point to, by appearing."
Oswald Spengler, Decline of the West, p. 6.

"To see one's own time or even one's own life as history is a doubtful privilege."
Werner Jaeger, Paideia, vol. 2, p. 74.

The history wars in Canada are over. You may be excused for not knowing that the war has come to an end. You may also be excused for not knowing that there was a war going on because the various and sundry combats of the history wars were fought over the soul of *Canadian* history, a subject which, when it is not spending its abundant free time in obscurity, regrettably passes away its days in oblivion.[1] Unpromisingly, the word "dull" appears in the very first sentence of Arthur Lower's classic and well-known history of Canada.[2] But a war there was and the Sociological-Progressivists vanquished the detested old guard, the Traditionalists.

The SocProg Triumph

According to Canadian historian Christopher Dummit, the war was won by self-styled progressive historians who practice something they like to call "history from below" and whose morally excellent purpose is to "open up the historical project to those traditionally excluded." [3] Dummit observes that, with a few "grumpy exceptions," history departments in universities across Canada have finally and at long last been "won over to a more inclusive history." [4] Give or take a year or two, the war lasted about four decades. It started in the late 1960s and ended, well, no one is really sure when it ended exactly. [5] We can only tell it is over because of the ghastly silence that now prevails, a silence where there should be spirited and energetic debate in the public realm. Indeed, one of the curiosities of this book is that, though it be written by a Canadian and though this chapter deals with the history wars in Canada, much of the research cited is American because Canadian historians and philosophers have written virtually nothing about these matters. [6]

Whilst the SocProgs are certainly enchanted by their victory for Liberty, Equality, and Justice, the grouchy and grumpy Traditionalists tend to paint that triumph in rather more sombre and muted tones. Traditionalists are uneasy about framing the end of the wars in terms of simple victory-defeat because that suggests two sides who were equally equipped and equally matched and who fought it out with the issue naturally going to the side that struggled hardest, longest, and fiercest; the side that was most deserving of victory. But that was not the case. Rather, we might enlist the explanation given by American historian Eugene Genovese who characterized the defeat of the Traditionalists in his country as a "general capitulation to destructive political pressures." [7] Thus, the victory that brought an end to the history wars was not at all like the grand and theatrical Battle of Waterloo, say. It was instead more akin to the French Foreign Legion's frantic and desperate last stand at Cameron Mexico in 1863, where a contingent of the Legion fought in a desperate battle almost down to the last man. They did not lose. They were overwhelmed. [8] Overwhelm: "*to crush with sudden or irresistible onset; oppress beyond endurance; overpower, hence to destroy; to roll with engulfing force*." [9] There is an ocean of difference between simply losing and being overwhelmed. Traditionalists in Canada did not lose the history wars. They were rolled with engulfing force.

There were three or four survivors from that last stand at Cameron, and evidently about as many survivors from the Traditionalists in the history wars. So thorough was the rout that, as of this writing, the SocProgs actually have no one left to fight and this has resulted in a turn of events that is almost kind of funny. Dummit observes that many of the SocProg veterans are still going into their classrooms acting as though the war is still on, still fighting against the Traditionalists and the "neo-conservatives," still fighting the battles of the 1990s.[10] And so today, we have the Quixotic spectre of the SocProgs out there on the plain, tilting at windmills, swinging at shadows and imaginary foes, excoriating "heterosexual white male elites," digging up the mangled corpses of old-guard Traditionalists and flaying them publicly before an audience of horrified, wide-eyed undergraduates. We can almost hear the depressing sigh in his voice as Dummit laments "we are still acting as if the old guys are still here."[11] The implication seems to be that those "old guys"—the Traditionalists—are in fact gone.

It's almost funny. But it's not, actually. It's the opposite of funny. SocProg historians in Canada are swinging at shadows and squabbling with and amongst themselves because they no longer face—never did face, actually—an organized opposition. The Traditionalists today are evidently keeping their mouths shut. Not only have they put away their swords, they have put away their pens, too. Or perhaps it is more accurate to say that even now, several years after the wars ended and more than forty years after they began, they still haven't even pulled out their pens.

One wishes that this silence was merely an expression of poisonous and destructive apathy, but it isn't. Mr. Dummit observes that one of the more pernicious results of our history wars was the fundamental transformation of history departments in Canada from disinterested centres of learning and knowledge into "a kind of activist organization [that is] just not friendly to conservatives."[12] This unfriendliness, then, takes the form of exclusion, exclusion results in the absence of debate, and this absence of debate, Dummit notes, is "increasingly striking."[13] The problem Dummit identifies here, however, is actually much larger than he is letting on.

English historian Robert Conquest argued that there is a general tendency today across the broader Western world toward an "increasingly irrational conformism" to SocProg ideals. And he notes that those of the SocProg stripe (anti-Western, anti-capitalist, what he calls "the new antis") are "often no longer open to, or even cognizant of, argument."[14] American philosopher John Hallowell elaborates on that theme. He explains that meaningful discourse is possible "only if the parties to the discourse presuppose the existence of a truth about the matter which may elude them both *but which they both seek*."[15] And since the SocProgs do not seek after anything at all—sociology has already discovered the answers and so the "science is settled" as they say—then what purpose could debate possibly serve? There is no reason for debate if the answers have already been found.[16] But we would do well to remember that dogmatism is not necessarily derivative of the truth but rather it is "an attitude of mind and a posture" which Mr. Hallowell more accurately calls a "personal failing."

It is helpful and clarifying to remember that the distant spiritual and intellectual cousin for many SocProg historians is the revolutionary Bolshevik party.[17] And like their cousins, who seized, shot, imprisoned, or exiled their opponents after their 1917 coup d'état in Russia, the SocProgs have seized control of the means of historical production, its journals and departments, and they have used their Virtue and their Justice to silence their opponents. But at least the Traditionalists are not being shot or imprisoned. Not yet, anyway. The macabre silence that Mr. Dummit and many others clearly discern grows directly out of an academic environment that is "hostile" to Traditionalists and who have, in turn, become, or rather remain, reluctant to raise their hand against the SocProgs. And so, there they stand: "these angry, maudlin, flabby, chinless [traditionalists] with limp moustaches, waving their shrivelled dicks at the cruel sky."[18]

The Wars: their origin, source, and early manifestation

The history and culture wars of the 1990s and 2000s were the culmination of a long and drawn out struggle that has its origins in the anarchy and chaos of the 1960s. That word "culmination" suggests that an end has finally been reached, that the struggles are now over and a consensus has in fact been achieved. Indeed Dummit himself calls it "the new common sense." But it is not consensus. What we appear to have, at least in Canada at any rate, is an imposition not an agreement. Here, our cultural consciousness has been saturated in and irretrievably warped by sociological thought and that to such a degree that there are, today, right and wrong ways to think.[19] And that itself grows directly out of the sociological project of making the world a better place according to their vision of it. Whilst people in the United States still seem to be debating the issue, which is good, here in Canada they are not, which is not good.

Think of the history and culture wars, then, as a delayed explosion, the backwash or by-product of the social and cultural revolutions that convulsed the Western world in the sixties. The issues at stake in each age were a carbon copy of each other mostly because the thing that caused the convulsions—sociology—was exactly the same. During the sixties, Hippies, student activists, and "youth" undertook a social and political project that, to their way of thinking, "exposed" the flaws and crimes of Western civilization. These "activists" directed their hostility at not just "the state" but everything associated with it: hierarchy, authority, and electoral politics.[20] Fresh from their introductory sociology classes, they hurled Marxian accusations that our society was blackened by and shot through with racial injustice, gender inequality, oppressive class divisions, human rights violations, moral and political bankruptcy, cultural vacuity. And what was worse, the activists claimed, was that these problems were "inherent" in Western society.[21] The problems were "systemic" as the sociologists would have it.[22] The West was, in their eyes, not just unjust but "corrupt from top to bottom."[23] A change was needed, a redemption; this world needed to be made better. And so beginning in the late 1960s, it became the self-appointed task of the New Left to make it so.

This broad social, political, and cultural upheaval—a revolution in every sense of the word—had a profound and, it seems, irreversible impact on historical thought itself. The most important of these changes to the discipline of history in most if not all Western countries was the death of the political history of the nation.[24] For much of the twentieth century down to the 1960s, many of the greatest historians in Canada were primarily concerned with the nation. They studied the country's political growth, maturation, and development and, often times, the tone of many of these works was celebratory. The New Left had very little patience for such works because the nation the Traditionalists were busy valorizing was the very same nation that the New Left was trying to renovate and redeem from injustice, tyranny, and oppression.

For those older historians, as caricatured by radicals and activists, the history of Canada was a triumphal march from colony to nation, from dependency through to responsible government and from thence to Confederation and on to the glorious present. This kind of "Whiggish" history revolved around great men, high politics, and the diplomatic arts. But the "youth" were naturally and temperamentally disinclined to practice a history whose basic plotline was: "and with sovereignty, everybody lived happily ever after."[25] It was an approach to the past wildly out of place in the 1960s. Not unlike John Diefenbaker.

The Canadian traditionalist most commonly associated with the Whig approach to history was Arthur Lower.[26] Lower wrote in glowing terms of the "stupendous crusade" by which Canada ascended from dependant colonialism to autonomous nation.[27] Lower took this celebratory approach not because he was intellectually addled and lame-brained as the New Left implied, but because one of his central preoccupations was with Canadian nationalism and his idea that all Canadians must share at least some sense of being connected, of having a shared past, and it was the job of historians to communicate that.[28] Lower wrote that an appreciation of our history and the self-knowledge which that implies was "necessary if [we] are to take [our] rightful place in the world and still more, if we are to be a happy people at peace with [our]selves."[29] It was merely his task (he charmingly wrote of "discharging a duty") to explain the nation to the people and in this way, historians acted as national sages of a sort. That impulse is, at bottom, a noble one for which Mr. Lower need not have been lambasted as he and others were. It has been a very long time since any academic wrote about having a duty to the nation. Too long.

Whiggish history of this type, though, tends toward oversimplification. The English historian Herbert Butterfield explained it this way: "historical personages [are] easily and irresistibly classed into the men who furthered progress and the men who tried to hinder it."[30] And so the execution of Louis Riel, say, was a Good Thing, because he was a hindrance to the development and progress of the nation and, indeed, was blocking the development of civilization itself.[31] As you can see, the Whig approach tends to see history as the unfolding of a plan and Butterfield argued (wrongly in some ways) that historians who embrace it are "riding after a whole flock of misapprehensions."[32] But curiously, after binning Whiggish history and cancelling the nation as a legitimate subject of inquiry, the New Left swiftly retrieved Whiggish history from the dust bin and promptly chased after their *own* flocks of misapprehension.

Having jettisoned Whiggish history in the 1960s, the New Left replaced it with Whiggish history. Only New Left Whiggishness was different from the other, badder kind. Instead of the celebratory tale of national awakening, development and progress, history in the hands of the New Left became the celebratory tale of the "awakening of the dispossessed and disinherited, a mounting struggle against racial, sexual and economic oppression."[33] In other words, they developed a schematic in which "historical personages [were] easily and irresistibly classed into the men who furthered progress and the men who tried to hinder it." Same old wine. Just a different wine skin.

National history, then, was arbitrarily cancelled in the 1960s. It was not because there was anything fundamentally wrong with what the political historians were doing; it was just that their approaches and their subject matter simply did not fit in with the spirit of the age. We have to remember that the sixties were always "less a movement than a mood," and that "mood" made political and national history almost impossible because that approach tended to celebrate and valorize the thing that perpetuated oppression, tyranny, and injustice.[34] Instead of the nation, then, the New Left historians found their new "units of analysis" (in the ghastly phrasing of the sociologists) amongst "the poor, oppressed, exploited and ignored."[35] And there was no shortage of work to be done there. There were, in no particular order, "blacks, Indians, Orientals, women, immigrants, slum dwellers, labour organizers, and political radicals... peasants, labourers, handicraftsmen, strikers, bandits, poachers...chiliasts, enthusiasts, criminals, madmen, slaves, peons, coolies, [and] fellahs."[36] To which we have since added lesbians, homosexuals, and the transgendered. And it is very likely that sociology will soon insist on the addition of "cisgendered" and "transabled."[37]

The Ideological Problem

Now, this turn of events, this emphasis on the people rather than the state, is not a bad thing in and of itself.[38] SocProgs will likely be surprised to learn that the lunatic Scotsman Thomas Carlyle—a lightly demented but beyond brilliant nineteenth century historian/prophet/essayist—not only foresaw but also *approved* of the very developments we are discussing here. He reckoned that the political historian, "once almost the sole cultivator of History," will soon find that his day is at an end.[39] Carlyle had argued that for too long historians have "dwelt with disproportionate fondness in Senate Houses, on battlefields, nay even in King's Antechambers forgetting that life rolled on" amongst the people. And there will come a time, Carlyle wrote, when "much of this has to be amended." [40] So here we are amending things, which is fine. But including the voices of the people in historical works is one thing; using history as an ideological tool to remake the world according to the vision of a strange and peculiar German economist is quite another. If there be a heaven, one thrills to the possibility of a meeting between Marx and Carlyle.[41]

It has always been the case that every solution creates its own unique set of problems.[42] And American historian Theodore Hamerow explains that the foremost and principal problem with this new emphasis on the oppressed and the marginalized in the 1960s was that it came with "unmistakeable" ideological and political baggage to which he should have added sociological baggage for sociology was (is) the principal tool and manifestation of the ideology here in question.[43] And of course the ideology in question derives from Karl Marx.

Obiter Dicta.[44] Ideology is not a good thing. The Truth is a good thing. Ideology is the opposite of that. The proof here is that people are hardwired to seek and desire Truth. That is what philosophy and history are all about. They are disciplines that developed organically and naturally and as a direct consequence of human beings seeking Truth. No one *seeks* Ideology. People adopt Ideology. People do not adopt Truth. And people usually adopt Ideology when they find out that Truth itself is difficult not only to find, but also to face and then to reckon rightly with. Ideology simply removes those difficulties. Ideology: "*The ideas or kind of thinking characteristic of an individual or group.*" The very definition itself has absolutely nothing to do with Truth. And, tellingly, the word "ideology" in the dictionary is only nine words away from idiocy. Idiocy: "*the condition of being an idiot.*"

At any rate, here is the essence of the ideological problem identified by Mr Hamerow. Marx: "Communism abolishes eternal truths; it abolishes all religion and all morality instead of constituting them on a new basis! The Communist revolution is the most radical rupture with traditional property relations! No wonder that its development involves the most radical rupture with traditional ideas!"[45] Clearly, there is a problem here.

Though we will have more to say about Marx in later chapters, it shall suffice here to roughly sketch out his broad vision. Marx had developed a "scientific" theory of history in the nineteenth century. He argued—sloppily as it turned out, for few people can manage the task of reading what he actually wrote—that throughout the broad sweep of Western history, humanity had moved from an apparently desirable "primitive communal" society to one in which "the elites" had monopolized not only political power and influence but they also dominated the realms of culture and religion.[46] And for Marx, these "elites" evidently had one fairly simple goal in mind: "to exploit and dominate the rest of the population."[47] In order to redeem these people from their bondage (a bondage of which, curiously, the people themselves seemed to have been most times unaware), Marx called for revolution, renovation, and redemption; for the wrecking, confusing, and undermining of Western society and its "bourgeois middle class values," values that were merely oppressive instruments and manifestations of an unnatural and perverse social and political order. That was what the sixties were all about, and the historical scholarship of that decade was heavily larded with these ideas.

Neither Marx nor the sociologists are exactly clear on what will replace what they destroy (again, there is that theme of negation, of *anti*-creativity), but still and despite that, the goal of both remains the same in its essentials: they seek "a final consummation of the historical process." And this consummation is to be a world—no, a *realm*—of social and political Equality, Harmony, and Justice.[48] And after we reach this utopia, Marx apparently believed, with astonishing credulity, that history would "come to a full stop."[49] Utopia: "*A visionary, impractical scheme for social improvement; excellent, but existing only in fancy.*" The word comes from the Greek *ou* which means "not" and *topos* which means "place." Thus *notaplace*, say. And Marx then and sociology today remain relentlessly determined to drag all of us to *notaplace* whether we want to go or not, because Marx then and sociology today believe that their beliefs, values, and ideas are representative of the beliefs, values, and ideas of humanity itself.[50] This, then, constitutes the core of the ideological problem.

It is worth pausing briefly here to consider Sigmund Freud's view of people who cannot accept reality as it is. Freud explained that people like Marx (and we might as well throw in the sociologists here, too), are displeased with the present and so engage in projects in which they wreck and negate the world currently on offer and try to build another better one in its place, "one in which the most intolerable features are eliminated and are replaced with others that accord with one's desire."[51] As a rule, Freud suggests that such people will, in the end, "achieve nothing" because they are animated by what he calls a "delusion." But it will take time for this reality to settle in to their minds because "no one who shares a delusion will recognize it as such." So, one expects we are in for a long and increasingly bumpy ride.

The Sociological Problem

In addition to the new history being distorted by ideology, that distortion was magnified still further by the principal tool of that ideology: sociology, which itself suffers from its *own* grievous inconsistencies that distort still further the history that grows out of it. In 1963, Peter Berger released his classic and foundational work, *Invitation to Sociology*, a title with unintentionally ghoulish and perverse qualities but a book that nonetheless profoundly shaped the subject and indeed the decade itself.[52] In that book, Berger explains how the sociological mind operates; he lays out the method by which sociologists go about "exposing" the lies, shams, and hypocrisies that govern our daily lives but which only they can see.

The first step in creating this better world envisioned by sociology is the development of what Berger calls the "sociological consciousness." This "consciousness" is characterized by what Berger over-glorifies as "the art of mistrust." This merely cynical "art" is rooted in the paranoid belief (Freud's "delusion") that there is more going on in society than appears at first glance; a reality more original than reality itself, to paraphrase philosopher Hannah Arendt's stinging little criticism.[53] This sociological consciousness is readily apparent in our introductory sociology textbook which, as we recall from the introduction, states that its central aim is to discover "what is really going on." Indeed, Berger observed: "it can be said that the first wisdom of sociology is this: 'things are not what they seem.'"[54] Well, "things" actually *are* what they seem—and what

Berger describes there as wisdom has nothing at all to do with wisdom—but let's never mind that for right now.

The fundamental problem with "sociological (un?) consciousness" is precisely this: the idea that there is something "more original" than reality itself. In simple terms, what Berger is getting at here is the idea that we are all of us in the West trapped and enmeshed in a reality that is thwarting us in some way. The world according to sociology looks something like this: an overarching system of capitalist oppression whose principal instrument, the bourgeoisie, has malevolently crafted a social, cultural, and political order that serves and satisfies its interests but which deliberately and intentionally thwarts and suppresses the liberty, autonomy, and individuality of the rest of us.[55] And Berger is suggesting that since we are all too stupid to understand this on our own, we therefore need a sociologist to explain to us "what is really going on." Indeed, Berger doubles down on the condescension, calling people in society "puppets on strings" and suggesting that sociology can save us because the study of it gives people the chance to finally see those strings and "in this act lies the first step toward freedom."[56]

But if we dispute this condescending idea—and we do—we inevitably arrive at a proposition which, while infinitely sad, seems to somehow make much more sense.[57] In rejecting the idea that reality is what it actually seems to be, sociology is therefore engaged in a totally *il*logical enterprise of undoing *un*realities. And from this it necessarily follows that a subject that begins in confusion can only sow confusion, which is precisely what modern sociology has done over the past forty years.

Beginning their path of destruction in the late 1960s—a path that would wind through the 1990s and 2000s with increasingly destructive results—sociologists have managed to wreak havoc and confusion on just about all of the traditional ideas, values, and beliefs which Western civilization developed over the course of centuries.[58] Marx would have been very pleased with what his progeny has wrought. These ideas include but are not limited to: our most basic understanding of what it actually means to be a human being, followed by family, marriage, sexuality, gender, power, authority, religion, truth, reality, objectivity, custom, convention, morality, ethics, deportment, behaviour, propriety, the nation, and patriotism. To name but a few.[59] Sociology has wrecked many things in its pursuit of Liberty, and so what sociology provides us is

Liberty through destruction and negation. Sociology gives us *negative* Liberty. But the New Left of the 1960s and the SocProgs today still have that goal in mind, that if we just push hard enough and far enough, if we just unmask and debunk and discard enough of those bourgeois middle-class ideas, those shams and lies and hypocrisies, we will arrive at the end of the historical "process" prophesized by Marx the Redeemer.

Of course, sociologists will likely reject the idea that they believe in any such thing. But we must counter that the whole point and purpose of their project is to "make society a better place to live" and the natural and obvious corollary to this is that at some point the end will be reached because one simply cannot go on and on making something better and better and better *ad infinitum*. That is a logical absurdity. Nor can something be made better to the point where it is the best that it can be and then simply held there at that best point. History does not stop for us like that. Never has, never will. Thus there is a "terminal-point mentality" that guides and directs everything that sociology does and which is built directly into sociological logic and it is a mentality that grows directly out of that Marxian conception of history moving toward a destination. Both the man and the subject share equally in the dangerous delusion that there is a terminal point to history, an end point and a desirable final goal. There isn't. Indeed, let's press the point: it is sociology that has the terminal point, not history.

Modern sociology has been debunking and unmasking now for more than forty years, but there is only a limited number of shams which it can unmask, and only so many hypocrisies that it can debunk. Whilst hypocrisy itself is limitless and knows no bounds (Marx's progeny the Bolsheviks capably demonstrated that), society's hypocrisies are limited. And so what happens, then, at this point, when there is, finally, nothing left to unmask or debunk and nothing left anymore to wreck? Will it be the utopia Marx envisioned or even that more modest "better world" promised by sociology? Or—and the smart money is on this one—will it simply be a general intellectual, spiritual, and moral collapse of Western civilization? Depressingly, so very depressingly, even sociologists are betting on collapse.

When modern sociology was launching its assaults on the Western soul in the late sixties and early seventies, British sociologist Stanislav Andreski made a compelling observation. He wrote that he had "no doubt that if the social sciences fall into total and irremediable decadence, this will be a part of a general collapse of civilization."[60] Twenty years after Andreski wrote that, Berger disowned modern sociology and, in doing so, he validated Andreski's claims of decadence. And so there is a very real caution we should be getting here from the words and actions of Andreski and Berger, a caution we should heed for the problems have grown much worse in the years since. The sociological consciousness, then: it originates in confusion, it sows confusion, and that confusion is animated by a delusion. Delusion: "*a false belief, especially when persistent.*"[61]

Sociology is dangerous but not in a good way and that is precisely because it is animated by a radical political ideology that has very certain and definite aims. The revolution that Marx always sought and desired—the wrecking of bourgeois society—is built directly into the sociological project. The social and cultural revolutions of the 1960s were a direct consequence of sociological theorizing. But sociologists both then and now did not and do not accept any responsibility for the destructive implications of their scholarship. Berger anticipates this very criticism in his book and he rambunctiously counters by arguing that sociology is not revolutionary but is actually "*inimical* to revolution."[62] Already saturated in illogic, Berger here sets sail onto a Pacific Ocean of unreason by arguing that sociology "sees not only through the illusions of the present status quo but also through the illusionary expectations concerning possible futures."[63]

Let's follow Berger's logic for a moment. Sociology exists to see through society's lies, shams, and hypocrisies. These shams are by definition wrong, false, or untrue in some way, and when sociology rids society of a sham it has thus gone some distance toward "making the world a better place." And then sociology congratulates itself. But using Berger's own logic, the destruction of Sham A only means that another sham, Sham B, will take its place. Valiant Sociology has the power to seek out and destroy Sham B, too, but will only then be confronted with still *another* sham, which would be Sham C. Thus does dreary sociology hack and tear away at things. *Ad infinitum.*[64] Quite apart from the pressing question of how these people actually sleep at night—Berger unintentionally ridicules them when he writes that "every sociologist is a potential saboteur or swindler"—what we learn from one of sociology's chief practitioners is this: *everything* is a sham.[65] And this is a problem. Australian writer and essayist Clive James explains: "In philosophy, the infinite regress is a sign that someone has made a mistake in logic. In ordinary life, it is a sign that someone is hiding from reality."[66]

But all of this confusion and disorder is simply the logical end point, the natural and inevitable destination of sociological thought. Marx had "abolished" not just truth, but also religion, morality, and human nature. Sociology has inherited and embraced those dismissals, those absurd cancellations. And when we cancel and displace those fundamentals and replace them with nothing, there is nowhere left to go but here. And here is nihilism. Nihilism: *"The doctrine that nothing exists or can be known...a political doctrine holding that the existing structure of society should be destroyed."* And so we see that the "sociological consciousness" is, like its ideological parent, wholly concerned with destruction, not creation, essentially. It is in every way concerned with negation, merely. And that was what the 1960s were all about: a physical manifestation of the negative liberty that Marx desired, sociology counsels, and the New Left then and the SocProgs today advocate in their scholarship.

Transition

The principal and lasting achievement of the 1960s was not Liberty or Justice or any other such thing. The triumph of that age lay in the cultural and social entrenchment of a worldview whose foundational ideas and philosophies openly and actively seek to wreck, confuse, and undermine traditional or transcendent values, beliefs, and ideas. And that worldview has saturated the moral, political, religious, and intellectual life of Canada and the Western world today. And it was the institutionalization of those corrosive Marxian ideas that created and generated the culture and history wars of the 1990s and 2000s.

But first there was a period of calm.

Things settled down in the seventies and eighties. Wham's gentle and pleasingly innocent *Wake me up before you go-go* provided the soundtrack for the peace which lay once more across our happy land. But the Western soul was not the same inside. It had been irrevocably changed—and that not for the better. We can get a bearing on the depth of those changes by considering the kind of history being produced then in Canadian universities. In 1985,

T.W Acheson, the president of the Canadian Historical Association, used this period of relative peace and calm to take stock as it were of the collective mind of the Canadian historical establishment. He compared the content of doctoral dissertations from history departments at Canadian universities in 1967 with those of 1985.[67] In 1967, right about the time the whole sixties thing happened, there were 236 doctoral dissertations and six out of ten concerned the operation of the state.[68] One is shocked but well pleased to hear that political biography, political processes, and political thought were the "most popular genres." And he observed that a "striking characteristic" of the 1967 studies was the "absence of any significant social history."[69]

But by 1985, the discipline was showing clear evidences of its sociological and ideological perversion. Political biography, long a staple in the writing of Canadian history, had by that time been "virtually eliminated." Of the 294 dissertations written in that year, fewer than half concerned politics and the majority of those were "scattered over a dozen topics."[70] These topics of course included gender history, labour history, medicine, poverty, and ethnicity.

Acheson was not hostile to these developments, not fundamentally. He approaches the issue with a gentlemanly aspect. He is cautious and circumspect even though his publications suggest he belongs, temperamentally at least, to that older generation of "ill-equipped" historians because he wrote virile, muscular, industrial-strength political history with titles like *The National Policy and the Industrialization of the Maritimes, 1880-1910*. Canadian history simply does not get any more Canadian than that.

Acheson admitted that he did have "concerns about the disintegration of the discipline." But he said we will have to live with it. "Like it or not" he said, "we have had our 'reformation' and must now live with the sectarian consequences."[71] That "reformation" and those "sectarian consequences" he mentions there are allusions to Martin Luther's Reformation of 1517, a grand event in human history but one which was followed by something like 150 years of war. And something similar happened after Acheson wrote those words in 1985: war broke out. Culture wars. History wars. "The rioting and riotousness" of the 1960s, as American jurist Robert Bork explains, were not dead.[72] The ideas that animated that decade had only gone into what he called "a fifteen-year remission" returning in the late 1980s "to metastasize more devastatingly throughout our culture than it had in the sixties." It was "more devastating" because this time, the activists, Hippies, and "youth" were not young kids and teenagers having free sex and smoking drugs and dropping out. They were now at the wheel. These people were no longer outside our institutions protesting: they were now inside our institutions, teaching.

The Last Stand or, Cameron Mexico (redux)

The wars of the 1990s—the language, dynamics, and disputes—were essentially no different than what occurred in the 1960s. The issues were again sociological and revolved around that subject's persistent and obsessive preoccupation with gender, race, class, power, and authority, etc. And so one important and fairly fundamental idea should be developing clearly by this point: sociology does not solve problems. Sociology *creates* problems. And that point should not be exceptional because sociology was birthed by a man who desired that very thing.

The resistance mounted against the SocProgs—the Charge of the *Really Light Brigade* if you will—was led by just two men: Messr's Jack Granatstein and Michael Bliss.[73] Mr. Bliss wrote his famous article "Privatizing the Mind" in 1991 and Mr. Granatstein wrote his wonderful little book *Who Killed Canadian History?* in 1998. Nothing had been written on the subject before; and nothing has been written on the subject since. To give you some idea of the "glacial pace" at which changes occur in the Canadian historical firmament, Christopher Dummit, as of 2013, still has the writings of both of these men on his reading list for his class on the writing of Canadian history.[74] Since we in Canada do not like dissent, we must take it where we can find it. As a side note here, we find in these works two of the greatest smack-downs in the history of the writing of history in Canada. Mr. Bliss called SocProg history "jargon-laden, lint-picking irrelevance" whilst Mr. Granatstein, after examining a historian's work on housemaids in nineteenth century Ontario, famously quipped "really, who cares?"

The core and essence of Bliss and Granatstein's attack was that the new historians were ignoring Canada's national past, its political narrative, for the sake of "exposing" the "social injustices" of our country's history. They charged that the SocProgs were relegating the teaching and writing of Canada's national story to the backroom while scholars, as Granatstein put it, chased down criminals from Canada's past and tried them in the court of Clio. "Everyone," he wrote, "is involved in an unthinking conspiracy to eliminate Canada's past."[75] Even the media, Granatstein charged, was only interested in using history not to understand our country but as a tool to "search for villainy" or, if not that, then they "mangle it beyond recognition to prove a contemporary argument."[76]

Michael Bliss shared the concerns of Granatstein. Mr. Bliss also spoke of the "disintegration" of the discipline and the "withering" of the sense of community in Canada.[77] Historians no longer occupied the venerable office of national sages like Arthur Lower, whose duty to an interested public was to explain the growth of our nation, to aid in our "self-understanding."[78] Instead, the Canadian historical establishment veered off into the turgid Marxian swamps of race-class-gender politics and they used history as a vehicle to get there.

The *Canadian Historical Review*, the flagship journal of the historical establishment in Canada, set the tone, publishing hopelessly dreary, obfuscatory sludge, sludge which Bliss correctly observed was "unreadable, and therefore unread by ordinary lovers of history."[79] That is still the case today. Only more so. The *CHR* editorial board explicitly recognized this problem in the 1990s because it seemed that ordinary citizens had stopped reading the journal. One assumes subscription rates plummeted because there were in fact concerns voiced over its "diminishing public stature."[80] The separation between academics and citizens was well in swing in the 1990s. And it has gotten much worse since then.

By and large, Bliss and Granatstein confined their arguments to the framework of "national history versus social history." It appears that the only disagreement registered over the actual intellectual content and substance of SocProg thought itself—and it is only a trace element of disagreement at best—was in an article written by Joy Parr in 1995.[81] Esteemed U of S historian Jim Miller had apparently argued at a historical conference in 1994 that there were many substantial, meaningful, and indeed existential problems represented by the new theories and ideas of the SocProg set. He took issue not with the content of the history that was being produced, but rather the Marxian sociological way of seeing, understanding, and explaining. The SocProg mind works like this: there is no hope of achieving any kind of objective certainty; there is no truth; human nature doesn't exist, but rather we all embody what are called "ideologies" which are, by definition, constructions of society; there are no facts, or rather no fact is independent of the observer which is to say a fact cannot exist outside of a necessarily subjective interpretation of it, etc.[82]

This dreary smorgasbord of intellectual and spiritual confusion naturally befuddled Miller. He observed that if everything is a social construction and a "mirage" then "there is no single truth that can be uncovered...if everything is socially or otherwise humanly constructed, then inquiry can never lead to truth."[83] But the sophisticated Joy Parr writing later in the *Canadian Historical Review*, dismissed Miller's concern as silly naiveté, an example of a historian who, as though it were a bad thing, wants to "cleave close to the roots of history in the humanities" which embraces beliefs in a human condition that are, for her, criminally, "absolute, enduring and universal."[84] They are, actually. Yes, Marx "abolished" them, true, but they're still there. Truth is funny that way. She doesn't go away simply because you want her to. But Parr explains that Miller is wrong in this traditional view of understanding because he is "taking as his guide" the ideas of German historian Leopold von Ranke. But Miller was doing nothing of the sort.

For the uninitiated, Ranke, was a stiff-necked, high-collared Prussian famous for saying (and it's usually the case that the following quote is the *only* thing that the gross majority of historians know about von Ranke) that history should be the recovery of the past "wie es eigentlich gewesen sie" or, in English, "as it actually was." The suggestion in this pithy quote is that there is a knowable past, a truth that can be faithfully articulated by the historian. Miller obviously agrees with that, while Parr does not. But Parr's equation of fact with dreary Prussian rectitude is what, in logic circles, is called a "straw man," for there is far more going on with von Ranke than Parr lets on.

If Parr had persisted past this single quote, she would have found that Ranke's idea about history "as it actually was" is merely the pointy tip of a very large iceberg whose largest portion she did not see. Ranke's ideal of history *beyond* "as it really was" is this: "To look at the world past and present, to absorb it into my being as far as my powers enable me; to draw out and appropriate all that is beautiful and great, to see with unbiased eyes the progress of universal history and in this spirit to produce beautiful and noble works. Imagine what happiness it would be for me if I could realize this ideal, even in a small degree."[85] Remarkable for its purity, dignity, and nobility of purpose, Ranke's ideal also reveals a touching and quaint humility, and these are virtues that, today, almost seem out of place; archaic somehow.

When Miller argued there are discoverable truths and Parr equated that with Prussia she was merely demonstrating her lack of understanding about what Miller had said and what Ranke actually meant. If Miller was channelling Ranke, then Ranke was simply channelling the spirit of the Greeks. The truths of the human experience (truths which sociology is busy denying and "refusing" and which Marx, anyway, had already "abolished") were a discovery or, better stated, a *realization* of the Greeks. The intellectual principle that guided all Greek thought was humanism: the study of humanity, its realities, as it really is.[86] When historians talk about truth, we are sometimes talking of this very thing: the realities of human existence, history as a manifestation of human nature, history as a mirror reflecting not who we *were*, but rather—and this is deeply disturbing and subversive for many SocProgs—who and what we actually *are*.

And anyway, just because the "modern" mind rejects notions of truths does not mean truths do not exist: we just live in an age where it seems silly to say so. It is more likely that it is the age that has the problem, not truth. Truth and her servant Clio will still be there waiting for us when we finally work our way through this moral confusion of ours. They say that each generation, each age, produces its own kind of history. The American writer and historian Brooke Allen wrote somewhere about this "morally confused" age of ours. An age of moral confusion, then, must produce morally confused history. Is it that simple? Carlyle thought so: "Know this also, that out of a world of Unwise nothing but an Unwisdom can be made."[87]

Of Perverts and Quirks

The history wars in Canada, then, were fought decently removed from public view, in classrooms and seminars where undergraduates with a more classical idea of history waged lonely, one-man battles against the anti-intellectual trends intrinsic in theoretical SocProg history.[88] And even though the works of Bliss and Granatstein provided the foundation for years of debate, you will not be surprised to hear that these two intellectual perverts (Pervert: "*an apostate;*

renegade") were labelled heretics and excommunicated by "the new hierarchy." The two men were "isolated" within the academic community and "dismissed as out of step with modern historiographical and political trends."[89] Not proven wrong mind you: just "dismissed" as no longer relevant. Granatstein captured the mood with wonderful Dickensian imagery: "[When the] few surviving political historians raise their head to plead for more...the social historians unite to swat them down."[90] Indeed, Granatstein's charge did in fact turn out to be "a last stand" because shortly thereafter, he retired.[91] Probably a good thing, too, for Western University historian Jeffery Vacante observed in 2010 that political history itself in Canadian universities—and by extension the historians who practiced it—has been more than remaindered; it has been "thoroughly displaced."[92]

Precisely the same attitudes that Bliss and Granatstein confronted here in Canada are manifest across the border in America (and, we can safely say, wherever else sociological thought is the prevailing orthodoxy). Historians Mark Malvasi and Jeffrey Nelson observed that those who go against the grain in their country, those who court "unpopular values," who "criticize approved methods, impugn cherished theories and question authorized conclusions" become "immediately suspect, their work regarded as illegitimate, disreputable, and worst of all, insignificant."[93] That is simply the way that the SocProg set deals with opposition: scorn, disdain, and contempt. Carlyle captures well this curious, incidental quirk so characteristic of Group Think: "It is indeed strange how prepossessions and delusions seize upon whole communities of men; no basis in the notion they have formed, yet everybody adopting it, everybody finding the whole world agree with him in it and accept it as an axiom of Euclid; and...taking all contradiction of it as an insult and a sign of malicious insanity, hardly to be borne with patience."[94] Carlyle marvels at what he calls "human swarms," and is amazed "with what perfection of Unanimity and quasi-religious conviction the stupidest absurdities can be received as articles of faith."[95]

Mao Tse Tung Thought, with Canadian Characteristics

In the absence of any published works, and in order to more fully appreciate the silence that prevailed then and today, we shall with profit here peer behind the curtain of the Canadian historical establishment itself in order to see "what is really going on." The Canadian Historical Association is just what its title suggests: an association that represents the interests of Canada's professional academic historians.[96] There is an annual conference which, most years, features a presidential address on the state of the discipline and the challenges facing Canada's historians. Not once in the twenty-five years between 1990 and 2015 did a president of the CHA ever question, dispute, or otherwise disagree with SocProg scholarship.

Not once.

Now, not all presidential addresses dealt with the issue of SocProg scholarship or even the state of the discipline itself. More recently, Mary Lynn Stewart used her 2011 address to examine the barriers (there were apparently four of them) that female historians had overcome since the 1960s.[97] One of the more recent addresses concerned the history of the RCMP's security service; another, the importance of the contributions Jewish people made to the treatment of minorities in Canada. But when the history wars were touched on, the issue was framed in such a way—not subtle, either; the opposite of subtle—that Traditionalists were made to understand that their way and their day were over and done.

At least one or two jaws would have dropped when CHA president Veronica Strong-Boag gave her address in 1994. She lamented that the profession was dominated by "middle-class heterosexual men" and argued that this state of affairs was intolerable (more poverty-stricken lesbians, then?) because the profession no longer represented the nation.[98] Not only was the "old guard" "white, heterosexual, and male" but, worse, they were mean and nasty too. Strong-Boag argued that the Traditionalists were so embittered by the SocProg advance, so morally soured and spiritually poisoned, that "women and people of colour" in some graduate programs across Canada reported being on the receiving end of "hostility."[99] So, not content with characterizing Traditionalists in Marxian terms as reactionary male, white, middle-class, and heterosexual, Strong-Boag also deployed the spectre of rancid, grumpy old white men running around history departments making women and immigrants cry.

In seeking to account for this "hostility" Strong-Boag explains that Traditionalists "do have a harder time" in this new world. The transition from old to new—this "fall from grace" as she phrased it—created "disenchantment" amongst the old guard.[100] But for her, the biggest problem facing "neo-conservatives" was their singular inability to undertake "self-criticism or even rigorous self-examination." (We will return in a moment to this very interesting but troubling theme of Bolshevist/Maoist self-criticism.)

The brilliant intellectual and cultural historian Jacques Barzun observed a quirk in modern scholars and artists of the SocProg persuasion. For them, he wrote, "whatever is old is obsolete, wrong, dull, or all three."[101] And that is where Strong-Boag goes in a dramatic swoop of SocProg self-regard when she consigns Traditionalism itself to the junk-heap:

> "In point of fact, the old history, like the old politics or the old literary and philosophical canon, with their preoccupation with white male elites and their common failure to interrogate power relations and address the reality of oppression within Canadian society, has rarely been adequately equipped either to characterize the reality of the past or to address the many pressing questions of the day. We do not need more assessments where concentration on a narrow range of political elites...ignores critical questions of oppression and injustice."[102]

And no one said a thing.[103]

Traditionalists said nothing then nor are they saying anything today. Still. Which begs the question. Noted American classicist Alan Bloom observed that the most dangerous tyranny is not the nightmare variety, the visible one with black shirts and horrid, twisted crosses and the "reptilian brain" that persecutes minorities.[104] The most dangerous tyranny, Bloom writes, is the one that "breaks the inner will to resist." Robert Conquest, himself a historian of the radical Bolshevik experiment, agrees with Bloom's assessment there adding that there is a distinct Bolshevikian tendency in SocProg circles "to silence those who disagree with one or another of the accepted beliefs." And so, the Traditionalists remained silent simply because they were "unwilling to face all the fuss and abuse" that would accompany objection.[105] We have repeatedly indicated that SocProgs write on behalf of Justice, which is precisely what makes them such slippery targets, and Bloom confirms this: "it is not so much power that intimidates, but its semblance of justice."[106] And that word "semblance"? "*A mere show without reality; pretense.*"

For Strong-Boag, then, history is wallowing in the filth and vileness of our national story, its abuses, its victims, and its national crimes. That impulse to wallow in criminality is another characteristic feature of SocProg history. They believe—and in many ways it is the whole basis of their conception of history—that the vile, the bloody, the brutal, *the unjust*, is somehow more "real" than, say, a celebratory history of the nation. Celebratory in their mind is somehow coeval with naiveté and general stupidity. Only the unjust is real. At any rate, Strong-Boag concludes that whatever future we have together in this country must begin with the recognition of "the responsibility for what actually happened in the past." For her, this included, but is likely not limited to, "theft of aboriginal land" and not just "the victimization of women," but also "children from all nations."[107]

As she brought her address to a close, Ms. Strong-Boag took the time to publicly engage in a kind of curious, Maoist self-criticism. Reflecting on her own earlier work, she says she saw many absences in it. Apparently, some of this work did not mention the sociological fetishes of race, class, gender, sexual orientations, "and other important signifiers of experience and power." Nowadays, though, she's much better. If she neglects to mention one or all of these (or perhaps combinations thereof), her listeners and students will evidently set her straight, and for that truthfulness and honesty she is "grateful!"[108]

This Bolshevistic-Maoist impulse to confess one's ideological impurity is a very real and very disturbing adjunct to SocProg thought. Some background here. History is well-familiar with Pavlik Morozov, a member of the ideological youth group the "Young Pioneers" in the former Soviet Union. He denounced his father to the local soviet who was then charged with crimes against the state. His crime was being sympathetic to the kulaks ("wealthy peasants"). But, since wealth was synonymous with the "elites" and since the "elites" had oppressed the lower classes for millennia, this sympathy made him an ideological enemy and he was shot.[109] The boy was later murdered by the villagers, but not before the young lad was publicly celebrated by the state for placing loyalty to an ideology above "bourgeois middle class values" like honouring your father (family values and, indeed, the family itself were something Marx and the Bolsheviks then and the SocProgs today treat with equal amounts of disdain). SocProg historians apparently feel the need to do something similar as young master Morozov: to confess and publicly purify themselves for ideological lapses, their bourgeois backgrounds, their middle-class values. SocProg historian Donald Finlay Davis does this in 1998.

Davis had written a history of "automobile elites" in Detroit.[110] The book examined the issue of "elites" and "the negative consequences of status seeking." As part of her 1998 CHA address, president Judith Fingard asked Davis why he entered the historical profession. For Davis, the issues were personal (and thus political). He reflected that it was only after he had written his book that he finally realized that he had been addressing "the issues of [his] childhood." As it turns out, Davis apparently disliked the new upscale neighbourhood he and his family moved to when he was a young boy. He wondered why his father wanted to live there. His father, evidently from a poorer neighbourhood, viewed the new place as a step-up, a neighbourhood in which he had aspired to live since he was a boy. But rather than seeing something fundamentally decent and honourable in what his father did, Davis instead earnestly confided to Fingard that "my father could be regarded as a status seeker."[111] Nothing like throwing Dad under the bus.

So at the annual meetings of the CHA, the Traditionalists had their approach to history dismissed by their association presidents as outdated, their minds characterized as ill-equipped, and their biological sexuality highlighted as evidence—nay, *damning proof*—of their ideological impurity. Recognizing on some basic and instinctual level that they would likely never get to speak in front of a meeting of the CHA again in their lifetimes, a group of Traditionalists apparently tried to rebel. A small group of historians in 1995 took tentative steps to secede from the CHA and form their own rival historical association. Something similar happened in America, too. Now, one might reasonably expect that the CHA president would exercise what is commonly called leadership and try to draw together both sides, to conciliate, to ratchet tempers down. One might *expect* that, but one would also be wrong. In fact, the secession barely rated notice.

Before addressing the secession itself, the president of that year, Mr. James Leith, took time to establish his ideological purity. Leith observed that he "personally welcomes" the "advances" made in social, gender, and labour history. And he pointedly reminds his audience that there is "no reason to look down" on political, military, or diplomatic historians "provided up to date approaches are used."[112] The qualifier "provided" suggests that if Traditionalists are not using "up-to-date approaches" (read: Marxian sociology), then it *is* okay to look down on them. And here once again we bump up uncomfortably, again, against Mao Tse Tung thought. During China's Cultural Revolution, an equally exasperated Chairman Mao wrote a pamphlet on how to handle "contradictions among the people," especially amongst intellectuals. We can hear the sigh in the Chairman's voice when he observed that "there are bound to be some who will always be ideologically reluctant" to embrace the new thought, and so he counselled patience.[113] "We should not be too exacting in what we expect of them" he wrote, so long as they try. But try they must, to "continue to remould themselves [and] gradually shed their bourgeois world outlook."

Leith then surveys the scene. He explains to his colleagues that the new methods of history, the new "novel approaches" had "enriched" the historical profession. But at the same time, he concedes, these changes made historians in this country "very sectarian and factious." While he obliquely and vaguely hints at a general disagreement here, he is rather more specific when he observes that "the defenders of the more traditional areas of study are often just as intolerant."[114] Please note here that he reserves use of the loaded epithet "intolerant" solely for the Traditionalists.

But the secession itself appears to trouble him little. These "intolerant" historians, he informed his colleagues, had taken steps to secede from the CHA and form their own association "so that they can do national history as they think it should be done." And he responds by offering the flinty observation that "it seems to me very ill-advised to form another organization when government funding for scholarly and learned publications is being drastically cut." Thus, fiscal probity, not professional unity is his argument against secession.

He does not offer an olive branch. He does not highlight the value of the traditional approach: indeed, he denigrates it. He does not appeal to a wider sense of community within the historical profession. He offers intransigent platitudes ("we should be working together to contribute to a synthesis," etc), and the secession gets almost none of the attention that such a turn of events would seem to require. In fact, the secession gets approximately six sentences, excluding the topic sentence. Having summarily dealt with the Traditionalists—and these six dismissive sentences suggest that, for Mr. Leith, the whole issue was janitorial rather than essential—he then moves on to more pressing matters: "I would like to discuss paper, food, flowers, and the environment."[115]

The remainder of his address was a banal inanity addressing the importance of globalization and the multicultural state so prized of academics in the 1990s. Boundless platitudes adorn his conclusion. Not only must we "better prepare our students for our multicultural society", we must do so because "only by trying to understand 'the other', can we really understand ourselves." His purpose in doing all this, his challenge to his colleagues, indeed his vision for the "Future of the Past in Canada," was this: "better preparation for our multicultural society and increasingly global world." And *that* "is my challenge to my colleagues." Stormy applause.[116]

Perversion, Unabated

And so there it is. Canadian historians wrote next to nothing about the disintegration of their discipline. The SocProg way has fully entrenched itself in universities. The *Canadian Historical Review* is today still unreadable, only more so. There are not fewer theories, there are more. And, citing American statistics because no Canadian statistics were available, Dummit suggests that the largest general fields in the study of history today are those associated with the SocProg project, which is to say social history, women's history, and gender history.[117] In fact, Dummit observes that gender history in America is the second-most-popular field of historical study.[118]

Too, we are also seeing the distressing growth of "masculinity studies," the most recent carbuncle to show up in the discipline. The pages of the *CHR* are full of this new "rootless and disinherited marauder."[119] Young men don't attend "masculinity studies" to learn how to be men (no one seems to know how to do that anymore anyway so a class in that might actually be helpful), they go there to learn that masculinity itself as an idea is actually a social construct and an artificiality.

The very few and limited calls for public debate about history in Canada still revolve around the national versus social paradigm of the type that characterized the history wars in the 1990s. Mr. Dummit laments (it is so awfully obvious, so crushingly *there*) that the "biggest thing we're missing is just the basic political history of Canada."[120]

And there is always that other perennial debate about how little Canadians know about their history, or even care. The research institute *Historica Canada* routinely publishes poll after poll revealing that only 50% of the population know who Sir John A Macdonald is, or that only 33% of Canadians know what Remembrance Day means, or that only 23% of Canadians know what a Loyalist was and why that even matters.[121] One of the essential features of being Canadian is our disinterest in and ignorance of our own history.

But the present work has absolutely no intention of re-igniting any of these debates. This work instead will focus on the dynamics and elements that were totally ignored or skipped over entirely during the history wars. And the task of first and utmost importance is dealing with the conceits of the SocProg set. It should be abundantly clear by this point that the SocProgs wallow in an unseemly self-wonderment which arises directly out of seeing themselves as new, advanced, progressive, cutting edge, and forward thinking. This tasteless self-glorification must be checked and challenged if for no other reason than simple decency and propriety demands it. We must understand that the SocProgs are nothing new but are rather something quite old and their appearance points toward a much larger issue concerning Western history itself.

Mr. Dummit observes that historians in universities today—and again we must remember that this is not an issue confined just to history departments in universities—are engaged in what he calls "[a] downward spiral of well-intentioned solipsism."[122] The interesting thing about Dummit's absolutely correct identification of the problem there is that it has happened once before in the West. Ancient Athens, our spiritual and intellectual home, was likewise ruined by what American philosopher Robert Cushman called "truth-destroying pluralistic solipsism."[123] Solipsism is defined as *"the theory that only knowledge of the self is possible and that for each individual, the self itself is the only thing really existent and therefore that reality is subjective."* It comes from the Latin *solus* which means "alone" and *ipse* which means "self." Thus *AloneSelf.*

This intellectual and spiritual connection between Athens and us is not superficial but rather essential and deeply meaningful and there is historical meaning, there, in that sameness. After all, the list of civilizations and societies that have been wrecked and ruined by Sophistry, solipsism, and *AloneSelf* is *very* short, and where Western civilization itself is concerned, we can comfortably say it has only happened on this scale twice: in Athens, where Western civilization was born, and today in Western liberal democracies whose direct inspiration is Athens. In order to establish, draw out, and explore these profoundly meaningful connections between the Athenian experience and our own, the next two chapters will escort the reader back to ancient Greece, for it is there where we will realize, finally, just who and what we are dealing with when we encounter a SocProg. SocProg historians do not just write history: they are history.

Endnotes

[1] The folks over at the *Dominion Institute* (now *Historica Canada*) seem to take a perverse and chronic glee in publishing poll after poll, year after depressing year, demonstrating how little Canadians know about their past. Please visit their website and check out virtually any poll on history. Any year will do.

[2] See Arthur R.M. Lower, *From Colony to Nation: a history of Canada* (Don Mills Ontario: Longman's, 1946), p. x. The first line of his preface reads: "Most of those who see this book will probably decide without opening it that it must be a dull one." And thus sadly even then, in 1946, was Canadian history considered dull. The SocProgs have done little or nothing to change that apprehension. In fact it is a certainty beyond doubt that they have worsened matters.

[3] Christopher Dummit, "After Inclusiveness: the future," in *Contesting Clio's Craft: new directions and debates in Canadian history* (London: Institute for the Study of the America's, 2009), p. 102.

[4] Dummit, "After Inclusiveness," p. 102

[5] I would put my money on 1998, the year Jack Granatstein published *Who Killed Canadian History*, the first, last, and only book published by the Traditionalists in the history wars. The debates generated by Mr. Granatstein's work echoed for years in seminar rooms across the country after he published his book. But of actual published work, there was none after 1998. Michael Bliss published a twelve page article in 1991.

[6] Just there I went and checked the bibliography and I see that there are almost no Canadian historians or philosophers cited in this entire book.

[7] Eugene Genovese "Heresy yes- sensitivity no," in *The New Republic* April 1991, p. 34.

[8] The book to read is Douglas Porch's wonderful history *The French Foreign Legion: a complete history of the legendary fighting force* (New York: HarperPerennial, 1991). For the Siege at Cameron please see pp. 138-142

[9] Interestingly, on some level, "whelm" comes from the German word *gehwelfan* which means "to bend over."

[10] Dummit "After Inclusiveness," p. 101. For the absence of debate, see also Terry Glavin, "Harper Tories don't trust historians—for good reason" in *The Vancouver Province* at: blogs.theprovince.com, February 14, 2013.

[11] Dummit, "After Inclusiveness," p. 101.

[12] Glavin, "Harper Tories." To give you an idea of how bad it got at times in the academy in the USA, a group of traditional historians at Duke University in North Carolina wanted to establish a National Association of Scholars, open to everyone who desired a return to the traditional principles governing historical research. They were apparently all denounced as "racist, sexist, and homophobic." See Roger Kimball, *Tenured Radicals*, p. 296.

[13] Christopher Dummit and Michael Dawson, "Introduction: Debating the Future of Canadian History: preliminary answers to uncommon questions," in *Contesting*, p. xiv.

[14] Robert Conquest, *The Dragons of Expectation: reality and delusions in the course of history* (New York: W.W. Norton, 2005), p. 45.

[15] John Hallowell, "Plato and His Critics," *Journal of Politics*, vol. 27, no. 2, May 1965, p. 283.

[16] Consider that idea for a second for it is truly and deeply disturbing. Sociology is the *only* subject in the academy that does not *seek* after anything. History and Philosophy seek Truth; Literature and Art History seek Beauty; Poetry seeks Transcendence; Science seeks Answers. But because it has already found out how to "make society a better place to live"—it's right there in their textbooks—sociology, then, only seeks its own validation.

[17] Most SocProg scholarship develops out of a confusing body of ideas called "postmodernism," and post-modernism is *heavily* influenced by the ideas of Karl Marx who, of course, was the ideological father of the radical Bolsheviks hence, "distant cousins." See Christopher Butler, *Postmodernism: a very short introduction* (London: Oxford University Press, 2002), p. 2.

[18] That gem is from Garrison Keillor in *WLT: a radio romance* (New York: Penguin, 1991), p. 6.

[19] Anecdotal evidence: frequently in daily news coverage one can hear/see/read reporters speak of a "right wing," whether it be a political party, a public commentator (hi Ezra), a movement or what have you, the press will often use that denigrating, patronizing, and dismissive phrase. But you could read, watch, and listen to the news for a year and never hear the phrase "left wing" uttered once. And this state of affairs tends to suggest that there is a consensus around what we might call a SocProg Centre and anything that deviates from that consensus is thus dismissed as "right-wing."

[20] Bryan D. Palmer, "New Left Liberations: the poetics, praxis, and politics of youth radicalism," in *The Sixties in Canada: a turbulent and creative decade* M. Athena Palaeologu, ed. (Montreal: Black Rose Books, 2009), p. 73. One is reminded of Marlon Brando's quip in the film *The Wild Ones*. A young woman asks Brando's character Johnny what he's rebelling against to which Johnny replies, "whaddya got?"

[21] Gregory Pfitzer, "History Cracked Open: 'New' History's Renunciation of the past," in *Reviews in American History*, vol. 31, 2003, pp. 143-151.

[22] I recall having a funny little conversation with a teacher of sociology. We were discussing sexuality and how it differs for men and women because evidently men and women have been "socialized into sex roles thought appropriate for their gender." Henslin, *Sociology*, p. 147. Cynically, I asked if these problems were "systemic." His eyes lit up and with great enthusiasm he said "Yes! Exactly!" At which point I sagged inwardly, fearing over the state of his mind and his soul.

[23] Robert Bork, *Slouching Towards Gomorrah: modern liberalism and American decline* (New York: Regan Books, 1996), p. 31

[24] Walter McDougall, "Mais ce n'est pas l'historie: some thoughts on Toynbee, McNeill and the rest of us," *Journal of Modern History*, vol. 58, no. 1, March 1986, p. 34

[25] JMS Careless, "Limited Identities," in *Careless at Work: selected Canadian Historical Studies by JMS Careless* (Toronto: Dundurn Press, 1990), p. 281.

[26] Carl Berger, *The Writing of Canadian History: aspects of English-Canadian historical writing since 1900* (Toronto: University of Toronto Press, 1986), p. 228.

[27] Berger, *The Writing*, p. 228.

[28] Berger, *The Writing*, p. 112. And in doing this Lower was simply trying to bring some measure of unity to a country that has had a very difficult time with that idea. All of our greatest prime ministers—and even some of the not-so-great—have tried in their own way to deal with this problem. Macdonald, Laurier, Borden, King, Diefenbaker, Trudeau, Mulroney, Harper: all have tried to bring some measure of unity or connectedness to Canada and so to excoriate Lower for doing so was (is) churlish, cheap, and carping.

[29] Lower, *From Colony to Nation*, p. xii. No one today can really make the case that Canadians are at peace with who we are and what we represent as a country.

[30] Herbert Butterfield, *The Whig Interpretation of History* (New York: Norton 1965), p. 11.

[31] The book to read on that particular issue is George Stanley's *The Birth of Western Canada* (Toronto: University of Toronto Press, 1936).

[32] Butterfield, *The Whig*, p. 10.

[33] Bruce J Schulman, "Out of the streets and into the classroom? The new left and counterculture in United States history textbooks," *The Journal of American History* vol. 85, no. 4, March 1999 p. 1533.

[34] Berger, *The Writing*, p. 264

[35] Theodore Hamerow, *Reflections on History and Historians* (Madison: University of Wisconsin Press, 1987), p. 164.

[36] Hamerow *Reflections*, p. 164.

[37] I have long loved words but in truth, I have absolutely no idea what "cisgendered" even means nor do I have any inclination to look it up. From what I can tell by simply looking at the word, it is a fabrication invented by fabricators. Fabricate: *"to invent fancifully, or falsely; concoct."*

[38] In my own little corner of the historical world—prairie history—the voices of the people who lived and worked the land formed the foundation of my first book *Happyland*. *Happyland* would not be *Happyland* without the voices of the people.

[39] Thomas Carlyle, "On History," in *Selected Essays* (London: T. Nelson and Sons, Ltd. no date), p. 238. Prophecy is not as lunatic as it might sound. Robert Conquest observed that "proper feeling for and judgment of history could indeed lead to the right conclusion" of what might possibly happen in the future. See Conquest, *Dragons*, p. 213.

[40] Carlyle, "On History," in *Selected*, p. 238.

[41] The phrasing there is from Martin Amis.

[42] I first heard about that dynamic from philosopher Isaiah Berlin.

[43] Hamerow, *Reflections*, p. 164.

[44] *Obiter Dicta* plural of *Obiter Dictum*: "A judge's expression of opinion uttered in discussing a point of law... generally, an incidental remark." *The Oxford Dictionary of Foreign Words and Phrases* edited by Jennifer Speake (New York: Oxford, 1997), p. 291.

[45] Karl Marx and Friedrich Engels, *The Communist Manifesto* (New York: Washington Square Press: 1964), p. 92.

[46] Paul Johnson, *Intellectuals* (New York: Perennial, 1988), p. 63.

[47] Richard Pipes, *Communism: a history* (New York: The Modern Library, 2001), p. 12.

[48] Karl Lowith, *Meaning in History* (Chicago: University of Chicago Press, 1949), pp. 33- 42.

[49] Pipes, *Communism*, p. 13.

[50] Johnson, *Intellectuals*, p. 72. The full idea reads: "Like many self-centered individuals, he tended to think that moral laws did not apply to himself or rather, to identify his interests with morality as such."

[51] Sigmund Freud, *Civilization and its Discontents* (London: Penguin Classics, 2002), p. 26.

[52] Peter Baehr, "The Undoing of Humanism: Peter L. Berger's sociology of unmasking," *Soc*, vol. 50, 2013, pp. 379-381. Berger is the fellow who popularized for us the Marxian untruth of "social construction." I asked a sociology teacher one day if he had a copy of the book. His eyes *gleamed* with joy as he proudly

showed me his copy. I didn't have the heart to tell him about Berger's 1992 renunciation. That just seemed mean.

[53] For Berger's comments on that "art of mistrust," see his *Invitation to Sociology: a humanistic perspective* (New York: The Overlook Press, 1963), p. 30. For Arendt's thoughts on sociology, see *Essays in Understanding, 1930-1954: formation, exile, totalitarianism* (New York: Schocken Books, 1994), pp. 33-34.

[54] Berger, *Invitation*, p. 23.

[55] By the way, who *are* these "elites" anyway? Do they have homes and families? Dogs? Do they go on vacations? Why have I never met anyone who has confessed to his or her part in this conspiracy? In immediate reflection here, I am struck by the eerie and uncomfortable parallels between "the elites," and "the Jews" as represented in *The Protocols of the Elders of Zion*, a ridiculous pamphlet that claimed to have found proof of a Jewish Conspiracy to Rule the World back in the day.

[56] Berger, *Invitation*, p. 176.

[57] In addition to Arrogance and Pride, Condescension too is an essential feature of sociology. Our introductory sociology textbook informs young students of the following: "You will see that the way you look at the world is the result of your exposure to specific social groups and your ignorance of others." See Henslin, *Sociology*, p. 4. One imagines trusting young undergraduates actually writing this down in their notes: "I am ignorant."

[58] I am just pulling daily news from memory here, but you should be able to recognize it and add to it: Sweden wants to ban the words "boy" and "girl" and replace them with gender-neutral terms thus ridding society of distinctions between boys and girls. The Alberta government is doing something similar with gender neutral bathrooms for kids. Sex-reassignment surgery is the New Normal. All of these kinds of things grow out of the Marxian untruth that gender is a "social construct."

[59] See Henslin, *Sociology*, pp. 2-424.

[60] Stanislav Andreski, *Social Science as Sorcery* (London: Andre Deutsch, 1972), p. 232.

[61] To continue with the definition of delusion: "a *delusion* is a mistaken conviction, an *illusion* a mistaken perception or inference. An *illusion* may be wholly of the senses; a *delusion* always involves some mental error." And, plowing further into that Marxian unreality of a Perfect World we may safely say that he was technically suffering from a hallucination because that word means "a false image or belief which has nothing, outside of the disordered mind, to suggest it." There is nothing in history itself to support Marx's visions of the future; there is "nothing outside of his disordered mind" that supports his ideas.

[62] Disingenuousness, too, is an essential characteristic of the SocProg worldview. Disingenuous: "*not sincere, artful, deceitful.*"

[63] Berger, *Invitation*, p. 47.

[64] Ad infinitum: "*to infinity; without limit; forever*" see *The Oxford Dictionary of Foreign Words*, Speake, p. 4.

[65] Berger, *Invitation*, p. 152. He got the "swindler" part right. Swindle: "*to cheat and defraud grossly or deliberately.*"

[66] Clive James, *Cultural Amnesia: notes in the margin of my time* (London: Picador, 2007), p. 677.

[67] T.W. Acheson, Presidential Address, "Doctoral Theses and the Discipline of History in Canada, 1967 and 1985," Historical Papers, *Journal of the Canadian Historical Association*, vol.21, no. 1, 1986, pp. 1-10

[68] Acheson, "Doctoral Theses," pp. 4-5

[69] Acheson, "Doctoral Theses," p. 6.

[70] Acheson, "Doctoral Theses," p. 8.

[71] Acheson, "Doctoral Theses," p. 9

[72] Robert Bork, *Slouching Towards Gomorrah: modern liberalism and American decline* (New York: Regan Books, 1996), p. 53.

[73] Please see their respective works: Michael Bliss, "Privatizing the Mind: the sundering of Canadian history, the sundering of Canada," *Journal of Canadian Studies*, vol. 26, 1991, pp. 5-17, and Jack Granatstein, *Who Killed Canadian History?* (Toronto: Harper Perennial, 1998).

[74] See course outline for Christopher Dummit, History 5118, Trent University, Department of History: www.trentu.ca/historyma/documents/HIST-5118H-GW2013. I cannot recall where the phrase "glacial pace" comes from but the writer who used it did so to characterize how slowly changes occur within the Canadian historical establishment.

[75] Granatstein, *Who Killed*, p. 3.

[76] Granatstein, *Who Killed*, p. 3. "The media" he refers to there, I am quite sure, is the CBC, Canada's state broadcaster and an important distribution point for the SocProg worldview. Dear CBC: your coverage of the 2015 federal election will almost certainly go down in history for what it actually was: a *coup d'état*. Coup d'état: "*a violent or illegal change in government.*" Speake, *Foreign Words*, p. 93.

[77] Bliss, "Privatizing." p. 5.

[78] Bliss, "Privatizing," pp. 5-8.

[79] Bliss, "Privatizing," p. 9.

[80] Marlene Shore, "Remember the Future: The Canadian Historical Review and the Discipline of History, 1920-1995," *Canadian Historical Review*, vol. 76, no. 3, September, 199, p. 451.

[81] Joy Parr, "Gender History and Historical Practice," *Canadian Historical Review*, vol. 76, no. 3, September 1995.

I have heard that Ms. Parr's nickname is "the Joy of History." After reading her history, we have to assume that the name should be taken ironically.

[82] Keith Windschuttle, "National Identity and the Corruption of History," in *The New Criterion*, Jan. 2006, pp. 7, 18-20.

[83] Parr, "Gender History," pp. 357-358.

[84] Parr, "Gender History," p. 358.

[85] Leopold von Ranke, *The Secret of World History: selected writings on the art and science of history* translated by Roger Wines (New York: Fordham University Press, 1981), p. 259. By the way I was taught by a man who breathed history through his eyelids such as the type as Ranke describes. My teacher was wise and brilliant in a way that many SocProgs can never be—since they reject truth they are, unwittingly, also rejecting wisdom.

[86] Werner Jaeger, *Paideia: the ideals of Greek culture* vol. 1 translated by Gilbert Highet (New York: Oxford University Press, 1945), p. xxiii.

[87] Carlyle, *The French Revolution*, p. 768.

[88] I recall the day my Canadian history professor, David DeBrou, consented to my request to read and comment in class on an essay concerning SocProg thought written by American historian Gertrude Himmelfarb. Up to that point, we had been going through articles concerning race-class-gender and

there was increasing frustration amongst the class about what we were reading. And, having stumbled across Himmelfarb's essay, I, *for the first time*, saw an alternative to the SocProg way. I asked Prof DeBrou if I could do this and, to his eternal credit, he said "You bet."

[89] Dummit and Dawson, "Introduction," in *Contesting*, p. xiii

[90] Granatstein, *Who Killed*, p. 66

[91] Jeffery Vacante, Review of Dummit, Chris; Dawson, Michael, eds. *Contesting Clio's Craft: new directions and debates in Canadian history.* H-Canada, H-Net Review. September 2010.

[92] Vacante, Review of *Contesting Clio's Craft.*

[93] In the preface to Lukacs, *Remembered Past*, p xxii. Historians can be nasty creatures. Writing about the new relativists and the "straight-line professionals" in the United States in the 1930s, historian Arthur Marwick says both sides lined up and "poured the burning oil of academic scorn upon each other's pretensions while nervously insisting upon the social or intellectual value of their work." See Arthur Marwick, *The Nature of History*, p. 227.

[94] Carlyle, "Shooting Niagara: and after?" *Selected Essays*, p. 407.

[95] Carlyle "Shooting Niagara," p. 407.

[96] By the way, the presentations at the *CHA* Annual Meeting in 2013 were a horror-show of SocProg scholarship. There were panels on "Beautiful Bodies in Pageants and Print: internal and external gazes," "Acts of Looking: cultural perspectives in Canadian Rural History," "Guarding the Threshold of the Body Politic: intersecting discourses of medicine, religion and the body in contemporary Canadian reproductive rights history," "Objects at Intersections: Between visual cultural studies, material cultural studies, and art history," "Our City Our Voices: citizen activism and urban planning in Canada, 1950-1908," etc & co. The conference was held in Victoria, an excellent location the organizers claimed, because, on Salish Territory near the Pacific Ocean "issues of indigineity, coloniality, and nationality resonate in a particularly compelling manner." I'll bet they do.

[97] Mary Lynn Stewart, Presidential Address, "Historians without Borders," *Journal of the Canadian Historical Association*, vol. 22, no. 1, 2011, pp. 1-34. Her address, though, was SocProggy in its themes and content. Too, we often hear of "periodization" in history and for the SocProg set there seem to be just two periods in the 2,500 years of the history of Western civilization: before the 1960s and after the 1960s.

[98] Veronica Strong-Boag, Presidential Address, "Contested Space: The Politics of Canadian Memory," *Journal of the Canadian Historical Association*, vol. 5, no. 1, 1994, p. 4.

[99] Strong-Boag, "Contested Space," pp. 4-5

[100] Strong-Boag, "Contested Space," p. 5.

[101] Jacques Barzun, "The Artist as Prophet and Jester," in *American Scholar*, vol. 69, no. 1, Winter 2000, p. 17.

[102] Strong Boag, "Contested Space," pp. 5-6.

[103] I have it on good authority that no one said a thing. Strong-Boag's taxonomy of those who came before her is more than a little off-point. It never occurred to Traditional historians to "interrogate power relations" because the whole concept of "power relations" is a Marxian sociological fetish; it is not a concept indigenous to the discipline of history—or even the human mind in its natural state for that matter—and the historians she lambastes for their failure to undertake this political project were singularly uninterested in dealing with politically charged sociological theory. "Exposing" the "reality of oppression in Canadian society" was simply not a part of the spirit of their age as it is today. Each age produces its own history,

reflecting its own values, and so it is arrogance of the most horrid sort to excoriate historians of the past for not being more like us.

[104] The phrase is from Martin Amis.

[105] Robert Conquest, *The Dragons of Expectation*, p. 50.

[106] Alan Bloom, *The Closing of the American Mind*, p. 247.

[107] Strong-Boag, "Contested Space," p. 6.

[108] Strong-Boag, Contested Space," p. 6. The full quote is "intermittently grateful!" and that "intermittently" suggests that she does still have a functioning mind of her own.

[109] Amis, *Koba The Dread*, p. 193.

[110] Donald Davis, *Conspicuous Production: automobiles and elites in Detroit, 1899-1933* (Philadelphia: Temple University Press, 1988).

[111] Judith Fingard, Presidential Address, "The Personal and the Historical," *Journal of the Canadian Historical Association*, vol. 9, no. 1, p. 7.

[112] James A. Leith, Presidential Address, "The Future of the Past in Canada on the eve of the Twenty-First Century," *Journal of the Canadian Historical Association*, vol. 6, no. 1, 1995, p. 1. Whatever is bad for traditional historians is generally three or four times worse for military historians. They are the kicked dog of the establishment. Some universities don't even have them on campus which is strange considering that war has been the catalyst of profound social, political, and intellectual change.

[113] Mao Tse-tung, *On the Correct Handling of Contradictions Among the People* (Peking: Foreign Language Press, 1966), pp. 42-43.

[114] James A. Leith, Presidential Address, "The Future of the Past in Canada on the eve of the Twenty-First Century," *Journal of the Canadian Historical Association*, vol. 6, no. 1, 1995, p. 6.

[115] Leith, "The Future," p. 17.

[116] The phrasing and tone of this paragraph have been borrowed from Martin Amis.

[117] Dummit "After Inclusiveness," p. 102. I was once told only half-jokingly by M. Polachic, an old university mate of mine, that I am likely the only history teacher in Canada who teaches Canadian constitutional history. Canada, or what became Canada, has had five constitutions: the Royal Proclamation, 1763; the Quebec Act, 1774; The Constitution Act, 1791; the Act of Union, 1840; and the one with which most people are familiar, the British North America Act of 1867. All of them fascinating; all of them wondrous.

[118] Dummit, After Inclusiveness," p. 102.

[119] That brilliant phrase belongs to Canadian historian Donald Creighton, who used it against the New Left crowd of the sixties.

[120] Glavin, "Harper Tories."

[121] Granatstein, *Who Killed*, pp. 8-9. Annually, I conduct my own little quizzes at the outset of each term. I compose ten simple questions (When is Canada Day? Who was our first Prime Minister? Who did Canada fight in the First World War? What animal prompted the French to settle in what became Quebec? What are the opening words to our national anthem? etc). I have all the students stand up after having written down the answers and then I go through the answers one at a time, asking each student to sit down when they get a wrong answer. Only once was I able to make it past the third question before everyone was seated.

CURTIS R. MCMANUS

[122] Glavin, "Harper Tories."

[123] Robert E. Cushman, *Therapeia: Plato's Conception of Philosophy* (Chapel Hill NC: University of North Carolina Press, 1958), p. 41.

CHAPTER TWO

THE SOPHISTS

"How did the mental distortions arise? How did the aversion to and alienation from reality come about? How did the destructive intellectual epidemic strike?"

Robert Conquest, on the rise of "progressive" thought in the twenty-first century, in Dragons of Expectations, p. 46.

"By the end of it, the clever were turning everything upside down and the simple felt that they had become out of date."

HDF Kitto on the impact that Sophistry had on Athenians by the end of the fifth century BC, in The Greeks, p. 166.

"The thing that hath been, is that which shall be; and that which is done is that which shall be done, and there is no new thing under the sun. Is there anything whereof it may be said See, this is new? It hath been already of old time, which was there before us."

Ecclesiastes, 1:9-10, King James Version

"This world was created by no God or man; it was, it is, and always will be an undying fire which kindles and extinguishes itself in a regular pattern.

Greek philosopher Heraclitus, in Classics in Translation, p. 108.

"He who sees the present has seen all things, both all that has come to pass from everlasting and all that will be for eternity."

Roman emperor Marcus Aurelius, Meditations, p. 53.

There are instances when history can actually be quite simple. This is one of those instances. The SocProgs of today are doing precisely what the Athenian Sophists did 2,500 years ago. And while today's Sophistry gains a peculiar animating energy, purpose, and direction from the ideas of Karl Marx, the substance of the thought itself and the ends at which the ideas aim, both then and now, are *exactly* the same. The SocProg project revolves around destruction and negation; it devotes itself to overturning traditions, customs, and conventions; to cancelling truth and objectivity; to refusing the very notion of timeless universals. And this is precisely what the Sophists did in ancient Greece.

The Sophists embraced and counselled relativity, the absence of truth, the arbitrary and so suspect nature of custom, morality, tradition, and convention, and the idea that there are no timeless universals all with the allied goal of liberating the individual from the bondage of society. It sounds all well and good; it even borders on sounding sophisticated somehow. But we would do well to revisit the meaning of that word. Sophisticate: "*to beguile with sophistry; mislead by false argument; to falsify by deceptive alterations; to disillusion.*" The dictionary philosophers here are painting a picture of a circumstance which is unappealing and undesirable, and if both the cause and effect of a thing are objectionable, then so too is the agent which set the whole thing in motion, and should likely be avoided. At all costs, too.

Introducing the Greeks

The Greeks may be foreign to many readers or, if not foreign, then a knowledge of the degree to which we are and remain indebted to them remains hazy and ill-focussed. This should not be the case, but it is. One wishes to write that it is impossible—but in this day and age we must settle with "difficult"—to not be moved and even changed in unalterable ways upon encountering the Greeks. Here is the quaint and donnish English historian HDF Kitto, who introduces us:

> "The reader is asked for a moment to accept this as a reasonable statement of fact that in a part of the world that had for centuries been civilized, and quite highly civilized, there gradually emerged a people, not very numerous, not very powerful, not very well-organized, who had a totally new conception of what human life was for, *and showed for the first time, what the human mind was for.*"

Kitto's words, then, should give us a bearing on the enormity of the thing we are dealing with here. And so, a few paragraphs on historical background and context are necessary for structure and in order to understand the appearance of the Sophists and, later on, the Cynics. The Greeks had organized themselves into a loose collection of city-states. Each city state—each *polis* as they were called—was an independent, self-contained community and Athens was the most famous of the bunch (there were hundreds). And it was here at Athens in the late sixth century BC that the Western soul was birthed and the first experiment in democracy set in motion.

Under the radical social and political reforms of Cleisthenes, the practice of full participatory democracy was established around 508 BC. This radical new social and political order was structured around the concepts of Liberty, Equality, and Justice. For the first time in history, people would govern themselves, and that is just one of the dozens of reasons why the Athenian experiment was (is) so thrilling: they were not subjects as so many peoples of the world were at that time. They were citizens with rights, duties, responsibilities, and obligations to the community. They did not have presidents or prime ministers; they had a democratic assembly in which each citizen was entitled to have his say and it functioned in a fashion not unlike our own. Through argument and persuasion based on logic and reason (hopefully), the citizen would make attempts at convincing his fellows of the wisdom of his recommendations.[2] This insistence on persuasion, on "presenting plausible reasons" for action was, regrettably, one of the entry points through which the Sophists would gain access to Athenian life.[3]

Life in Athens revolved around the public sphere in an almost total sense. Every man over the age of eighteen was entitled and indeed expected to participate in this democratic experiment. Such responsibilities included making oneself available as a juror in the law courts (Athenians were a notoriously litigious bunch), organizing annual festivals, volunteering for military duty, and all the other seemingly innumerable public offices to which every Greek citizen was expected to give his time and energies.[4] The influential statesman Pericles told his fellow Athenians during that radiant golden age of the fifth century BC that what really matters is "not membership in a particular class, but the actual ability a man possesses." "No one," Pericles observed, "so long as he has it in him to be of service to the state, is kept in political obscurity because of poverty."[5]

Pericles hints directly there at that wonderful spirit of public mindedness and civic virtue that animated the Athenians. He remarked that "here each individual is interested in not only his own affairs but also the affairs of the state." And, pandering just a little to Athenian pride, he goes on to observe that "we do not say a man who takes no interest in politics is a man who minds his own business; we say that he has no business here at all."[6] Intriguingly, the word "idiot" which we use today to mean "*a human being conspicuously deficient in mental powers*" comes from the Greek word *idiotes* which means "a private person," someone who did not take part in public affairs.

Now of course, not all citizens took to this social and political order with unblinking enthusiasm—there were bad citizens then as there are today.[7] But the Athenian experiment was predicated almost entirely on the basic idea that all hands should be on deck rowing in the same direction. The Ephebic Oath which young men took on their eighteenth birthday gives us a pretty good indicator of the Athenian spirit:

> "I will never bring reproach upon my hallowed arms nor will I desert the comrade at whose side I stand but will defend our altars and our hearths single handed or supported by many. My native land I will not leave a diminished heritage but greater and better than when I received it. I will obey whoever is in authority and submit to the established laws which the people shall harmoniously enact. If anyone tries to overthrow the constitution or disobeys it I will not permit him but will come to its defence either single handed or with the support of all."[8]

Athenian life, then, was open-air, it revolved around the public sphere and this helped to foster and perpetuate a vibrant and bracing intellectual and cultural atmosphere. Since a large part of that public life revolved around the democratic assembly and the law courts, men found it crucial to be able to clearly develop and articulate arguments. The Greek way, then, gave rise to a group of teachers and thinkers who, for a fee, would teach the art of persuasion.

Enter the Sophists

The word "Sophist" is derived from the Greek word *sophia* which means either wisdom or cleverness, depending on context. Where wisdom means *"the power of true and right discernment"*—a power so obviously on the decline in the twenty-first century—cleverness means something much less elevated: *"ready and adroit with hand or brain; dexterous, capable, quick-witted, talented."* The Sophists were indeed quick-witted, capable, and talented, but they had no interest whatever in developing the powers of true and right discernment. History and philosophy would become responsible for that. Instead, Sophists taught people how to win an argument without regard to truth. Our modern definition of Sophism captures their substance: *"a false argument intention-ally used to deceive."* Neither now nor twenty-five centuries ago was the word Sophist a good thing (at least for most people; certainly not for Plato). And in the eternally changing world of the meaning of words, it is interesting that the meaning of Sophist has not really changed at all: they were, and remain, bullshit artists.

Princeton University philosopher Harry Frankfurt wrote a tiny but deeply thoughtful little treatise entitled *On Bullshit*, a scholarly examination of the concept of "bullshit" and the "artists" who propound it. Frankfurt here explains the essential differences between truths, lies, and bullshit:

> Someone who lies and someone who tells the truth are playing opposite sides, so to speak, in the same game. Each responds to the facts as he understands them, although the response of the one is guided by the authority of the truth, while the response of the other defies that authority and refuses to meet its demands. The bullshitter ignores these demands altogether. He does not reject the author-ity of the truth. He pays no attention to it at all. [9]

The Sophists, then, appear to possess qualities that allow us to classify them as liars *and* bullshit artists. And of course this has all kinds of disturbing impli-cations for SocProg scholarship.

The Sophists were a natural fit for Athens. In a community whose citizens formed and developed government policy based on argument and discus-sion, and whose legal system was likewise structured around persuasion, the

Sophists thrived. And, as Athenians grew increasingly wealthy throughout the fifth century, more and more men could afford to purchase the services of the Sophists.[10] Persuasion was all, argument was all, and thus whatever served those ends was a good thing, and the Sophists eagerly and with enthusiasm satisfied that demand.[11]

There is, however, much more going on with the Sophists than merely developing the skills necessary to win an argument. These men were "philosophers" after all, and philosophers have ideas and the Sophists' principle and foremost contribution to the history of Western thought should be entirely and thoroughly familiar to us today because we are so completely and utterly saturated in it once again: the primacy of the subjective consciousness. Solipsism. *AloneSelf.*

Up to this point in Athenian/Greek history, many philosophers had assumed that there was an objective order to this world, and that the human mind could, if suitably trained, apprehend that order.[12] But when the Sophists arrived, they cancelled truth and objective reality and instead argued the opposite: that things are only as they appear to the individual and so universally valid truths do not exist. In other words, the Sophists "abolished" truth 2,400 years before Karl Marx got around to doing it. And this "philosophy" that was taught by the Sophists circulated and, as ideas are wont to do, it "struck its roots into the whole moral, political, and religious life of that time."[13] And this is precisely what has happened with sociological thought today: it has saturated our moral, political, intellectual, and religious life. Or at least what is left of it.

The man most closely associated with the cancellation of truth and objectivity was Protagoras. He developed a body of ideas which held that perceptions, sensations, and impressions are as diverse as the subjects that experience them.[14] Or, in other words, the world is only as it appears to the individual. And from this position it follows that there are no timeless universals, there is no right or wrong, there is no good or bad, there is only relativity and interpretation according to individual perception.[15] This idea was given clothing in what is sometimes referred to as the "two-sides" doctrine and it works like this: war is bad for the soldiers but good for the armourers; sickness is bad for the patient but good for the doctor; a broken pot is bad for the house wife but good for the potter.[16] You see? There is nothing objectively or absolutely wrong or bad, it merely depends on your perspective, your point of view, perhaps even your opinion. For Protagoras, if person A believes in X but person B holds Y to be true and so each thinks they are right, then it stands to reason that everyone speaks the truth.[17]

This "two sides" doctrine was memorably captured in the dialogues of Plato. Engaging in a debate with Socrates over what is Good, Plato has Protagoras argue the point: "I know plenty of things—food, drink, drugs and many others—which are harmful to men, and others beneficial; and others again which, so far as men are concerned, are neither." Indeed Protagoras claims, "so diverse and multiform is goodness that even with us the same thing is good when applied externally but deadly when taken internally."[18] So dense and long-winded does he become that Socrates threatens to leave if Protagoras doesn't start making sense.

Plato, though, was capturing an important part of the intellectual kit of the Sophists. Protagoras denied the existence of transcendent truths, or "trans-phenomenal reality," on the basis that such reality was entirely beyond our capacities to apprehend.[19] And since there is no reality beyond our perception, no higher order that we can apprehend with any degree of certainty—nothing timeless which can be solidly grounded and explained—we inevitably come back around to subjective interpretation.

Protagoras claimed that there are, in the end, at least two possible positions on every question. And that is true in so far as it goes. But what the Sophists failed to do was take the next step. Yes, there are at least two possible positions on every question, but those positions then need to be weighed and measured and evaluated because the relative *value* of each position is not the same. Determining that value might be done by examining what each position will generate, produce, or result in and thus reveal what is good or bad, perhaps even what might be true or not true. But again, the Sophists, like the SocProgs, never got that far.

Summing up Sophistry, Aristotle, in that crisp and bracing logical fashion of his, observed: "Sophist thought is apparently wisdom but it is not; and the Sophist is a man who practices what is apparently wisdom, but really is not."[20] And it was not wisdom for the single reason that, at its very core, Sophistry moves against both truth and being and anything that moves against truth and being—sociological thought, for example—lacks wisdom in an absolute sense because wisdom requires a reckoning with both.[21]

Once the idea of truths and timeless universals are cancelled, and once we can no longer establish or even agree upon what is good or bad or even what is right or wrong, it is a very short step to questioning, challenging, and then overturning the morality, laws, and ethics of society. And that is precisely where the Sophists focussed their energies: on the contradictions and tensions between what they designated Nature and Convention. And their efforts in these areas have in fact been called the first expressions of "sociological theorizing" because that is precisely what it was: an effort to wreck and negate truth, morality, custom, and convention in the pursuit of a greater Liberty.[22]

Sophists argued that following the demands of nature was much more important than adhering to the mere conventions of society. Conventions, customs, and traditions, they argued, were deliberate creations and they are by definition—but only superficially—arbitrary and so not "true" not as such, and thus they can be subject to personal whim or subjective discretion. The Sophist Antiphon argues the point: "For it is laid down by the law for the eyes what they may see and what they may not, and for the ears what they may hear and what they may not, and in the case of the tongue what it may say and what it may not, and what the hands may do and not do and where the feet may go and not go and in the case of the mind what it may desire and what it may not." And thus he concludes: "The advantages which are prescribed by the law are shackles upon nature, whereas the advantages prescribed by nature make for freedom." Sociologists make exactly the same argument in much of their scholarship. Indeed, there is no difference here between Antiphon's "shackles" and Berger's "puppets on a string." They use almost the same words to describe *exactly* the same idea.

Antiphon's intellectual speculations here are all well and good but they brought into question the "naturalness" and thus the legitimacy of just about every element of Athenian life: the family, private property, gender differences, the distinction between Greek and non-Greek, as well as religion, morality, and the law itself.[23] Before the arrival of the Sophists, for example, a man defending himself in court was content to show that his conduct was right and good and in accordance with customary Athenian law. But as the Sophists attacked morality, custom, and law, and as they made all things relative and suspect (as they "unmasked" falsehoods such as they were), men actually began showing up in court arguing that the *law* was wrong not the behaviour in question.[24]

We should not have a very difficult time here understanding the nature of the moral, spiritual, and ethical crisis the Athenians were confronting.

The charge against the Sophists is that they created and fostered an atmosphere in which moral indifference and moral confusion thrived because nobody could tell anymore what was right and what was wrong. It seemed that people were becoming "moral morons."[25] In Plato's dialogue, *Meno*, the character Anytus says of the Sophists, "I hope no relative of mine or any of my friends, Athenian or foreign, would be so mad as to go and let himself be ruined by those people [Sophists or sociologists]. That's what they are, the manifest ruin and corruption of anyone who comes into contact with them."[26]

And thus it was that *AloneSelf* began its long tear through the West's first experiment in democracy. And it was the very principles of democracy—Liberty, Equality, and Justice—that had allowed and enabled the growth, development, and perpetuation of ideas that weakened and corroded it. Democracies are like that. But the Sophists did not see it in this way. Instead, as German philosopher Albert Schwegler put it, the Sophists "bustled about, enjoying with childish delight, the exercise of this new power of subjectivity, and destroying by means of a subjective dialectic all that had previously been objectively established."[27] Westerners are like that.

As the spiritual corrosion and moral confusion proliferated, there were ripplings of disquiet in Athens. The statesman Pericles was fully aware of the Sophists and what they were doing. At the same time as he seemed to enjoy their company and encouraged them in their endeavours, he also desired boundaries.[28] He warned against the dangers of "excessive intellectualism."[29] And he also spoke feelingly of the importance of Athenian customs and traditions, reminding citizens of the importance of upholding "those unwritten laws which it is an acknowledged shame to break."[30]

The Comedians Fight the Philosophers

It was not just statesmen and philosophers who quickly grew alarmed at what the Sophists were doing. In Athens, even the comedians waded into philosophical debates. Aristophanes was one of the great comic playwrights of his day and he wrote his play *The Clouds* as a direct challenge to destructive Sophistry.

The play could *easily* be situated in the twenty-first century. The playwright was deeply troubled by what he saw happening in Athens as the Sophists quietly and with words and ideas corroded and destroyed traditional Athenian values. And so *The Clouds* is an expression of Aristophanes' anger, of his "passionate hatred [of] the increasing sham-wisdom which went hand in hand with a degenerating democracy."[31] Whereas Socrates and later Plato used philosophy to fight the Sophists, Aristophanes instead deployed his brilliant satirical skills.

The play centres around Strepsiades, a man who owes money for debts incurred by his son who spends too much on horses and chariots. "Already because of you" the father muses to his sleeping son at the outset of the play, "I've been dragged into court more than once and ordered to pay up or else. Now some of them [his creditors] are even threatening to have my goods seized if I don't." But the father knows his son doesn't care: "Do you think" the father asks aloud of his sleeping son, "he's going to wake up before its day? Not he; he's still farting merrily away wrapped up in his five blankets." The young lad was also apparently growing his hair long.

So, the frisky but simple-minded father enrols himself at a place called "the Thinkery" where "if you pay them well, they can teach you how to win your case, whether you're in the right or not."[32] Strepsiades' goal is to be taught The Wrong Argument and thus get out of paying his creditors even though he knows he owes them money. Ultimately, Strepsiades proves to be too hilariously slow-witted and dull to learn the new thought and so he sends his son to learn in his place.[33]

The son is secluded in "the Thinkery" for a time and at the end of his learning he emerges full of the new thought which the Sophists taught him about Nature and Convention and he promptly goes home and starts beating his father. His reasoning went like this: since the father had beaten the son for his own good whilst he was growing up, the son naturally enough felt that he should beat his father for *his* own good. The horrified father pleads to his son, "Look at the laws! Can you name a city where the laws allow you to do this to your father?" To which the son replies with perfect Sophist-SocProg insouciance: "But what is a law anyway? It must have been made at some time and made by a man just like you or me." And since laws are arbitrary and thus shams, the son quite sensibly reasons: "why shouldn't I make a new law allowing sons to beat their fathers in return?"[34] The father tries to remonstrate with his son who replies that his father had better watch his words otherwise "Mom's next on the list for a bashing." The play ends pleasingly, with the father burning down "the Thinkery," saying: "[it was] no more than they deserved; people who cock snooks at the Gods and argue about the back side of the moon must pay for it." Indeed.

To this point in *The Clouds* we see Aristophanes pushing back against several key elements of Sophistry and which are readily apparent in the sociological consciousness. There is the radical relativizing of thought; a rejection of convention and traditional customs; a defiance of established law; the dismissal as unimportant the plainly intelligible yet rationally inexplicable hierarchy of families; and an embrace of the idea that laws and customs do not reflect timeless and universal ideals but instead are merely arbitrary, man-made creations, false and illusory and hence shams and so subject to personal discretion. The time and the context of the play are different but the intellectual substance, animating spirit, and philosophical content are precisely the same as the problems the West is confronting today.

It was not just the Sophists' attack on law and custom that enraged Aristophanes, but also their attack on the very morality of Athenian society as well. In *The Clouds*, Aristophanes has a character named Wrong (he represents specious argument) argue against simple modesty and decency. Wrong says of those Virtues: "Another curse of our time! Come on, prove me wrong; tell me of anything good that your modesty or decency has ever done."[35] Wrong even takes a swipe at Virtue itself by listing all the pleasures a man will forfeit if he embraces a good and disciplined life lived in accordance with traditional values. Wrong argues: "Listen to all the things that Virtue can't do for you my lad...No boys. No women. No gambling. No fancy stuff to eat. No booze. No belly laughs."[36] Wrong argues against the character of Right (who, sadly, turns out to be a bit of a pervert), and claims that his way is better because "you can do what you like and get away with it—indulge your desires, laugh and play, and have no shame."[37]

Wrong here is attacking what the Greeks called *sophrosyne*, a "value word" that means moderation and self-discipline.[38] We might use the related word propriety. Propriety: "*The character or quality of being proper; especially, in accordance with recognized usage, customs or principles.*" But for Wrong and the Sophists (and the sociologists), being "proper" is an empty, meaningless proposition because it is merely a Convention that gets in the way of satisfying individual wants and desires, or Nature. And what is worse, propriety is rooted in "recognized usage and custom" which is, by definition, arbitrary and so in some fundamental way, false. A law, especially one concerning notions of propriety is, for Wrong, simply a law "made at some time and made by a man just like you or me" and so he rejects it. It is clearly not hard to understand how the Sophists in Athens came to be seen as frivolous and immoral.[39]

Aristophanes never would have guessed it, but SocProg historians would take the substance of Wrong's argument—or at least his cavalier beliefs and attitudes about right and wrong—and use it in a defence of the gross and sensual over-indulgences of the Hippies of the 1960s (we will examine that article in detail in Chapter Five). And while we're here, it is worth mentioning too that Wrong perfectly prefigures the attitude that characterized the Hippies. Wrong said: "do what you like and get away with it—indulge your desires, laugh and play, and have no shame." And so the Hippies did. And they didn't.

Aristophanes' play is not just brilliant satire but it is also and more importantly an incredibly valuable document from a society struggling with the very same corrosive intellectual and spiritual problems with which the West is struggling today. Every single theme of the play—moral and intellectual relativism, the tensions between nature and convention, traditionalism against progressivism, the old education versus the new, the unrequited longing for the "good old days"—is immediately relevant to us right now because we today are dealing with precisely those very problems. Indeed, we even share Aristophanes' ironic fatalism. For as much as he hated the new sham wisdom and the Sophistic politicians who had "trampled without conscience upon everything which had come down from the past," Aristophanes was clever enough to know that a return to the old ways was impossible.[40] Aristophanes fully realizes that he too is a product of his own age and from which he cannot escape.[41]

It may not have been the Sophists' intention to "let loose unprincipled monsters on Greek society."[42] But yet that seems to have been precisely what they did. Historian H.D. Rankin suggests that the Sophists achieved this degeneration by "undermining value words." Traditional Athenian values of probity, courage, decency, and virtue, along with loyalty, duty, and obligation to the *polis*, came to be seen as merely arbitrary and customary social constructions and so subject to personal whim and discretion. And this is how it came to be that Athens "lost her spiritual foothold." The Sophists arrived and proceeded to "talk all the traditional values out of existence."[43] Sound familiar?

The really maddening thing was that the Sophists carefully avoided taking responsibility for what they were doing. A Sophist immortalized by Plato seems to have argued that what he was doing was actually "value free." Gorgias suggested that he taught no set doctrine, but rather he merely taught people how to argue and as such ought not be responsible for the effects of what he was doing. [44] He argued that one can teach a young man to wrestle but if that wrestler then goes home and strikes his father, the teacher certainly cannot be held to blame; one can teach a young man the arts of combat, but if he then goes and strikes his friends, the teacher cannot be held accountable for that either. And so he concludes: "it is not the teachers that are bad, nor does this mean the art is responsible or bad but rather I think those who use it incorrectly."[45] The sociologist Peter Berger would argue precisely the same point about the subject he taught in 1963.[46]

Socrates

Naturally, there had to be a more robust challenge to the Sophists, something other than just brilliant and hilarious comedies. This is roughly the point at which Socrates enters the picture. Socrates laid the foundation for Western philosophic thought, a foundation built upon and added to by his most famous student Plato (that foundation was of course challenged by Plato's most famous student, Aristotle, a philosopher who in later life would tutor Alexander the Great). Socrates was born around 470 BC, the son of a stonemason and he himself picked up his father's trade.[47] He came of age during that time when Sophistry was wrecking the Athens that he loved and to which he remained devoted all his life. He saw the traditional Athenian morality was changing. No one was beating their fathers or mothers yet but that did seem like a very real possibility. He saw it as his divinely ordained mission to arrest that slide into moral and intellectual anarchy. The Spanish historian of philosophy, Julian Marias, describes the Socratic mission this way: "to re-establish the meaning of truth in Greek thinking."[48]

Socrates was, on the face of it, a highly unlikely candidate to undertake such a task. He was chubby if not fat, his eyes were not pleasing and well set but rather "bulged," and he evidently walked with "a rolling gait not unlike that of a pelican."[49] He was a living, breathing violation of all those transcendent Greek ideals concerning beauty, proportion, and symmetry. He was "a squat, ugly, barefoot man who did not bathe too often."[50] So no, he was not a ladies' man but the picture we do have of him suggests a man with a love for life and a "humorous toleration for human weakness."[51] Humans can be weak. It is a part of our nature. Socrates accepted this and revelled in it. As a general rule, SocProgs do not accept this idea that humans have intrinsic natures which certainly helps to explain their lack of toleration for it, in addition to their lack of humour about it.

Now, Socrates understood that not all of the ideas of the Sophists were bad. The German philosopher Albert Schwegler observed that the truth of Sophistry lay in its embrace of "the freedom of subjective conviction" or the idea that everything we believe must first be shown to be rational before our own subjective consciousness.[52] We might call it intellectual individualism or a way of thinking in which we are free to adopt a belief or an idea but only after rigorous thought and careful consideration. The problem, though, was that very many people were (are) disinclined to deploy that kind of intellectual rigour to their thought and so what we are left with, then, is not thought at all but rather the "accidental will and opinion" of the individual. And it was this kind of "accidental thought" with which Socrates had a problem.

For Socrates, it was not a matter of "*my* thinking" but rather "my *thinking*" that decides matters of truth and good and right and wrong.[53] Thought is everything, not the individual who has the thoughts. As Schwegler explains, what is true, right, or good does not depend on accidental and unthinking opinion but rather on our *rational* faculties. Active thought and reflection were everything. And so the mission of Socrates was to encourage men to think and to know themselves, and so here we arrive at the core of Socratic philosophy where the idea of virtue resides.[54]

The word "virtue" in the Socratic sense is being used as a kind of substitute for the word "essence." And this virtue or essence, broadly defined, seeks after ultimate purposes. And for Socrates the virtue or essence of being human was knowledge. And it was our purpose in this life not to change the world to make it accord with our desires but rather to gain this particular self-knowledge which would then lead us to a better understanding of our own virtue, our own essence or, in a word, our purpose, our excellence. We have all heard the Greek/ Socratic injunction to "Know Yourself." And that is what it means, as summed up here by Julian Marias: "it is a moral imperative, whereby man may gain possession of himself and be his own master, through knowledge."[55] It is a deeply aspirational philosophical ideal, and a profoundly moving and human one, too.

This injunction to begin one's quest for knowledge in knowledge of the self may sound similar to Sophistic solipsism, but similar does not mean same. Socratic self-knowledge differs from solipsism in one fundamental way: solipsism is a closed loop. Solipsism gives up before it even gets going. Protagoras argued there is nothing outside of the self and so his variant of self-knowledge, then, stops there *in* the self; it is not looking for anything because apparently there is nothing to look for. But for Socrates, knowledge of self was the first step toward a Universal Wisdom. Protagoras sought to see, and he sought to see through, but he did not seek to see through *to* something as Socrates did. And there is a big difference between seeing, seeing through, and seeing through to. Indeed, Sophistry as a way of seeing and understanding—with its counsel of relativity, the refusal of objectivity, and the rejection of truth—is, in the end, "*incapable* of being anything more than opinion."[56] But with Socratic knowledge, there are loftier goals. As the American philosopher Robert Cushman later phrased it, we can get to reality, to the real and the true, *only* through an understanding of who we are as human beings.[57]

This, then, was the mission of Socrates and later his student Plato. Both men desired to find through thought and reflection those realities of our world that were *not* subject to caprice, fancy, or whim; that were not susceptible to perversion, corrosion, or "abolishment" by men like the Sophists.[58] Whereas Plato undertook this project in a series of heart-achingly beautiful philosophic prose dialogues, Socrates went straight to the *agora*, the marketplace, and talked to people, questioning, probing. Socrates wanted to drill down to the truth and the biggest part of that process involved questioning. If an Athenian claimed to believe in Justice, for example, Socrates would ask him what he meant by that. The Athenian would reply that Justice meant doing no harm. Socrates would then ask him to define harm and on and on it would go. The person would stutter or stammer or otherwise be at loss to explain what Justice was or what

Harm was, and thus the "abysmal ignorance" of the person being subjected to what we today call the Socratic Method would be "gradually, painfully, inexorably" exposed to public view."[59]

His goal was not to humiliate (although the Platonic dialogues suggest he probably did enjoy that and, given the end he met, perhaps too much[60]), but to burrow down into truth, to the eternal and the changeless. It was his followers who, lacking his mental acuity and high moral purpose, turned the Socratic Method into a byword for smart-assery and back-talk.[61] And that is the likely reason behind Aristophanes' decision to have Socrates act as the principal Sophist in his play *The Clouds*, when in fact Socrates was not a Sophist at all. Where the Sophists pursued the infinitely roomier path of simply negating and cancelling the truth, Socrates sought to find it. Both he and Plato questioned and probed to find the core, or the essence of what it meant to be a just man, a courageous man, a moral man, a virtuous man; in other words, what was good and right, true and just.[62]

Neither Socrates nor Plato doubted the existence of these transcendent elements because we daily see evidences of them in the particular. Indeed, it seems to follow from their very existence that there is "trans-phenomenal reality," a larger order to this world of ours. Consider: why is it that self-righteousness *always* boomerangs back on its subject? Why is it that Pride always results in disaster? Why is it that imbalances are always set back to balance? And why is it that we can so clearly discern disharmony in music but not in thought? Why, when that wrong note is struck on a piano, can we know with one-hundred-percent certitude and in our very being that it is wrong; that the struck note is out of place and does not belong there? But yet, when a wrong moral note is struck or a wrong intellectual note sounded we have great difficulty admitting it?[63] Perhaps it is because finding that trans-phenomenal reality, locating it, understanding it, knowing it, basing our conduct around it, was (is) not an easy thing to do. And so we swap out philosophy with ideology. At least there are clear answers in ideologies; certainly removes the difficulty of looking for the truth. Too, it offers us the comfort of being right which is always satisfying.

For Socrates and Plato, though, our traditional modes of apprehension, our senses, are tools that are simply not powerful enough to perceive this realm of the True or the Good. Sense perceptions can deceive. And so for Plato, learning to see with the eye of the *soul* is the way to truth. Plato suggests that the Good will be found only by the man who "pursues the truth by applying his pure and unadulterated thought to the pure and unadulterated object cutting himself off as much as possible from his eyes and ears and virtually all the rest of his body as an impediment which, if present, prevents the soul from attaining to the truth and clear thinking."[64] This method, he says, is for "real lovers of learning," for those who wish to gain knowledge and thus understanding and wisdom and it is an approach precisely the opposite of that counselled by the Sophists (and the sociologists).

The problem with the Platonic-Socratic approach to understanding is that it is difficult. It demands rigorous self-discipline, painful honesty, active thought, and persistent reflection and thus it is a way to knowledge and understanding which moves against the natural inclinations of human nature. Human nature is like water. It will usually—or if not usually then quite commonly—seek out the path of least resistance or the path that requires least effort. And this is especially true where matters of intellectual or philosophical truths are concerned because the very pursuit of those things must be animated by an "act of self-compulsion," a deliberate harnessing of the energies of the mind toward the attainment of an intellectual or philosophical goal.[65] And one is reasonably comfortable in arguing the point that most people then and today are singularly uninterested in intellectual or philosophical self-compulsion. The truth of this can be seen everywhere. We are seeing the depopulation of history and philosophy programs right across the Western world as young minds migrate to the social sciences, especially sociology.[66] For it is easier there. The climate is warmer, the rigours less, the demands pleasing and simple. All that sociology asks of its students is that they submit to what it has to offer. And, once having surrendered themselves, students can then become expert in the flaccid and impotent art of seeing through the sham of things, and unmasking and debunking things, just like the Sophists did.

Too, our culture places great emphasis on politics and ideology, not philosophy. But politics is not philosophy. Politics is colour-by-numbers thought which, in most if not all instances, does not even require thought; it, like sociology, only requires conviction or submission. Philosophy though, begins in thought; it begins in self-knowledge and aims at self-mastery, discipline, and wisdom.[67] It takes a lifetime to develop what we might call a "philosopher's soul," but once on that path—a path along which Plato counsels us to follow reason and "abide always in her company"—reason will "bring calm to the seas of desire" and wisdom to those who seek it.[68] The Socratic-Platonic way holds out the promise of truth or, as Robert Cushman put it, philosophy "rightly disposes" men and women to the realization of truth.

The really interesting thing is that neither Plato nor Socrates ever said they found these truths. It has been said of Plato that he is the least dogmatic of Western philosophers. And it has been said of Socrates (and we might also add Plato here) that he was "a servant of the truth, not an oracle of it."[69] Indeed, Socrates' only claim to fame was that his wisdom consisted in fully realizing how little he actually knew, a modest and charming humility that stands in marked contrast to the *monstrous* arrogance of Karl Marx who not only claimed to have discovered the "scientific" laws which govern our world, he called on people to change the world to reflect his own understanding of it. And what's even worse is that they tried to.[70] And sociology is still trying to.

Plato has been carelessly and thoughtlessly lumped in with Marx as an example of Western utopianism. But Platonic utopianism is not the same as the Marxist variant. The perfect city Plato envisioned in *The Republic* was *an* answer; *The Communist Manifesto*, by contrast, was *the* answer. Full stop. After Marx, the science was settled. As historian Paul Johnson observed: "[Marx] was not interested in finding the truth but in proclaiming it."[71] And that terrible and booming proclamation echoes throughout our world today. Governments form policy based on sociological untruths.[72]

Still more, Plato was not concerned with creating the ideal or perfect city not as such. He wanted to construct a model of the "right social order in the image of a well-ordered soul."[73] He felt that a soul operating in harmony with itself would create a climate out of which better politics would then follow.[74] But as for his hopes as to the full and perfect realization of such a city? No. He poignantly committed only to this: "Perhaps there is a pattern set up in the heavens for one who desires to see it and, seeing it, to found one in himself."[75] Imagine the better world that could come out of that.[76]

By the way, even though Plato wrote next to nothing about history and certainly never went to a university for a PhD in it, he still somehow managed to develop a better understanding of it than Marx who spent his entire life studying it. Plato clearly recognized that all political and social orders created by human hands are subject to inevitable decay.[77] We humans can create nothing permanent and that includes democracy. Marx, though, thought the opposite, believing that once he had renovated and redeemed society, there it would stay, perfect, forever. And that is just ridiculous. Ridiculous: "*absurdly comical; unworthy of consideration.*"

Perhaps, then, in some kind of larger cosmic sense we should be thankful for the Sophists for their appearance led directly on to the philosophy of Socrates and Plato. Socrates has been called the "embodiment and the first example of the new form of moral and intellectual individualism."[78] He sought with the aim of discovering, not destroying, and so his project was positive, not negative. He did not wreck the customs and traditions of Athens. He accepted the Athenian order as he found it.[79] He was a citizen soldier who, when asked to fight in its wars, did. He revered Athenian law; he lived by it, revelled in it, and submitted himself to it even after he had been sentenced to death by it.[80] But for all of his evident virtue, though, and despite his mission, Socrates was simply not enough to save Athens from herself.

Athens: a cautionary tale

The great spiritual and political leader of Athens, Pericles, had once told his fellow citizens that their city was "an education to Greece."[81] Each citizen, he proclaimed was "the rightful owner and lord of his own person," and with a feeling for posterity Pericles claimed that "future ages will wonder at us as the present wonders at us now."[82] He was right. But by the fourth century, the wonder was gone because the bracing and "white-hot" spiritual energy was gone.[83] The wonderful public spiritedness which characterized Athens in the fifth century disappears in the fourth. Wrong's admonition to live according to the dictates of personal liberty was apparently fulfilled as Athenians "only sought enjoyment" and all those traditional and religious ties that had previously bound men to the state were, as Jacob Burckhardt explains, relaxed if not non-existent.[84] The Athenians had come to see the will of the people, not tradition or religion, as the source of all custom and law.[85] Robert Cushman observes that Athenians had, over time, developed a mentality in which "private satisfactions" were the goal of life. But that begs the question: what sort of laws and customs will issue forth from a culture in which private satisfactions, solipsism, and *AloneSelf* are the gold standards of conduct?

We cannot attribute the wrecking of Athens solely to the Sophists but their efforts certainly did not help. Those "new sages" as Moses Finley called them, turned over and wrecked as many accepted beliefs and values as they could find, especially where religion and morals were concerned.[86] And we would do well to remember that the destruction of moral and ethical codes does not occur without cost and without consequence. The philosopher Isaiah Berlin observed that philosophical concepts, "nurtured in the stillness of a professor's study" can in fact destroy civilizations.[87] There is a bill to pay for all things. Athens paid that bill in the fourth century with the erosion of public spirit, the withering of community, and the decay and degeneration of democracy leading to their ultimate conquest and subjugation. It seems that even the sons of Socrates "were apparently stupid."[88]

Some of the more sensible Sophists were actually frightened by the consequences of their own project. Protagoras especially was apparently quite anxious about the moral, spiritual, and intellectual destruction he and his fellow Sophists had wrought. And so, in the end he came to counsel a kind of pragmatic "philosophy of self-interest" which held that the people of the community should still live by those arbitrarily constructed social and moral codes because it was expedient to do so.[89] Expedient because without standards, morals, traditions, and conventions, there are no bones left to hold up society; it becomes formless, shapeless, spiritless; a blob, merely. Albert Schwegler, with his hi to Hegel, describes the effects of Sophistry this way:

> "The subject viewed himself as superior to the objective world, especially as higher than the laws of state, customs, religious traditions and popular creeds. He sought to apply his own laws to the objective world; and instead of seeing in the given objectivity the historical realization of reason, *he recognized in it only a dead, unspiritual matter upon which his arbitrary will might be exercised.*"[90]

And let's be honest with ourselves: can anything good ever really come out of that?

The Greeks in the fourth century had become trapped in subjectivity. The Canadian born philosopher-historian Will Durant called it "a disintegrating individualism."[91] Edith Hamilton picks up on this theme. With an eye on the past but her mind firmly on her particular present, she wrote in her fantastic book, *The Greek Way*, that "everywhere we are distracted by the claim of the single man against the common welfare."[92] And she adds that "it is not that we perceive too clearly the rights and wrongs of every human being but that we feel too deeply our own, *only to find in the end that what has meaning only for each one alone, has no real meaning at all.*"[93] Once we jettison, debunk, and unmask our shared values, beliefs, and faiths in the larger community and once the subjective will becomes its own standard, and once *AloneSelf* becomes the aspirational ideal of a culture, we are then left living in a world without meaning. And so it should come as no surprise, then, that in a world without meaning, we see the appearance of the Cynics.

Endnotes

[1] HDF Kitto, *The Greeks* (London: Penguin, 1991), p. 7. I was introduced to the Greeks by this man and his love for them showed through on every page. I experienced precisely the same thrills and joys as Kitto. And there are many others who have also had the same experience. I taught students who likewise found real and meaningful nourishment in the Greeks. A couple of exceptional ones who spring to mind are D. Veenstra and A. Delorme the latter of whose writing has, I see, become super-charged and muscular as it always wanted to be, so, well done. It is also important to note here that there is real historic meaning in these experiences. After all, why is it that, even after 2,500 years, we are *still* so deeply and profoundly moved by the Greeks?

[2] Thomas R. Martin, *Ancient Greece: from prehistoric to Hellenistic times* (New Haven: Yale University Press, 2000), p. 88.

[3] Martin, *The Ancient Greeks*, p. 88.

[4] Kitto, *The Greeks*, pp. 73-74.

[5] Thucydides, *The History of the Peloponnesian War* translated by Rex Warner (London: Penguin, 1972), p. 145. In an early rejection of the idea that poverty is a "systemic" problem, rather than a manifestation of a personal flaw or failing, a still-understanding Pericles observed of poverty: "No one need be ashamed to admit it; the real shame is in not taking practical measures to escape from it." Really, if you only ever read one thing from Thucydides, read Pericles' Funeral Oration. It is moving, profound, and inspiring.

[6] Thucydides, *The History*, p. 147. Some translations have Pericles saying, "We say that such a man is useless."

[7] Historian Matthew Christ deserves a medal for being able to develop his excellent explication of this theme out of scanty texts. See *The Bad Citizen in Classical Athens* (London: Cambridge, 2008).

[8] John Wilson Taylor, "The Athenian Ephebic Oath," *The Classical Journal*, vol. 13, no. 7, April 1918, pp. 495-501.

[9] Harry G. Frankfurt, *On Bullshit* (Princeton: Princeton University Press, 2004), p. 54.

[10] Jacob Burckhardt, *The Greeks and Greek Civilization* (New York: St Martin's Press, 1998), p. 239.

[11] H.D. Rankin, *Sophists, Socratics, and Cynics* (London: Croom Helm, 1983), p. 20.

[12] Albert Schwegler, *A History of Philosophy in Epitome* translated by Julius H Seelye (New York: D. Appleton and Company, 1880), p. 52.

[13] Schwegler, *A History*, p. 53.

[14] Schwegler, *A History*, p. 58.

[15] Burckhardt, *The Greeks*, p. 265, see also Dillon, *The Greek Sophists*, p. xvi.

[16] Martin, *Ancient Greece*, pp. 143-144

[17] Dillon, *The Greek Sophists*, p. 18. I recall reading in a first-year philosophy textbook that beaches do not exist, which is in fact true (if you're a Sophist). One grain of sand does not make a beach. Neither do two or three grains of sand, nor one hundred for that matter. Therefore, beaches do not exist. While the textbook did not say so, the exercise, I learned in reflection many years later (for the problem it outlined never left my mind), demonstrated the crucial value of Arbitrary Distinction: that a line, finally, *must* be drawn somewhere.

[18] Plato, *Protagoras and Meno* translated by W.K.C. Guthrie (London: Penguin, 1956), pp. 67-68.

[19] Robert E. Cushman, *Therapeia: Plato's Conception of Philosophy* (Chapel Hill NC: University of North Carolina Press, 1958), p. 40.

[20] Julian Marias, *History of Philosophy* translated by Stanley Applebaum and Clarence C. Strowbridge (New York: Dover, 1967), p. 36.

[21] Marias, *History*, p. 37.

[22] John Dillon and Tania Gergel eds., *The Greek Sophists* (London: Penguin, 2003), pp. xv-xvi.

[23] Dillon, *The Greek Sophists*, p. xvii.

[24] Werner Jaeger, *Paideia: the ideals of Greek Culture,* vol 1 translated by Gilbert Highet (New York: Oxford University Press, 1945), p. 374.

[25] I thank my mother Carol McManus for this phrase.

[26] Plato, *Protagoras and Meno*, p. 146.

[27] Schwegler, *A History*, p. 52.

[28] Bertrand Russell, *History of Western Philosophy* (London: Routledge, 1996), p. 85.

[29] Jaeger *Paideia, vol. 2*, p. 137. Pericles here was likely channelling the sentiments of the more conservative elements of Athenian society who wanted to restrict that "excessive intellectualism." A man known only as the Old Oligarch is perhaps the most well-known exponent of Athenian conservatism. No one knows who the Old Oligarch was—only that he left behind for posterity a highly reasoned and very well organized tract in which he rails against democracy and liberty. The Oligarch felt that one of the flaws of democracy was this: "The Athenian people forbid anyone to satirize them." That may be still another intrinsic quirk of democracy because, really, when was the last time you saw a movie or a television show in which the buffoonish character was a working-class man and the noble character was "rich and pedigreed"? See "The Constitution of Athens" by the Old Oligarch, translated by Paul MacKendrick, in *Classics in Translation* vol. 1, pp. 224-228.

[30] Thucydides, *History of the Peloponnesian War* translated by Rex Warner (London: Penguin, 1972), p. 145.

[31] Schwegler, *A History*, p. 66.

[32] Aristophanes, *The Clouds* translated by Alan Sommerstein (London: Penguin,, 1973), p. 116.

[33] Just prior to the father's expulsion, Socrates sends the father to bed so that he can think and in thinking generate an idea of how he might be able to get out of the mess he's in. It didn't work out exactly as planned. Socrates appears later and asks "have you got anything yet?" to which the father, laying underneath the sheets which are revealing an enormous bulge in the region of his crotch, says "no." Socrates, exasperated, asks if he is serious, to which the father replies, "Well, I've got my prick in my hand if that's what you—no, I suppose you don't." See *The Clouds*, pp. 142-143.

[34] Aristophanes, *The Clouds*, p. 170. Frighteningly, this is a reasonable question. Really, why *shouldn't* one beat one's father, if not for the biblical injunction to honour one's parents.

[35] Aristophanes, *The Clouds*, p. 155.

[36] Wrong there mentions "No boys" which reveals a dynamic of Greek culture that was enthusiastically homo-erotic, at least amongst the upper classes. Male love was a central part of Greek culture. See Thomas Cahill, *Sailing the Wine Dark sea: why the Greeks matter (New York: Nan Talese, 2004)*, pp. 168-170. For an extended discussion on the theme, please see Plato's *Symposium*. For an intriguing examination on men who love other men but who don't wish to engage the Gay Lifestyle with its inherent political

themes and wretched cultural dross, please see the interesting work by Jack Malebranche, *Androphillia, a Manifesto: rejecting the gay identity, reclaiming masculinity* (Dissonant Hum Press, 2012).

[37] Aristophanes, *The Clouds*, p. 156. The Cynics made a "cult" of that very thing: "shamelessness."

[38] Marvin Perry et al, *Western Civilization: ideas, politics, and society* (Boston: Houghton Mifflin Co., 1996), p. 78. The *Online Etymology Dictionary* defines *sophrosyne* as "prudence, moderation in desires, discretion [and] temperance." *Sophrosyne* is pronounced suh-*fross*-ah-knee.

[39] Russell, *History*, p. 84.

[40] Schwegler, *A History*, p. 67.

[41] Schwegler, *A History*, p. 67. We see evidence of this in Aristophanes' portrayal of the character Right, a pervert and apparent pederast who, having been defeated by Wrong, gives himself over to a life of Sophistic debauchery which he begins by "accidentally-on-purpose" falling into the arms of a man in the audience. Too, there is also the old saying: "A man will resemble his own age more than he will ever resemble his own father."

[42] Rankin, *Sophists*, p. 14.

[43] Jaeger, *Paideia,* vol 2, p. 28.

[44] Dillon, *The Greek Sophists*, pp. 55 and 61.

[45] Dillon and Gergel, *The Greek Sophists*, p. 6. That quote comes from Plato's dialogue *Gorgias* but both Dillon and Gergel agree that the observation is a fair and fairly wrought estimation of Gorgias' own views on the matter. Plato, it seems, was quite fair in his dealings with the Sophists, taking pains to accurately represent their thought which again underscores the rigorous intellectuality that underpinned much of the Athenian experiment.

[46] Berger, *Invitation*, p. 174. The idea reads: "It is one thing to dispense the sociological poison to...graduate students" but quite another to dispense this poison to those who have no chance "to proceed to a deeper understanding." In other words, no problems would occur if the subject was studied correctly.

[47] Cahill, *Sailing*, p. 158.

[48] Marias, *History*, p. 38.

[49] Rankin, *Sophists*, p. 147.

[50] Cahill, *Sailing*, p. 158.

[51] MacCunn, "The Cynics," p. 189.

[52] Schwegler, *A History*, p. 61.

[53] Schwegler, *A History*, p. 61.

[54] Marias, *History*, p. 41.

[55] Marias *History*, p. 41. See also Hallowell, "Plato and his Critics," pp. 285-286. Hallowell writes that Socrates would try and lead men toward this understanding but then leave the final choice up to those individual men as to "whether they will continue to live in perpetual disagreement with themselves or live in self-accord."

[56] Marias, *History*, p. 40. Italics added.

[57] Cushman, *Therapeia*, pp. 242-243.

[58] "Selections from Plato", translated by William C. Greene, in *Classics in Translation volume one: Greek Literature*, edited by Paul MacKendrick and Herbert Howe (Madison: University of Wisconsin Press, 1952), 316.

[59] Cahill, *Sailing*, p. 159.

[60] The closing lines of the dialogue "Euthyphro" clearly show how exasperating Socrates could be, and the glee he took in running ragged his interlocutors to the point where they would just want to get away. See *The Last Days of Socrates* translated by Hugh Tredennick and Harold Tarrant (London: Penguin, 1993), pp. 25-27.

[61] Cahill, *Sailing*, p. 159.

[62] John Hallowell, "Plato and His Critics," *Journal of Politics*, vol. 27, no. 2, May 1965, p. 282.

[63] I would like to hail former student R. Falcon ("*Fal*con!"). One day she and I were engaged in a Socratic back-and-forth about what it means to be a good person. In pursuing her line of thought, she mentioned playing a piano and instantly the idea there described was dislodged and kicked loose. "The Socratic Method: it just works."

[64] Plato, *The Last Days*, p. 119. For an excellent demonstration of this approach to inquiry, please see the disquisition on Love and Beauty in Plato's *The Symposium* translated by Walter Hamilton (London: Penguin, 1951), especially pages 92-95.

[65] The words there come from philosopher Michael Polanyi as cited in Hallowell's "Plato and His Critics," p. 287.

[66] Harvard University no less reports that enrollments in the humanities between 1966 and 2010 has fallen from 14% of all degrees taken, to just 7%. See "Addressing a Decline in Humanities Enrollment," in *Harvard Magazine*, June 6, 2013. As well, of the number of students who declare their intention to study in the humanities (history, philosophy, literature, art, languages) at the outset of their degrees, fully 50% end up in a social science. The very same thing was true when I taught history. Students who, in my classes logged Ds and Fs could simply cross the hall, enroll in a sociology course, and there soar to great intellectual heights because the only thing necessary for intellectual excellence was submission.

[67] We see Socrates at his most hilariously disciplined in Plato's *Symposium* where he resists all entreaties to sensuality offered by Alcibiades, a character perfectly wanting in discipline. For Plato/Socrates, the physical life with its physical delights was a poor substitute for thought, reflection, and contemplation, because the soul desires and so seeks Wisdom—it is the body which seeks Pleasure.

[68] Plato, *The Last Days*, p. 143. The ancient Chinese philosopher Confucius put it this way: "At fifteen, I set my heart on learning. At thirty, I was firmly established. At forty, I had no more doubts. At fifty, I knew the will of heaven. At sixty, I was ready to listen to it. At seventy, I could follow my heart's desire without transgressing what was right." See *Sources of Chinese Tradition* vol. 1 edited by Wm. Theodore de Bary (New York: Columbia, 1960), p. 22.

[69] Cushman, *Therapeia*, p. 8.

[70] Both Socrates and Confucius arrived at roughly similar points on this matter of knowledge: "Confucius said: 'Shall I teach you what knowledge is? When you know a thing, say that you know it; when you do not know a thing, admit that you do not know it. That is knowledge." In *Sources*, de Bary, p. 24.

[71] Paul Johnson, *Intellectuals* (New York: Perennial, 1988), p. 54.

[72] The most egregious recent example is in Ontario, where it appears that Premier Kathleen Wynne ransacked a sociology textbook, repackaged it as a new Sex Ed Curriculum, and now young children are being

educated in sex by sociology. I must close my eyes for I do not wish to witness the damage that is being done to young minds.

[73] Hallowell, "Plato and his Critics," p. 282.

[74] Cushman, *Therapeia*, p. 30.

[75] Hallowell, Plato and His Critics," pp. 280-281.

[76] On this point too, Greek and Chinese philosophers were coming to roughly approximate conclusions about being human. The Confucian philosopher Mencius wrote in the fourth century BC: "A gentleman steeps himself in the Way because he wishes to find it in himself. When he finds it in himself he will be at ease in it; when he is at ease in it he can draw deeply upon it; when he can draw deeply upon it, he finds its source wherever he turns. That is why a Gentleman wishes to find the Way in himself." *Mencius* translated by D.C. Lau (London: Penguin, 1970), p. 130.

[77] R.G. Bury, "Plato and History," in *Classical Quarterly* vol.4, 1951, p. 88.

[78] Jaeger, *Paideia vol. 2*, p. 75.

[79] MacCunn, "The Cynics," p. 190.

[80] MacCunn,"The Cynics," p. 190.

[81] Thucydides, *History,* p. 147.

[82] Thucydides, *History* p. 148.

[83] The phrase "white-hot" energy comes from Edith Hamilton.

[84] Burckhardt, *The Greeks*, p. 282.

[85] Cushman, *Therapeia*, p. 34.

[86] Moses Finley, *The Ancient Greeks* (London: Penguin, 1963), p. 138.

[87] Isaiah Berlin, *Four Essays on Liberty* (London: Oxford University Press, 1969), p. 119. One cannot understand the twentieth century without understanding two writers: George Orwell and Isaiah Berlin. Titans, both.

[88] Burckhardt, *The Greeks*, p. 289-290.

[89] Thomas R. Martin, *Ancient Greece: from prehistoric to Hellenistic times* (New Haven: Yale University Press, 2000), p. 142. See also Bertrand Russell, *History of Philosophy*, (New York: Routledge, 1996), pp. 80-86.

[90] Schwegler *A History,* p. 52. Italics added.

[91] Will Durant, *The Story of Philosophy* (New York: Washington Square Press, 1966), p. 7.

[92] Hamilton, *The Greek Way*, p. 315.

[93] Hamilton, *The Greek Way*, pp. 315-316. Italics added.

CHAPTER THREE

THE CYNICS

"Away with all modesty and decency and moderation...do boldly in front of everyone things that no decent person would ever do, even in private and choose the most absurd ways to satisfy your lusts. Such is the happiness that we can promise you."

Diogenes the Cynic as portrayed in a comedy written by Greek
writer Lucian, cited in Diogenes the Cynic, p. 5

"With a more decided contempt for all knowledge, and a still greater scorn of all the customs of society, the later Cynicism became a repulsive and shameful caricature of the Socratic spirit."

German philosopher Albert Schwegler in A History of Philosophy in Epitome, p. 81.

"A man who knows the price of everything and the value of nothing."

Oscar Wilde's definition of a Cynic in The Oxford Dictionary of Quotations, p. 99.

"Our modern, virtually unqualified, enthusiasm for liberty forgets that liberty can only be 'the space between the walls,' the walls of morality and law based upon morality. It is sensible to argue about how far apart the walls should be set but it is cultural suicide to demand all space and no walls."

American jurist Robert Bork in Slouching Towards Gomorrah, p. 65.

If the Sophists provide us with a preview of much of what constitutes socio-logical thought today, the Cynics help us round out that picture and allow us to see more clearly not just the ideas but also the attitudes which animate the SocProgs. The Cynics like the Sophists both shared a disdain for custom, tradition, and any and all notions of settled or permanent values, of truth. But here the two groups may be said to part ways. Whereas a few of the Sophists actually grew concerned and backtracked a little over all their negations and destructions, the Cynics held no such reserve. The Cynics loudly and brazenly challenged and ultimately rejected any and all conventions, customs, and traditions they could get their hands on. They even went so far as to imagine a new world, a better world, a world in which there was no property, no custom, no tradition, no morality, and no religion; a world in which everyone was free to have sex with whomever one wished whenever one wanted. And of course the reader will note that these are precisely the themes and ideas that would form the basis for the "revolt" against "society" which would erupt 2,500 years later in the 1960s. Plato and Aristotle notwithstanding, historians of Greece cite the fourth century as a period of decline and decay. Indeed, Thomas Cahill refers to the "debased intellectual climate" of that time.[1] If it be true—it isn't, but let's go with it for right now—that we study history in order to learn from it, surely there are lessons to be learned here.

Diogenes and Socrates

Diogenes was a wrecker. Socrates was a seeker. And there is an enormous difference between one who wrecks and one who seeks. And so to begin here, we'll compare and contrast the philosophical project of each man to gain a better appreciation for, and understanding of, what has come to be called positive and negative Liberty. We have already seen how the thought of Socrates is immediately relevant and meaningful to us today, but so too, sadly, is the thought of Diogenes. Dioegenean thought, like Socratic thought, is not a dusty relic of the ancient world: it is "modern" thought, for it is not at all difficult to immediately identify the moral and spiritual distemper at play here in the philosophy of Diogenes.

Diogenes is generally credited with being if not the founder of the Cynic "school," then certainly the most recognizable and famous exponent of it. He was born in a community on the Black Sea and, according to tradition (for the story is murky), came to Greece after either Diogenes himself or his father "defaced the coinage" of his *polis*, a charge associated with counterfeiting. Diogenes arrived in Athens sometime in the fourth century, after the death of Socrates in 399 but right about the time when his most famous pupil, Plato, was developing his philosophy. The two of them frequently butted philosophical heads. The story has it that Diogenes once asked Plato for a few figs and Plato sent a bushel, an act of generosity to which Diogenes responded: "The same old story—ask him one thing and he'll reply with a thousand."[2] At any rate, Diogenes, disinclined to embrace the rigorous and difficult Platonic way of finding the Good, seems to have been more temperamentally suited to learn at the feet of the philosopher Antisthenes from whom he learned the much less demanding "art of mistrust" so characteristic of the Cynic way.

Antisthenes apparently did not like the young Diogenes very much. When the lad persisted in hanging around, Antisthenes—and this was in the days before student evaluations—apparently "beat him with his stick."[3] But Diogenes stayed on and, as he matured, his purpose in life gently swam into view. Diogenes wanted to deface the culture and values of the Athenians.[4] And it is thus that he comes to us across time: "criticizing conventional values, exposing shams, unimpressed by reputation of any kind."[5] Like the SocProgs, his project also revolved around negation and destruction.

Some modern historians, revealingly, have tried to legitimize Diogenes by placing him within the Socratic tradition.[6] And while one must regrettably admit that there are in fact many similarities—both men were fiercely independent thinkers, both were frank and open, both prized freedom of speech, both disregarded mass opinion, and went against the grain and substantially, both Diogenes and Socrates embraced a kind of personal austerity and an indifference to worldly honours and successes—there remain, however, fundamental differences that are too profound and fundamental to ignore and which reveal the essential *dis*similarities of the two.[7]

First, there is a sincerity lacking in Diogenes, a sincerity which, through Plato, we clearly divine in Socrates. Sincerity: *"free from hypocrisy."* The word comes to us from the Latin *sin* which means "without" and it combines with the word *caries* which means "rottenness." Thus sincerity means "without rottenness." Socrates was without rottenness. Diogenes was not. Socrates, for example, dressed and lived simply, and rejected the pleasures of this life so that he might better seek understanding and wisdom. For Socrates, the soul is the seat of reason and in order for the soul to be able to gain the wisdom it seeks it must be cut off from the daily pleasures and pains of life "[else] it loses its way and becomes confused and dizzy."[8] Learning to see with the eye of the soul requires and demands austerity and discipline.

Diogenes, though, took Socratic austerity and then exaggerated it. He set up his "home" in the streets of Athens in a "jar" or "tub" as it has been variously called. He begged in the streets, had only a well-worn toga and his only possession was a stick. And while Diogenes patterned his approach to philosophy on Socrates in that both men probed and questioned, the former used deliberately shocking language and tactics to challenge people, forcing his ideas on them in what has been called a "constant performance."[9] This is unSocratic.

And the ends at which Diogenes aimed were wildly different. Where Socrates sought truth, which is an essentially positive goal in that it is looking *for* something, Diogenes' aims were fundamentally negative, in that he "dismissed almost everything that people value and pursue" not only luxury and pleasure but also civic duty and responsibility.[10] And anyone can do that. Sociology does that.

So, since exaggeration is always deliberate (the word means "*to represent extravagantly; to overstate*" and it comes from the Latin *ex* meaning "out" and *agger* meaning "'heap" thus to "out-heap"), and always aware of itself, Diogenes is less a philosopher and more the original self-conscious, cynical, ironic Westerner. Cynicism, self-consciousness, and irony are, of course, three of the *essential* spiritual characteristics of the Western world in the twenty-first century. Plato once remarked of Diogenes: "How pleasing your simplicity would be if it was not a sham."[11] Funny. The man who claimed to be able to see through the sham of things was regarded by the founder of Western philosophy as a sham. And here, one muses as to what Plato might think of sociology.

Perhaps the biggest difference between the two, though, was their level of devotion to something larger than self. In Socrates, we see a man who upheld and was faithful and devoted to the legal, political, and social order of the Athenian state. He did not want to wreck it. The speech Socrates gives in defence of Athenian law after it had sentenced him to die is so moving precisely because of his touching and perhaps even tragic devotion to it.[12] In the brilliant dialogue, *Crito*, Athenian Law personified appears and addresses Socrates. And the speech of The Laws reveals why Socrates so valued it: "We have brought you into the world and reared you and educated you and given you and all your fellow citizens a share in all the good things at our disposal."[13] And the gratitude

Socrates feels for receiving those benefits, for living under Athenian law, is one of the reasons he refuses to escape jail. Escaping his imprisonment would be unjust because it would be an offence against The Laws and Socrates had lived his life according to the principle of being Just. And according to that principle, in no instance is injustice justified. While Socrates lived life according to a principle, the Cynics lived life according to an attitude and those are two very different things. A principle is "*a settled law or a rule of conduct.*" But an attitude is synonymous with a pose which is defined as "*a position studied for artistic effect or considered with references to such effect.*" Thus, Diogenes was not only the first cynical, ironic, self-conscious Westerner: he was also our first poser.

And by the way, very likely thinking of the Sophists and Cynics, Plato has The Laws suggest the following: "any Athenian who...seeing for himself the political organization of the State and us, its Laws, is permitted, if he is not satisfied with us, to take his property and go away." Diogenes did not go away. He stayed and undertook his mission: "a thoroughgoing onslaught on convention, custom, [and] tradition in all aspects."[14]

Ultimately, the difference between the two is largely one of attitude and spirit. Socrates tried to see *through to* the truth, to the eternal and the unchanging, whilst Diogenes sought merely to see *through* the sham of things.[15] Diogenes appears to have been sneer made manifest. Sneer: "*A brief satirical utterance that throws a contemptuous light on what it attacks without attempting to prove or disprove.*"[16] This is not philosophy; it is attitude, merely. And it is a sneering contempt which Diogenes and the Cynics have evidently bequeathed to later agents of social and political change in the West. Indeed, it was this very attitude of the Cynics that gave them their name.

The word "Cynic" is a Greek word which means "churlish, doglike." And even Greek writers at the time observed that there were many similarities— four to be precise—between Cynics and dogs. To wit: like dogs, the Cynics eat, make love in public, and go barefoot. Like dogs, they are shameless and indeed "they make a cult of shamelessness not as being beneath modesty but superior to it."[17] Dogs make good guards and the Cynics guard their philosophy. And dogs discriminate between friends and enemies, as do the Cynics, who receive their friends kindly "while those unfitted, they drive away like dogs by barking at them."[18] And of course on this last point we are reminded of certain former presidents of the Canadian Historical Association.

Liberty, Positive and Negative

The whole aim, point, and purpose in rejecting social conventions, refusing morality, and wrecking customs and traditions revolved, for the Cynics, around some kind of hazy and ill-defined notion of the sovereignty of the Individual and the pursuit of a greater Liberty rooted in some solipsistic sense of Justice. Customary beliefs, traditional forms of behaviour, and social expectations rooted in some sense of shared or community values—in a phrase, "bourgeois middle-class values"—are all restrictive in some way because they all require or demand of the individual a thought, belief, or an action that he or she would perhaps not otherwise think, believe, or do. Too, customs, conventions, and traditions are also often arbitrary. Arbitrary: "*Fixed, made, or done capriciously or at pleasure.*" Arbitrary by definition means that a thing is not true, not as such. And so if there is no *rational* reason for the prohibition against X then it follows that the prohibition itself must be illegitimate. This is what Diogenes was on about and it is referred to as negative liberty. And it is precisely this type of Liberty that animated Marx's worldview. His entire political vision was built on it.

The philosopher Isaiah Berlin explained the concept of negative liberty in an essay written, tellingly, in 1969. Negative liberty seeks the removal of restraints. This ideal, Berlin wrote, holds that "I am free to the degree to which no man or body of men interferes with my activity." And he further explained that "if I am prevented by others from doing what I could otherwise do, I am to that degree unfree."[19] This type of freedom is potentially troublesome. While the ideal is underwritten by an entirely rational definition of freedom as 'not being interfered with' it is an ideal being wielded by a fundamentally and essentially *ir*rational creature. Negative liberty operates on this principle: "the wider the area of non-interference, the wider my freedom." And since freedom is essentially good, more of it, then, should be better. And, when stretched to its logical and in most cases totally unavoidable endpoint, we get Cynics. We get Hippies.

Of course positive liberty is the corollary to its negative cousin and we have already been looking at that in quite some detail and for quite some time now. Both Socrates and Plato are excellent examples of what this ideal represents. Berlin defines positive liberty this way: "The wish on the part of the individual to be his own master." He elaborates: "I wish to be the instrument of my own, not of other men's, acts of will...I wish to be self-directed and not acted upon by external nature or by other men as if I were a thing."[20] Positive freedom is essentially Socratic-Platonic freedom because it suggests and assumes that "a man is divided against himself" and so the struggle for *real* freedom occurs there, inside, when what Berlin calls the "transcendent dominant controller"—Plato's "charioteer of the soul"—moves against those passions and desires that are to be "disciplined and brought to heel."[21]

Now these two conceptions of Liberty may appear similar in some ways, but if we burrow down here we see that each ideal revolves in a fundamental way around a totally different conception of what it means to be human in this world. Positive liberty seeks discipline in self-abnegation in the pursuit of that larger goal of independence whilst negative liberty relies on "total self-identification with a specific principle or ideal" in order to achieve the same ends as its positive counterpart.[22] Negative liberty, then, sees the problems of the world out there, external to man. But positive liberty sees the problems inside, internal to man. In so many words, positive liberty is the "freedom to," as opposed to its negative and adolescent counterpart which desires merely "freedom from." And there was much that the Cynics wanted freedom from.

The Cynics were critical of and thus sought to wreck, confuse, and undermine just about every idea or institution they could get their hands on: political institutions, property, the family, luxury, culture, democracy, patriotism, and especially religion ("a temple is no holier than any other place"[23]). All these institutions and ideas received the contempt of the Cynics because they restricted or impeded the thoughts and actions of the individual.[24] Even relationships with other people seemed to have been frowned upon for the Cynics are quoted as saying "when you worry about another, then you neglect yourself."[25] Charming, that.

Diogenes and the other Cynics buttressed their contempt for morality and social conventions by embracing Sophistic relativism of the type we saw in Aristophanes' play *The Clouds*. They argued that customary behaviours and traditional morality differ at different times and places and so they have no universal validity and in the absence of that universality it follows, then, that morality itself is not true, not as such.[26] The dangerous consequences of this idea were, of course, given full reign and expression in the 1960s. But to give you a sense or a flavour of how all these sophisticated ideas played out in the real Athenian world, we might consider a few examples here.

The Cynics were apparently offended by the prohibition against eating in the *agora*, the market place and the traditional space for discussion in Athens. So they courted the anger of citizens by flouting the convention and ate in the *agora* and, in doing so, achieved a completely unnecessary and utterly meaningless victory for Liberty.[27]

Temple sites were of deep religious significance for the Athenians. It was frequently the case that both public and private valuables were stored there and thus stealing from a temple bordered on sacrilege not only because such acts violated community laws concerning private property but also because they transgressed religious boundaries. But for the Cynics it was no big deal. Diogenes held that there was "nothing improper" in stealing from a temple because there was, really, nothing special, nothing sacred about them.[28] It was just an inanimate object to which we humans had affixed arbitrary and meaningless sanctity. Indeed, it seems to follow that sanctity itself must be simply a "social construct."

The Cynics were also observed masturbating, defecating, and urinating in public. Their argument was simple (and it also perfectly prefigures the logic of the Hippies): these acts are natural and therefore good and so it follows that it is the law against their practice in public that is unnatural, not the act in question. Diogenes marvelled at his own social precociousness exclaiming after publicly masturbating: "If only one could put an end to one's hunger by rubbing one's stomach!"[29] We didn't invent moral, intellectual, and spiritual confusion—the Greeks beat us to it by about 2,500 years.

At the same time as the Cynics were proudly denouncing morality by masturbating in public, they also contentedly busied themselves with the task of rejecting not just the laws of Athens but also the duties and responsibilities that came with citizenship there.[30] It should not surprise us that the Cynics were not good citizens and so we might pause with profit here to consider the word "anomie." Anomie is the word we give to the modern urban condition in which man feels separate, cut-off from his fellows, alone and isolated. The word itself is Greek and means "without law." And since the law was provided by the *polis*, the word "anomie" technically means a man without *polis*, without community. And as HDF Kitto reminds us, Aristotle had long argued that a man without *polis*, a man without community and thus without law and custom, is nothing, something less than a man.[31] And so it seems, then, that the Cynics favoured Nothing over Something. Or perhaps it might be more clearly stated this way: Nothing is what we gain when we pursue Liberty through the destruction of Morality, Tradition, Custom, and Convention.

At any rate, neither the state nor its laws and customs mattered to Diogenes. Their very creation and existence was arbitrary and so illegitimate.[32] Diogenes defiantly proclaimed, "I am not a citizen of any of your cities."[33] And he once famously asked, "Why should I be proud of belonging to the soil of Attica with the worms and the slugs?"[34] But since every human being needs to believe in and be connected to something larger than just self merely, the Cynics gave over their allegiance to some hazy concept about the "brotherhood of man" rather than directing that desire toward the *polis*. And in this way, the Cynics became the first cosmopolitans, the first sophisticated internationalists.[35]

Here is yet more appealing sameness between the Cynics, sociology, and Karl Marx. The latter we know emphasized not the local but the global; not the nation, but rather the international proletariat, the working men of the world. And of course this cosmopolitan attitude of the Cynics is likewise characteristic of the sociological worldview. The postmodern ideas that underpin SocProg scholarship have been called "a doctrine of the metropolis" which is to say they are urban and global, not local and parochial.[36] And even Peter Berger observed that sociological consciousness is fundamentally "cosmopolitan" because "it is not only urban but urbane" with its "broad, open, emancipated vista." The perfect sociologist, Berger dreamily reflected, will be "a man with a taste for other lands."[37]

But the funny thing is, at the same time as the Cynics were flinging contempt and contumely on the *polis* they never strayed very far away from it, which is odd. They ridiculed and rejected the state and its laws and its customs but the very thing at which they directed their scorn was the very thing that they could not do without. The *polis* protected them from harm with its laws.[38] Too, the *polis* kept the Cynics fed because they were beggars and it's hard to beg in the countryside.[39] But also and perhaps most importantly for our purposes here, a Cynic could simply not be a Cynic without someone there to watch them being Cynical and here again we bump up against that theme of artificiality, of self-consciousness and self-awareness, states of being which do not conduce to either sincerity or honesty. Cynicism, absent spectators, would simply evaporate. As Robin Hard observed, one must give credit to the Christian ascetics. When they retreated from society, they retreated fully out of public view, grew their own food, and at least tried to support themselves. And one is reasonably sure that they masturbated in private.

"Imagine"

Sophists and SocProgs can be easily criticized for failing to replace what they destroy. But Diogenes, to his credit, actually had a positive idea of what his ideal society might look like. Diogenes is credited with writing a book called *The Republic* (perhaps entitled such as a sneer at Plato) and in it he envisioned a better world than the one on offer at Athens, and that world—not unlike the world Marx and sociology envision—was a world that bore no relation to the actual world. But still and happily, it accorded nicely with Diogenes' personal quirks, oddities, and interior fevers.

In this Diogenean Republic, women would dress the same as the men "differing from them in no way at all," perhaps because different dress denoted different genders and classes and thus different power relations, and so if we do away with different dress then surely it must follow that we will do away with socially constructed ideas of gender and class.[40]

Further, we need not be surprised that Diogenes also wanted to do away with rank and hierarchy in all of its forms.[41] Maybe the Cynics recognized that rank and hierarchy are "social constructions" which upset and pervert the balance of power between individuals.

Marriage, too, was to be taken to the chopping block. Since marriage itself was not natural but rather a custom merely—one whose legitimacy had already been questioned and "debunked" by the Sophists—the only marriage in Diogenes' Republic was the union of "a man who had persuaded a woman who in turn let herself be persuaded."[42]

And in the absence of marriage, then, sex and free love would flower. Prefiguring the sociologist Herbert Marcuse and his counsel in the 1960s of sex everywhere and all the time, Diogenes counselled the beauty and importance of "promiscuous sexual intercourse."[43] In the world of the Cynics, "the women make advances to the men and seek to persuade them in every way to have intercourse with them."[44] There would be no restrictions on sexual intercourse: "everyone misbehaves with everyone else, husbands have intercourse with their maidservants, wives abandon their husbands to go off with those that better please them." Incest was not proscribed.[45] As the Hippies would deliriously trumpet: "If it feels good then go ahead and do it." It doesn't matter with whom.

Diogenes never got his Republic but the Hippies in the 1960s, without even knowing who Diogenes was, erected what amounted to a Diogenean Republic in their communes filthily littered across Canada and the United States. And they did so for *exactly* the same reasons as Diogenes. The Cynics, we must remember, were all about attacking what they saw as the "hypocrisy and inconsistency" of the Athenian moral and ethical code, its conventions and traditions.[46] And so it was for the Hippies. According to a *Time* magazine reporter writing in 1967, Hippies were "unable to reconcile themselves to the stated values and implicit contradictions in contemporary Western society."[47] So, the Hippies cut themselves off from "society" and established communes where they were going to show the world how to live a better, natural life. Like the Cynics, what was natural was also by definition good and so the key "ethical element" to the Hippie experiment was love "indiscriminate and all-embracing...making love, however and with whomever they can find."[48] The Mounties observed Hippies having unrestrained sex with whomever they could find and were "not ashamed to make love anywhere."[49] Diogenes would've been pleased and so would Marx have, too.

The framework for Diogenes' Republic was actually laid out by his teacher Antisthenes, and that worldview perfectly prefigures the world Karl Marx would envision 2,400 years later. Antisthenes argued that wealth lay at the root of most evils; that private property was loathsome; that morality and conventions were artificial and should be eliminated because they violated the natural law of man.[50] For Antisthenes, the only way to resolve these "contradictions" was to destroy that which was not natural and rid society of those traditional customs and conventions that kept people "shackled." English philosopher Bertrand Russell sums up the vision of Antisthenes this way: "There was to be no government, no private property, no marriage [and] no established religion."[51] And we can safely presume that Antisthenes also meant to do away with the ethics, behaviours, codes of conduct, and moral standards associated with those institutions. Pure negative liberty: a promising and bountiful land containing nothing but self.

But still the big question lingers. What happens when all of this is achieved? The Sophists and the Cynics and the Hippies and the Marxists and the SocProgs, all of them partake of this essentially negative vision of destruction. But what about after? What happens then? Seeing *through* a thing is *not* the same as seeing *through to* a thing. Writing of both the Cynics and the Hippies, historian Efraim Shmueli observed with accuracy and precision that both groups were "oblivious of, or negligent about, and unable to foresee and less so to control the re-establishment which inevitably follows disestablishment," which is to say that after they destroyed, they had nothing else to offer other than self.[52] Socrates, too, clearly divined this particular strain of anti-creation in the Sophists as well who, like the Cynics, attacked and wrecked the old ways but had absolutely no idea of what to put in the place of the thing they destroyed.[53]

This strange talent for anti-creation holds true for the SocProgs as well. The "post-modern" ideas which animate the SocProg set create what Christopher Butler calls a "disabling" world view. It works like this: they adopt an attitude or worldview in which all phenomenal life is seen as a sham or a lie or an untruth, and that very outlook and attitude precipitates destruction (of a custom, a tradition, a value, a belief, a moral). But that very same attitude *dis*allows them to create anything in its place because as Butler points out, their worldview "lacks a settled external viewpoint." This is to say that the Cynics, Sophists, and SocProgs cannot conceive of anything timeless, universal, unchanging, and stable—of anything "settled"—and as a direct consequence they have absolutely nothing at all to offer in a positive sense.

We clearly see this absence of a positive goal in sociology. We recall Peter Berger's absurd comments from Chapter One in which he argued that *all* things are shams which sociology can apparently just go on and on and on debunking and unmasking and for the very same reason as Butler identified: sociology lacks that crucial and critical "settled external viewpoint." Sociology simply cannot conceive of anything as timeless and universal outside of its own ideas, and those ideas concern destruction and negation, merely. And destruction and negation as Universal Principles around which to structure human life just doesn't sound too terribly satisfying. Such ideas do not nourish human life;

they weaken and sicken it. Cynics, Hippies SocProgs, Marxists, sociologists, take your pick—none of them have anything to offer outside of destruction.

American jurist Robert Bork sensibly argued that Liberty is "the space between the walls." Those walls are law and morality. Bork sagely observes that we can and should argue about how far apart the walls should be set, "but it is cultural suicide to demand all space and no walls."[54] The Sophists did not want walls; Cynics did not want walls; the SocProgs do not want walls. But once the walls are removed, what is left? There is nothing left but self. Solipsism. *AloneSelf.*

Taking Stock of the Cynics

Perhaps we might try to find in the Cynics some redeeming features and qualities that might help to balance our picture. After all, one must give even the devil his due. The optimist might argue that they were engaged in a noble project of what historian Jacques Barzun called "primitivism." This desire seeks at reducing or destroying or rejecting the norms of society and embracing instead the demands of our nature and in doing so we thus become "liberated from bourgeois inhibitions and social practices."[55] And Barzun says this impulse toward primitivism is a chronic and persistent feature, an essential characteristic, of the Western mind.[56]

We might also profitably consider the fact that Cynicism was a product of its society. The Cynics were an urban phenomenon and had their roots in Athens.[57] Athens in the fourth century was still a quite wealthy and sophisticated city despite her decadence and lack of public spiritedness, and thus the Cynics appeared as "a reaction against an overdeveloped civilization."[58] That is a point which needs to be emphasized. The Cynics—and we might include the Hippies here as well—were a reaction against increasing wealth and luxury.[59] Cynicism met the growing demand for a "simpler creed," a creed which advocated austerity, simplicity, and a rejection of what we might call "conspicuous consumption" or the "consumer society." And the same was true of the Hippies as well. One Hippie wrote in the 1960s that "faced with the choice of the vacuum-packed, artificially sweetened, freeze-dried insanity that passes for success, I for one would rather become a head rather than get ahead."[60] In other words, this young man rejected the ostentatious and wealthy consumer-driven society into which he had been born and that was a sentiment shared by many of the Cynics as well.[61] And it is also likely that many regular citizens feel that very same thing today.

In sympathetic hands, Diogenes and the Cynics even lay out some general tenets of living with which most of us would agree. Happiness is living in agreement with nature; happiness is available to any person willing to engage in sufficient physical and mental training; and there is even value in the idea that wealth, say, ought not be the goal of life because it has no actual value in nature.[62] Diogenes and the Cynics can be seen as people who "challenged, often in astonishing ways, the norms and conventions of society." Diogenes railed against the world because "the human world was in a state of moral bankruptcy and intellectual vacuity and it required a systemic defacing of its values."[63] Indeed, the Cynic attachment to the concept of self-sufficiency, an indifference to suffering, their "blunt freedom of speech," these are all noble goals and ideals.

But we simply cannot ignore the obvious. If we set aside their intentions and their ideals and look squarely at their actions all we see is "a slump towards animalism and a retrogression from civilization."[64] Like the SocProgs, the Cynics were bent on the destruction of repressive morality, as well as traditions, customs, and conventions with the aim of liberating the individual and that has a Heroic cast to it. But if one looks at what they actually did, the Heroism is wanting; all one sees is someone defecating, urinating, masturbating, and having sex in full public view for no other reason than they felt that proscriptions against it were unnatural and unjust. And in the end, all of this plain living and railing against the world simply cannot be squared. This way of life, as would be the case for the Hippies, naturally, inevitably, and implacably led to "unredeemed beggary, squalor, and indecency."[65] We would do well to consider historian John MacCunn's summation:

> "The incentives in daily life which we all share, the affection for friends, the kindliness of daily life, the stimulus of public spirit, the love of country, these incentives may look commonplace beside the passion for saving souls, the heroic spirit of renunciation, the rupture of all ties, the hating of father and mother...yet it is at our peril that we try to cut out these incentives, and, like the Cynics, cast them from us. For...the risk is that the mass of mankind, bereft of the ordinary motives

that are the permanent safeguards of morality, may find nothing to check their descent toward the brute."

There, too, is yet another warning from history.

MacCunn argues that yes, in the end, the Cynics were in full possession of their Liberty, their own selves, their own true souls. They had emancipated themselves from bourgeois values. But MacCunn adds, with some measure of wisdom, that "their souls could hardly be said to be worth the possessing."[66]

The Cynic Project Withers...

When Diogenes died and the worst excesses of the Cynics were curtailed, Cynicism itself went on to become a kind of popular philosophy; it has been called a "philosophy of the proletariat."[67] The watered-down Cynicism after Diogenes became a kind of superficial, everyday approach to life, more an attitude than anything, and it was never really anything more than that anyway. It's funny. When fabulously rapacious Rome took Greece as a province in the second century BC, Rome took what she wanted from Greece but she did not take Cynicism because "Rome did not want Cynicism."[68] The stern and litigious Roman character—with its *frugalitas*, and its *dignitas*, and its *gravitas*—found Cynicism to be intellectually puerile and deemed it "an offensive vulgarity." Rome was just not the place to be a Cynic. The men of the Roman Senate would not have responded very well to the Cynics, at least in the days before the Republic lost its way.

For as much as Rome did not want Cynicism, though, ideas cannot be checked at a border. Cynicism did in fact leak into the Roman consciousness here and there, although given the hostility to Cynicism in Rome, the expressions of those ideas remained literary rather than actual until well after the Augustan age in the first century AD.[69] The most famous of the Roman Cynics was Demetrius. He was simply a reheated version of the earlier and original Diogenes. These Roman "opponents of convention" had, by the end of the Augustan Age, "standardized both the manner and the matter of their assault" into a fairly conventional form which required no originality of thought as such but merely required the right attitudes, the right pose as it were.[70]

The Roman writer Lucian couldn't stand the Cynics mostly because they—not unlike the Sophists and so not unlike sociology—pretended at philosophy. Lucian composed a story, *The Fugitivi*, in which Philosophy personified comes weeping to Olympus and pleads with Zeus and Apollo to do something about these Cynics. In between choking and tearful sobs, Philosophy finally makes clear her problem. She complains of a "race of half breeds" on earth who dress like Philosophy and claim to be operating under her command "but their life is an abomination, full of ignorance, boldness and depravity and of great insolence." She complains that these Cynics are "just like Aesop's donkey who thought he was a lion when he put on its skin and brayed." Gallant, philandering Zeus sets Hercules to the task of clearing these characters out and Hercules remarks that such a task will be worse than clearing out all those horse stables.[71] And on that last point, Hercules was more correct than he knew. The RCMP observed that the Hippies in the 1960s lived amidst squalor, filth, and "pet excrement."[72] So, perhaps the Hippies too needed a Greek or Roman God to clean their homes. Evidently, they couldn't. Or perhaps it's not that they couldn't do it themselves but rather, taking the higher ethereal Cynic plane, felt that concepts of cleanliness were too closely associated with arbitrarily constructed bourgeois middle-class values. Because you see, for the Hippies, even house cleaning was political.

...and waits.

Both Sophistry and Cynicism mellowed after the decay and subjugation of Greece and both philosophies disappeared entirely after the fall of Rome in the fifth century. The necessary pre-conditions for the development of such philosophies were absent throughout the Western world for centuries following the collapse of Rome. Through the Dark and Middle ages, the West transitions into its Christian phase, and this period is "the most profound division in the history of Western philosophy."[73] Philosophic speculations turn from "world and man" toward creation and the Divine. The Magna Carta notwithstanding, there were very few moves taken toward social and political orders in the West of the type that had existed in Greece and Rome. As historian Francis Fukuyama points out, in 1790, there were only three or four democracies of that general description on the planet: Britain, the United States, and France.[74] By the way—and it has the appearance of being an oddity—Switzerland is on that list, too.

Democracy bloomed late in Canada, for we do not like dissent.

And so the history of the West after the collapse of Greece and Rome refracted through the prism of the church and that remained true, though in steadily declining degrees, all the way down through to the Enlightenment and into the great modern democratic revolutions of 1776 and 1789, just a little more than two centuries ago which, in historic time, is like nothing. Then, in that century, after a hiatus of millennia, Western civilization once again began a slow creep toward the establishment of liberal democracies. And the modern democrats were very much taken with and inspired by their forebears in Greece and Rome. *Very* much so.[75] Indeed, the spirit of antiquity was anxiously hovering in the rooms as though a nervous parent, looking over the shoulders of the French and the American statesmen as they wrote their constitutions.

Interesting big-picture stuff here. It took from 1776 to 1992 before historian Francis Fukuyama could tentatively suggest that there appeared to be, at that time, the development of a consensus which held that liberal democracies were the only truly viable and legitimate social and political order. But it only took another twenty-two years after Fukuyama's book *The End of History* appeared for the whole issue to be flipped on its head when the *Economist* newsmagazine was compelled to ask: "What's Gone Wrong with Democracy?"[76] And the time in between Fukuyama's book and the *Economist* article was precisely the time during which Marxian sociological thought had entrenched itself in Western democracies. And so the quick hit and run: apparently it takes democracies about 250 to 300 years to waste themselves.

At any rate, it takes some time for these democratic principles we are discussing here to go from being aspirational goals to commonly accepted ideals, but they do. Gradually, slowly, and over time, enabled by growing ease, comfort and prosperity, principles like Liberty have gone from being revolutionary in the eighteenth century to being the very air that we breathe in the twenty-first century. Imagine for a second here our life without Liberty, our lives absent all of the personal Freedoms we have. It is scarcely possible to do so. We are drowning in Liberty. And Sophistry and Cynicism are philosophies that are built directly in to the ideal of Liberty itself.

We have already examined the two broad and contending visions of Liberty and the philosophies that develop out of those two distinct visions of being human. And it would seem here that negative liberty, which counsels "freedom from," will always win out against its positive counterpart, which counsels rigorous self-knowledge instead. Positive liberty is rooted in an act of self-compulsion. Negative liberty, at its core, simply means "stop bothering me." Negative liberty asks very little of its subject; positive liberty does, and a good deal of that, too. Negative liberty is a philosophy which seeks to extend what Isaiah Berlin called that "wider degree of non-interference." Negative liberty holds that freedom is good and so more of it must be better and so into the sixties we go.

Endnotes

[1] Thomas Cahill, *Sailing the Wine Dark Sea: why the Greeks matter* (New York: Nan Talese, 2004), p. 250.

[2] *Diogenes the Cynic: sayings and anecdotes* translated by Robin Hard (London: Oxford, 2012), p. 33. And, prefiguring Marx's repudiation of the Platonic Way, Diogenes is quoted as saying that the philosophy of Plato was "a waste of time." See Hard, *Diogenes*, p. 32.

[3] Bertrand Russell, *The History of Western Philosophy* (New York: Routledge, 1996), p. 222.

[4] Russell, *The History*, p. 222.

[5] Donald R. Dudley, *A History of Cynicism: from Diogenes to the 6th century AD* (Hildesheim, Germany: Georg Olms Verlagsbuchhandlung, 1967), p. 27.

[6] R. Bracht Branham and Marie-Odile Goulet-Caze eds. *In The Cynics: the cynic movement in antiquity and its legacy* (Berkeley: University of California Press, 1997). See introduction and pp. 1-23. See also Hard's introductory essay in *Diogenes the Cynic*, pp. vii-xxvi, p. x.

[7] Russell, *History*, p. 95.

[8] Plato, *The Last Days of Socrates* translated by Hugh Tredennick and Harold Tarrant (London: Penguin, 1993), p. 138.

[9] Hard, *Diogenes*, p.viii.

[10] Hard, *Diogenes,* p. viii.

[11] Farrand Sayre, *Diogenes of Sinope: a study of Greek cynicism* (Baltimore: John Furst Co., 1938), p. 79.

[12] See especially Plato's dialogue "Crito" in *The Last Days of Socrates* translated by Hugh Tredennick and Harold Tarrant (London: Penguin, 1993), pp. 76-92.

[13] Plato, *The Last Days*, p. 88.

[14] Dudley, *A History*, pp. 27-28.

[15] Dudley, *A History*, p ix.

[16] To continue with the many shades of the sneer: "The *jeer* and *gibe* are uttered; the *gibe* is bitter...the *jeer* is rude and open. A *scoff* may be in act or word and is commonly directed against that which claims honour, reverence or worship. A *fling* is careless and commonly pettish; a *taunt* is intentionally insulting and provoking; the *sneer* is supercilious; the *taunt* is defiant." All of this underscores my insistence on calling them "dictionary philosophers" because of their brilliance in unpacking the many subtle shades of meaning in our language.

[17] Dudley, *A History*, p. 5.

[18] Dudley, *A History*, p. 5.

[19] Isaiah Berlin, *Four Essays on Liberty* (London: Oxford University Press, 1969), p. 122.

[20] Berlin, *Four Essays*, p. 131.

[21] Berlin, *Four Essays*, p. 134.

[22] Berlin, *Four Essays*, p. 134. In China, a variant of positive and negative Liberty was explained this way: "Confucius said, 'The gentleman makes demands on himself; the inferior man makes demands on

others.'" See *Sources of Chinese Tradition* vol. 1 edited by Wm Theodore de Bary (New York: Columbia, 1960), p. 30.

[23] MacCunn, "The Cynics." p. 185.

[24] Sayre, "Greek Cynicism," p. 114.

[25] Hard, *Diogenes*, p. 63.

[26] Sayre, "Greek Cynicism," p. 115.

[27] I am reminded here of Gwen Jacobs, the celebrated Ontario woman who, in the 1990s, removed her shirt and walked topless through the streets of her city. The laws against woman going topless, she argued, were unfair because they made arbitrary distinctions between men and women where none should be made. Quoting from memory, the judge in her case said that anyone who thinks male and female breasts are the same is "not living in the real world." But the point: sociology counselled that such restrictions were arbitrary because there is no fundamental difference between men and women—we are not just equal, we are *alike*—and so Jacobs sought to remove the restriction. It was not because it was oppressive but because it was a restriction merely, and Liberty necessarily seeks the removal of Restriction. There are now, in the twenty-first century, topless movements right across North America.

[28] Hard, *Diogenes*, pp. 48 and 202; note 215.

[29] Hard, *Diogenes*, 16.

[30] Dudley, *A History*, p. 34.

[31] HDF Kitto, *The Greeks* (London: Penguin, 1991), p. 11. The full idea from Kitto reads: "If you did not do this [live in a *polis*] you were something less than a man at his best and most characteristic." Also, Kitto explains: "The city-state was the means by which the Greek consciously strove to make the life both of the community and of the individual more excellent than it was before." The Cynics, of course, did not share this idea of the Individual and the Community operating in mutually beneficial ways.

[32] Sayre, "Greek Cynicism," p. 115

[33] Dudley, *A History*, p. 34.

[34] As cited in MacCunn, "The Cynics," p. 185. Attica was the region of Greece in which Athens was situated.

[35] Efraim Shmueli, "Modern Hippies and Ancient Cynics: a comparison of philosophical and historical developments and its lessons," *Cahiers D'Histoire Mondiale*, vol. 12 1970, pp. 490-514, p. 498. That idea of the "brotherhood of man" may in fact be *homonia*, a Greek word associated with the harmony of mankind.

[36] Christopher Butler, *Postmodernism: a very short introduction* (London: Oxford, 2002), p. 5.

[37] Peter Berger, *Invitation to Sociology: a humanistic perspective* (Woodstock NY: The Overlook Press, 1973), p. 53.

[38] Shmueli, "Modern Hippies," p. 500

[39] Hard, *Diogenes,* p. x.

[40] Hard, *Diogenes*, p. 50. I think that was the whole idea behind Chairman Mao's little blue suits.

[41] Dudley, *A History*, pp. 36-37.

[42] Hard, *Diogenes*, p. 49.

[43] Sayre, *Diogenes*, p. 6.

[44] Hard, *Diogenes*, p. 49.

[45] Hard, *Diogenes*, p. 49.

[46] Branham, *The Cynics*, p. 35.

[47] "The Hippies," *Time Magazine*, July 7, 1967, vol. 90, no. 1, p.22.

[48] "The Hippies," *Time Magazine*, pp. 25-30

[49] Marcel Martel, "'They Smell Bad, Have Diseases and are Lazy': RCMP Officers' reporting on Hippies in the late Sixties," in M. Athena Palaeologu ed. *The Sixties in Canada: a turbulent and creative* [turbulent yes, creative no] *decade* (Montreal: Black Rose Books, 2009), p. 181.

[50] Shmueli, "Modern Hippies," p. 495.

[51] Russell, *History*, p. 222. One here is reminded of John Lennon's beautiful song *Imagine*.

[52] Shmueli, "Modern Hippies," p. 512.

[53] Marvin Perry et al, *Western Civilization: ideas, politics, and society* (Boston: Houghton Mifflin Co., 1996), p. 80.

[54] Robert Bork, *Slouching Towards Gomorrah: modern liberalism and American decline* (New York: Regan Books, 1997), p. 65.

[55] Branham, *The Cynics*, p. 35.

[56] Jacques Barzun, *From Dawn to Decadence, 1500 to the Present: 500 years of western cultural life* (New York: Perennial, 2000), p. xix.

[57] Dudley, *A History*, p. 143.

[58] Dudley, *A History*, p. 143.

[59] Dudley, *A History*, p. 124.

[60] Shmueli, "Modern Hippies," p. 493.

[61] MacCunn, "The Cynics," p. 187.

[62] Branham, "The Cynics," p. 30.

[63] Luis E. Navia, *Diogenes the Cynic: the war against the world* (Amherst New York: Humanity Books, 2005), p. 7.

[64] Sayre, *Diogenes*, p. 1.

[65] MacCunn, "The Cynics," pp. 197-198.

[66] MacCunn, "The Cynics," pp. 197-198.

[67] Dudley, *A History*, p. 118.

[68] Dudley, *A History*, p. 118.

[69] Dudley, *A History*, p. 118.

[70] Dudley, *A History*, p. 127.

[71] As cited in Dudley, *A History*, pp. 145-146.

[72] Martel, "They Smell,'" p. 177.

[73] Julian Marias, *History of Philosophy* translated by Stanley Applebaum and Clarence C Strowbridge (New York: Dover, 1967), p. 105.

[74] Francis Fukuyama, *The End of History and the Last Man* (New York: Perennial, 1992), p. 49.

[75] If you're into constitutions and you ever get the chance, please read the Pennsylvania State Constitution of 1776. It is a remarkable document: a modern reimagining of the direct democracy of ancient Greece with a little of the Roman Republic (or is it Sparta) sprinkled in. It was a constitution which sadly did not last long because it proved to be a little too radical, a little *too* heavy on the "democracy" (democracy is a Greek word that means "people rule" so, yes, a little too much "people rule," there, in Pennsylvania, in 1776). The French Constitutions of the revolutionary period too all bear the *direct* stamp of antiquity, especially the Constitution of 1792. The British—well they're just different. They just simply refuse to write things down.

[76] Check out the story in the March 2014 edition.

CHAPTER FOUR

THE HIPPIES

"In the West, it is the 'exceptions' which break through the universal [and]
in this is rooted the perpetual disquiet of the West, its continual dis-
satisfaction, its inability to be content with any sort of fulfilment."

Karl Jaspers, The Origin and Goal of History, p. 64.

"Do you know that I actually went away to school and took a class in the
culture of the sixties just to try to understand the way you lived, the choices
that you made; just to try and make sense out of all that new freedom and
upheaval and fucking anarchy! And the problem is you tore everything down
but you were too lazy to actually build anything as an alternative!"

Actor Edward Norton in the film Leaves of Grass. The scene revolves around a
young professor of Greek philosophy confronting his aging Hippie mother.

"Get your motor runnin'/head out on the highway/looking
for adventure/and whatever comes our way!"

Steppenwolf, Born to be Wild, circa 1968.

"Hey Hippie! You don't pay taxes so why don't you walk in the ditch!"

The author's maternal grandfather, Floyd Mellum—a farmer, landowner,
and businessman—addressing a Hippie hitchhiking on Highway 41
in rural Saskatchewan in 1968 after slowing down his car to do so.
The story was related by the author's mother, Carol McManus.

The time is now at hand when we must reluctantly though of necessity but
mercifully only briefly explore the gross indulgences—sensual, intellectual, moral, and otherwise—of the 1960s, the most bloated, overblown, and
overrated age of "modern" times. Our excursion here will be brief because the

purpose of this chapter is to merely draw out the obvious and many parallels and connections that the Hippies share with the Sophists and Cynics. This spiritual and intellectual sameness will in turn enable us to gain a much firmer and deeper understanding of, and appreciation for, who the SocProgs actually are. Since the SocProgs take their philosophies and worldview *directly* from this decade, they are, as a consequence and in every meaningful way, the institutional embodiment of the Hippies, Cynics, and Sophists.

The laudatory tomes written about the 1960s generally credit the age with being new, advanced, progressive, creative, and original, but it was none of those things. Indeed, let us be clear: it was the *opposite* of those things. One of the only real and substantial differences between the Hippies and the Cynics was simply the presence or absence of the music of Jimi Hendrix.[1] And so rather than beginning at the beginning here, we'll begin at the end.

It's funnier that way.

Sociology: seeing what's really going on

Sociology is amusing in many ways but perhaps sociology at its most hilarious was its total inability to later explain this cultural and social revolution, an inability which is made even stranger when we consider that sociology exists in the first place to explain cultural and social revolutions and that strangeness is multiplied by a factor of ten when we understand that sociology was a hugely important causal factor in this particular cultural and social revolution. Sociology is funny like that.

Writing in 1992, Peter Berger attempted to unpack this mammoth intellectual confusion. First, Berger here "innocently" wonders at the developments of the sixties themselves: "How could it be," he asked, "that some of the most privileged people on earth, indeed in history, turned violently against the very society that had made them thus privileged?" Good question. He presents another: "The question is, 'why have sociologists been so inept in dealing with as massive a phenomenon?'" Another good question which results in this: "The failure of sociology to either predict or at least apprehend [the sixties] indicates that something is seriously wrong."[2] Really?

The short answer to Berger's first question there about causation is simply bad sociology. But that answer reflected back, and it reflected poorly, on sociologists and so in the years that followed the sixties, they apparently went looking for causal explanations elsewhere, places, one assumes, that did not have mirrors. They bounded hither, thither, and yon, searching under every Marxian theoretical rock for causes and explanations. Some sociologists tried to "squeeze" it into "the proletarianization of the middle class." Apparently, that didn't work. Some others, according to Berger, "mumbled something about 'status politics.'" That didn't work, either.

And so Berger was finally compelled to point out the obvious to sociologists almost thirty years after the fact (that he had to explain this at all suggests that even then, still, sociology was reluctant to admit its part in what he himself called a "cataclysm"): "The best interpretation is probably that most sociologists were very much a part of the phenomenon. The generation that entered the profession in those years had all the peace signs emblazoned on their hearts. To them, this was a conflict between the good guys and the bad guys."[3] And it was these "good guys"—the sociologists—who were determined to make this world better. You didn't really believe, did you, that one morning in 1968, the "youth" of the Western world collectively realized—at the same time and using the same language while living in different countries and on different continents—that their parents, their society, their religion, and their civilization were shot through with "hypocrisy and inconsistency"? No. They learned this stuff in their introductory sociology classes. Same thing goes for all that "free love" preached by the Marxian sociologist Herbert Marcuse. That comes right out of Karl Marx's *Communist Manifesto*. It's right there on page eighty-nine.[4] (And to make the point absolutely clear, many of the sickly perturbations afflicting the West today—political correctness, history wars, culture wars, language wars, transgender bathrooms, expunging statues of dead white men from university campuses, "slut-walks," arranging class-rooms in a circular fashion so that "power" is "decentred"—can be traced directly back to sociology and sociological theorists.)

And so Berger explains sociology's failure to understand and explain the decade it substantially caused with this strange and inverted weirdness: "People are reluctant to accept sociological explanations of their own commitments—even if they are professional sociologists." The people who claim to be able to see through the "shams" of "society" were totally unwilling and unable to see through their own.

Yes, sociology is funny like that.

The problems Berger was addressing in his article were actually much larger. He was openly lamenting a much wider sociological failure to apprehend, explain, and understand not just the sixties but other major post-war developments as well. He writes "each of these developments surprised most if not all sociologists. What is more, sociologists found themselves unable to explain them or to make sense of them." But where the sixties in particular are concerned, he explains that "the failure of sociology to apprehend this development is largely due to ideological blinders."[5] We can totally accept the point Berger is making, mostly because, once again, it is true. But the problem worsens the deeper we probe into it.

Those "ideological blinders" that Berger identifies as the principal reason for sociology's monumental failure to explain the sixties are essential to the subject of sociology itself. To make the point clear, sociology *needs* "ideological blinders." Berger: "Sociology is not so much a field as a perspective, and *if this perspective fails, nothing is left.*"[6] History is not a perspective; it is a discipline that invites other perspectives. Nor is philosophy a perspective; it too is a discipline which invites other ways of seeing. But sociology is the way of seeing itself, and the sixties clearly and plainly revealed the perversity of that perspective. Sociology was forced by its own hypocrisies and inconsistencies to put on those ideological blinders in an effort to avoid the truth thereby preventing, or at the very least forestalling, its own collapse. It is more than a little revealing here that our introductory sociology textbook has an entire twenty page chapter on "Social Movements and Social Change" and nowhere are the sixties mentioned, which is strange because it was, after all, *the* seminal social movement seeking social change since 1789.[7] Maybe they're just still a little embarrassed about the whole thing.

And so here, amidst all of this intellectual and spiritual confusion, we can clearly see and understand how and why it was that Berger finally turned his back on sociology at the end of his career. He suggested in 1992 that it was a "bankrupt enterprise" whose "obsolescence" was at that time readily apparent and whose "dissolution" would, in the end, "not be a great intellectual disaster."[8] People would miss philosophy, history, poetry, literature, science, and mathematics for they are essential. Berger here is suggesting that if it disappeared (and we pray, *fervently*, for that day[9]), no one would really miss modern sociology, for it is not essential. It is merely a perspective, and the chaos and anarchy of the sixties clearly revealed the bankruptcy of that perspective. Once again and for emphasis: sociology does not solve problems. Sociology *creates* problems.

There is no other subject in the academy that suffers from such grievous structural hypocrisies and perverse intellectual inconsistencies, but that should not be surprising since sociology was birthed by Karl Marx. There is bad history, but history itself is not bad. There is bad philosophy, but philosophy itself is not bad. There is bad sociology because sociology itself is bad. The problems from which sociology suffers are "systemic," not unlike the "systemic" problems in "society" which sociology has claimed to have uncovered as part of its *self*-proclaimed and *self*-defined goal of "making the world a better place to live." And that too is part of the problem: nobody ever asked sociology to make the world a better place. It simply does what it does for its *own* reasons, its *own* goals, and its *own* purposes.[10] It is a certainty beyond doubt that, in the long annals of time and in the history of ideas come and gone, sociology will one day be held to account for what it has done.[11]

And so the Hippies (what's the word here then?) "appeared" in the 1960s and tried to do what Marx had wanted and sociology had counselled: live life absent truth, religion, and morality. Too bad neither Marx nor the Hippies had read Aristophanes.[12] If they had, they might have been reminded of that gentle and sober suggestion from Athenian Law who, we recall from Chapter Three, said, "If you don't like what we have to offer, then you are always free to pack up your things, and leave."

In substitution for all of the destruction that was set to occur on this journey outward to that new and better world, Marx promised our young revolutionaries this: "In place of the old bourgeois society, with its classes and class antagonisms, we shall have an association in which the free development of each is the condition for the free development of them all!" In other words, Marx promised pure negative liberty taken to its full, sad, illogical, irrational end. An end at which there is, finally, nothing left at all but the self. Solipsism. *AloneSelf*.

Welcome, then, to the 1960s.

"Units of Analysis"

The Hippies arrived on "the scene" right across the Western world in the 1960s. Very much like prolific fungi, they popped up in Canada, the United States, Britain, Australia, and wherever else sociology was taught. Fungi: "*non-flowering plants of wide distribution and great variety...reproducing chiefly by asexual means and obtaining nourishment as a parasite on living organisms.*" The Hippies came from the generation that was born in the 1940s and 1950s. Generally speaking, they were raised in affluence, isolated in suburbia, swaddled in comfort, and lacked any experience with war or conflict.[13] Although admittedly they lived on the edge of nuclear annihilation, the fact remains that they were "devoid of historical awareness" and thus lived in a kind of "dream world" as a consequence.[14] And it was out of this dream world that their visions of a new world developed, and that new world did in fact resemble a dream world. French philosopher Raymond Aron breathlessly explores their vision: "It is *beyond* affluence that there lie spaces to be explored, riches to be discovered. What spaces? What riches? No one knows. The future belongs to action, not to foresight; it must be forged, not imagined. For the future which our young revolutionaries want is prefigured by no existing society."[15] Not a bad vision for teenagers and twenty-something undergraduates with no grounding in history or philosophy and who frequently experience difficulty completing research papers longer than five pages.

In any event, they were, it seems, determined to, like Marx, "act in contradiction to all past historical experience!"

There were actually three types of "activist" in the 1960s.[16] The first was "the student radical." This creature was the Enlightenment-inspired actor who cleaved to the age old delusion of progress and the perfectibility of man, as well as the elimination of those social, economic, and political inequalities perpetuated by an unjust economic and political system. These "activists" had learned in their sociology classes that the customs, values, and traditions of that system were created by, and only served the interests of, the capitalist bourgeois "elites." The second type of activist evidently held the same values of the first type but tried to effect change not through political action but through "moral exhortation." It was the third type, though, that is most recognizable and most associated with that decade: the Hippies. They shared the same values as the first and second varieties, but they rejected political activism, preferring instead to show by doing, through example. All three types, however, were "liberal intellectuals" who were in fact "unified in [their] rejection of society" and all of them had some kind of vision of a "totally new social framework."[17] Amongst the radicals of the age, though, the Hippies represented "the most radical protest against the establishment."[18]

There were a handful of general concerns unrelated to the tyranny of bathing that seemed to animate the Hippies and activists in the West. There was the Vietnam War and the consequent peace movement; there was the civil rights movement which focussed on those sociological fetish-themes of race-gender-class-sexuality-power; and there were the protests on campuses whose aim was to "reform" the universities and push them toward freer and more democratic structures.[19] Within this broad framework, the activists and Hippies also apparently had "a grievance against and refutation of the dominant social structure."[20] And they also were "against" "social conditioning, indoctrination, mass-taste, [and] whatever narrows down the individual human potential and its creative spontaneity."[21] Or in the Cynic estimation of it, whatever interferes with Liberty.

Befuddlement and Confusion

It is quite easy to forget how the Hippie movement shocked the world when the whole thing broke across the West in the sixties; how strange, new, and utterly befuddling it all was. Of a sudden, there were these strange creatures wandering the land, with outlandish clothes, long hair, drugs in their pockets, and zero sense of personal hygiene. They hitchhiked on roads, sat on streets, harassed conventions and traditions, and made themselves odious to citizens.

Teachers, family members, professors, and university administrators were quite at a loss to determine what this movement was, how to deal with it, what it meant, or even why it appeared. It was as if the historical firmament had opened up and spewed forth moral and spiritual wreckage from another world, another time. We might revisit Thomas Carlyle here, and what he wrote about the proto-SocProg Jacobins and their muscle the *sans-cullotes* during the French Revolution: "On a sudden, the Earth yawns asunder, and amid Tartarean smoke, and glare of fierce brightness, rises SANSCULLOTISM, many-headed, fire-breathing, and asks: what think ye of me? The Age of Miracles has come back! Behold the World Phoenix, in fire consummation and fire creation: wide are her fanning wings; loud is her death-melody, of battle thunders and falling towns; skyward lashes the funeral flame, enveloping all things: *it is the Death-Birth of a World.*"[22] Okay, yes, perhaps a little much, but it does point us in the right direction: the death-birth of a world.

But back to befuddlement. Members of the American Psychiatric Association met in Boston in 1968 to discuss "youth" problems.[23] The professors and doctors in attendance had conflicted attitudes toward this new movement: some saw it as a sign of a sick society, some as a society struggling toward health. A certain Dr. Dana Farnsworth lamented that it was "depressing to be in a country where personal inhibitions and customary restraints have broken down." But Dr. Farnsworth was at a loss to explain how and why this had even come to pass. The psychiatrists could find neither a political nor an economic reason for it, for these elements are the usual precipitators of revolutions. But there were none of Carlyle's starving "millions" living in their "hovels" "emaciated" as on the eve of the French Revolution. The Englishman Lord Chesterfield wrote just prior to the outbreak of the French Revolution that "all the symptoms which I have ever met within history, previous to great Changes and Revolutions in Government, now exist and daily increase in France."[24] But none of that existed in the 1960s. Berger has already indicated that they were some of the most privileged people in history.

In Britain, too, there was confusion. Like their counterparts in Canada and the United States, the Hippies in Britain had come from good homes where a kind of modest affluence had been gained by their parents and whose stability and security had been attained by "an unremitting endeavour that the Hippie cannot bring himself to emulate."[25] This inability to put themselves to the task and actually work was celebrated and valorized by Canadian "activist" Dimitrios Roussopoulos who observed that "the most promising development in the factories today is the emergence of young workers who smoke pot, fuck off on their jobs, drift into and out of factories, grow long hair...steal, harass all authority figures, go on wildcats, and turn on their fellow workers."[26] Indeed.

"Fighting the Man"

The counterculture movement was, in broad form, intolerant and suspicious of the values and mores of the society in which they grew up. You see, there were hypocrisies and "inconsistencies" in "society" and the "youth" had "discovered" these hypocrisies and inconsistencies and that discovery had apparently occurred in their introductory sociology classes. They could not tolerate the glaring discrepancies between the stated ideals of society and the way it actually functioned.[27] Canada, for example, proclaimed a devotion to democracy, but that democracy did not function as it should. The flaws of Canadian democracy were and are well known. There is the unrepresentative nature of the first-past-the-post system, the naked grasping for power for power's sake, and the totally ridiculous concept of "responsible government" whose proper functioning requires "party discipline," itself a concept that sounds (actually *is*) positively Stalinesque.

But the point is that there was nothing *new* in the Hippie critique of Canadian democracy. The real animating problem for the "youth" was neither the presence of "discrepancies" nor the lack of adherence to an ideal. The real problem was that these "youth" were encountering for the first time the age-old conflict between the Ideal and the Actual and, not knowing how to process these contradictions because they lacked the mental and intellectual acuity to do so, demanded a "new world" instead.

For the Hippies, their society was "contradictory" and "without meaning." They viewed the older generation (and it helps to remember that "the older generation" on which they "flung their contempt" was the generation that had fought and vanquished the Nazis in the most righteous war in history), with derision or pity, seeing them as "hypocrites."[28] The old pillars of society—"country, religion, scientific progress, and modern government"—were institutions in which the "youth," with all the wisdom that can possibly accrue to a teenager just months removed from living in his parents' basement, had evidently examined the system and had "lost faith" in it.[29]

Having discovered—or rather, having been told by their sociology professors—that the system was corrupt and hypocritical, Hippies refused to become a part of it and instead dropped out. They apparently "dreamt of expressing their uniqueness or of creating."[30] The Hippies set up "pads" or "communes" right across North America. In 1967, only a year or so after the explosion of the Hippie counterculture, a *Time* magazine investigation into this "bizarre permutation from the middle class" revealed that as many as thirty communes existed in Canada and the United States.[31] On these communes, the "nature-loving hippie tribesmen" set up a kind of alternate society, a Bizarro-world if you like. They lived the good life on "turnips, brown rice, fish, and bean curd."[32] Most Hippies, like the Cynics, were "insatiable hedonists" having sex "with whomever they can find." Indeed, love was one of the key elements of the Hippie ethos. "Superzap them all with Love!" was the cry.

"Love, Sociologically"

Ahh, free love. If the sixties are known for anything, it is that. The age in which the tyranny of Christian prudery was overthrown, sexual morality valiantly liberated from the clutches of the bourgeoisie, and the traditional concept of the family eroded, confused, and very nearly discarded as we lurched toward gluttonous self-satisfaction and the perfect realization of negative liberty. We collectively and mistakenly hold a kind of halcyon, rose-colored view of the whole free-love thing seeing it as a kind of Spontaneous Ejaculation of a Love for Humanity by Nature Loving Hippies. But we forget that free love was not really a spontaneous idea, nor was it a manifestation of any kind of loftier benevolent principle. Free love was a direct and debauched consequence of sociological thought.

Free love develops straight out of Marxian sociology. It works like this: Marx argued that marriage and indeed the family itself, as an idea and an institution, were not decent and honourable but rather by-products of capitalism. He makes the point: "On what foundation is the present family, the bourgeois family based?! On capitol [and] private gain!"[33] (By the way, sociology today has slightly modified its view on the family. It is still oppressive, but the oppressor is different. Rather than the family being a creature of capitalism and so by definition oppressive and unnatural, the family today is characterized by "patriarchy" which, the sociologists tell us, is "a social system in which men dominate women."[34] Essentially, the sociologists appear to have swapped out economics for gender; more current and up-to-date, I suppose.[35])

At any rate, we have here an idea which holds that the oppressive socio-economic system against which our rebels in the sixties were told by sociology to fight was apparently also responsible for the creation of the institution of the family itself. And if the socio-economic system was unjust, then the same was doubly true for the family and family values. Now, since Marx argued that the "internal contradictions" of capitalism would lead to its collapse, the same would hold true for the family itself. Marx: "The bourgeois family will vanish... with the vanishing of capitol!" Unmindful or more likely uncaring of the fact that a family unit of some kind transcends time, borders, politics, *and* economic systems, Marx revealed his spitting contempt for the family before arguing that after its destruction free love would flower: "Bourgeois marriage is, in reality, a system of wives in common and thus, at most, what the communists might possibly be reproached with is that they desire to introduce, in substitution for a hypocritically concealed, an openly legalized system, of free love!" For Marx, any talk of the family or family values or even the sanctity of the parent-child relationship was little more than "bourgeois clap-trap" designed to conceal "what was really going on."[36]

What was really going was that, in Marx's estimation, capitalists were apparently behaving poorly. Marx's hostility to the family was rooted in part in what he saw as the hypocrisy and inconsistency of capitalists who "not content with having the wives and daughters of the proletarians at their disposal, not to speak of common prostitutes, take supreme delight in seducing each other's wives!" This, then, was his view of the family: an unjust and perverse institution—nay, an instrument of capitalism—rooted not in love and decency but in hypocrisy and inconsistency. And today, sociology remains committed to wrecking the family only for different though equally incoherent reasons. Sociology tells us that our traditional definition of family (a family consisting of a man, woman, and child), is wrong. Such an idea, the sociologists tell us, reveals a "monolithic bias [?]" which "not only lends itself to a very incomplete approach but also tends to support **a conservative bias**." And really, does it seriously surprise you at this point that the bold type is in the original?[37]

But the simple and most basic mistake he makes—The Obvious is, here, glaring at Marx, menacingly—is at the same time a quite fundamental one. In his distorted and perverse understanding of the family, he saw only what sociology still seeks: "systemic" problems that are "inherent" in the "unit," "system," or "institution" under investigation, as though finding a sham was the same as finding a truth. It isn't. Seeing *through* and seeing *through to* are not the same. Marx had to force himself to believe that the hypocrisy to which he claimed to have been a witness was a "systemic" problem rather than simply just being a human problem because he had little or no understanding of being human. And it was out of this gross misunderstanding of what a family is, and of what it means to be a human being, that he arrived at his even grosser prescription for it: free love. The family was not natural. The Sophists and Cynics had already proved that. And, like the Sophists and the Cynics, Marx, too, also argued that it was free love that was natural. Marx: "The Communists have no need to introduce free love; it has existed almost from time immemorial!"

Funny. Marx spent a life time railing against hypocrisy and inconsistency (and sociology, still today, trots out this mission as one of the principal reasons for its existence). But hypocrisy and inconsistency are bedrock elements of those who buy into Marxian untruths. Marxian ideas cannot exist without the life-giving support of hypocrisy. Hypocrisy, for example, became the spiritual and intellectual foundation of Marx's Bolshevik progeny. Hypocrisy was the fuel that activated and energized the Bolshevik mind. And as Martin Amis reminds us, Bolsheviks did things with hypocrisy that even hypocrisy didn't know was possible:

> "Hypocrisy boomed under the Bolsheviks like hyperinflation. I do not intend it as a witticism to say that hypocrisy became the life and soul of the party—indeed, this understates the case. Hypocrisy didn't know what had hit it in October 1917. Until then, hypocrisy had had its moments, in politics, in religion, in commerce; it had played its part in innumerable social interactions; and it had starred in many Victorian novels and so on; but it had never been asked to saturate one-sixth of the planet.[38]

And so no, free love was not a spiritual movement by nature-loving Hippies. Free love, in the end, was a fanciful idea predicated on an untruth, that the family itself and the values enshrined in it were oppressive "social constructs" and merely manifestations of an illegitimate capitalist order. Free love had nothing to do with any sort of organic eruption of cosmic brotherly love which had been suppressed by rigid 1950s morality as the caricature goes. Free love or, in a phrase, ruinous promiscuity, was the debauched consequence of young and impressionable men and women being pardoned by sociology from "bourgeois, middle-class sexual morality." In reflection here, free love seems to lose most if not all of its appeal when its origin and source are identified. The Hippies had cried "Superzap them all with Love!" But since love does not exist in the reductive and mechanistic universe of Karl Marx, perhaps the Hippies adopted that ethos because they simply could not bring themselves to shout out what was *really* going on: "Superzap them all with Sexual Economics!"

The Marxist theoretician who was most responsible for the moral decadence of that decade was Herbert Marcuse. He was a kind of godfather figure to the Hippies. Canadian historian Bryan D. Palmer calls him "one of the New Left's most esteemed theoreticians."[39] Somewhat more sensibly, British sociologist Stanislav Andreski calls Marcuse's thought "defective by any reasonable intellectual standards."[40] At any rate Marcuse, a sociologist (and yes, studies do show that the majority of activists and Hippies were from what French philosopher Raymond Aron called those "disciplines of refuge," sociology and psychology; one cannot help but smile here at the wonderfully comforting fact that, amongst the radicals and Hippies, there were "very few engineers"[41]), counselled this: "negation of the entire establishment, its morality and culture; affirmation of the right to build a society in which the abolition of property and toil terminates in a universe where the sensuous, the playful, the calm, and the beautiful become forms of existence and thereby the form of society itself."[42]

Okay. This is not philosophy. It is not even thought. It is a Flight of Fancy, merely. It is flighty-*ness*, manifest. Flighty: "*Given to light headed fancies or caprices; volatile; slightly delirious.*" It deals nowhere with consequences mostly because it is painting a picture of a world that does not and cannot exist. It is an amoral counselling that bears no relation to the human condition and human nature but since sociology rejects the existence of both, it is only natural that the sociological mind comes up with junk like this, ideas totally unhinged from any kind of connection to the *actual* world. And yet Marcuse's sociological thought formed a not insubstantial portion of the intellectual spirit of the 1960s.

But when we strip away Marcuse's pretensions—the PhD, the books, the university appointments, his membership in the equally destructive "Frankfurt School" of Marxists—we see that he is merely counselling a way of life advocated by Antiphon, Antisthenes, Diogenes, and even Wrong who, we recall from Chapter Two, had told the young men of Athens 2,500 years ago to abandon restraint, modesty, and decency and instead "do what you like and get away with it—indulge your desires, laugh and play, and have no shame." Is it really any wonder here that later sociologists had such a difficult time explaining this decade? Of course they mumbled stuff about "status politics."

There were worries of course about what was going on and into the minds of the young people at that time. The president of the American Psychiatric Association observed in 1968 that these young people were "very bright, but also unformed," and that made it quite easy for teachers to fill the souls of their students with an "uninformed radicalism" with no thought to consequence.[43] And most of that "uninformed radicalism" that was going into their minds was sociological theory. Stanislav Andreski watched the whole thing unfold with horror and he placed the blame squarely and directly on "bad sociology." He said that the Hippies were doing their "thing" as a result of "an exposure to a sloppy pseudo-science" that had evidently "stultified their powers of logical reasoning."[44]

The dangerous implications of sociological thought were well-known by their peddlers in the 1960s. Andreski comes right out and says that the decade was caused by bad Marxian sociology. But even the sensible and venerable Peter Berger felt worried enough about the potential damage that could be wrought by sociology that he, too, expressed his worries. He asked in 1963, even before things went bad, by what right does the sociologist "peddle such dangerous intellectual merchandise among young minds?"[45] He says that it is one thing to "dispense the sociological poison ["dispense"? "poison"?!] to graduate students" but he adds that it is quite another thing to "dispense" it to those who have no opportunity or inclination to develop their understanding further.[46]

Berger is tacitly admitting here that sociology does in fact counsel ideas which do have dangerous implications for society, animated as it is by Marxian visions of progress, revolution, and renovation. But he is very careful here to deflect the criticism that sociology causes problems rather than solves them when he implies that no problems would occur if the subject is studied correctly. The Sophist Gorgias made exactly the same point about his teachings 2,500 years ago. Sophistry ruined Athens, but Gorgias deflected the criticism by using precisely the same argument as Berger: "it is not the teachers that are bad, nor does this mean the art is responsible or bad, but rather I think those who use it incorrectly." But let's be clear here—if problems issue forth from the art, or the teacher of the art, or the students of the art, but in all cases the problems can be traced back to the art, then perhaps it would be well and sensible to reconsider our position on the art itself.

Liberty, Running Amok

Where the faculty of universities did not encourage or actively participate in this revolution, they did capitulate to youthful pressure. They "publicly confessed their guilt and apologized for not having understood the most important moral issues" of the day.[47] And thus the professoriate agreed to change and reform the goals and functioning of the university, what was taught, what was expected of students. And students were "determined to be heard," whether it was teaching methods, or even the material being taught.[48]

At one school in New York, students rebelled and stopped attending classes until their "voice" was heard. The students claimed to be "uptight" about "a lot of things." They demanded a say in administrative control, for example. But when the administration agreed to the proposition and established meetings to flesh out the details, very few students showed up.[49] With some wisdom, teacher Joe Lobenthal suggests that the students had merely seized on this notion of administrative reform and student voice "mainly for its purity." It sounded good.

These particular students did of course publish a manifesto. But manifesto is perhaps too grand a word. Their programme is a childish tantrum, a horror show of adolescent petulance run amok. "We want to decide what we learn" the students declared. "The faculty must serve us and serve as consultants to us—but as equals not as final arbiters. How can they know what we know when they teach and test on only what they know?"[50] Go on. Read that last sentence there. Ponder it for awhile. They all simply needed a good spanking.

But even this capitulation of teachers and elders to "youth" is nothing new. We have been here before. The kind of attitude and spirit we are seeing here in the sixties had already been seen and done in Athens and Plato captures the mood brilliantly.

Under the pressures exerted by Liberty, he wrote, society will change. The people infused with "the neat spirit" will "abuse as servile and contemptible, those who obey the authorities."

And this attitude will move into the private lives of citizens where "it becomes the thing for the father and son to change places, the father standing in awe of his son and the son neither respecting nor fearing his parents."

And from the family, rampant Liberty moves into the schools where "the teacher fears and panders to his pupils, who in turn despise their teachers."

And from the school, Liberty moves into the social life of the community where the young disrespect their elders "while their elders try to avoid the reputation of being disagreeable or strict by aping the young and mixing with them on terms of easy good fellowship."[51]

And with tongue firmly in cheek, Plato observes that ultimately Liberty "will permeate private life and infect even the domestic animals with anarchy."[52] Horses and donkeys, he says, will "walk about the streets with a grand freedom and bump into people they meet in the streets if they don't get out of their way. Everything is full of this spirit of liberty."[53] And Plato's interlocutor, the indefatigable Glaucon, wholeheartedly agrees, exclaiming, "you're telling me! I've often suffered from it on my way out of town."

Both amusing and *painfully* relevant, Plato's observations here can also be read as a kind of warning from history, still another one. In explaining the nature of democracies here and what Liberty does to people, Plato's larger purpose was to try and understand how and why social and political orders change from one condition to another, in this case from democracy to tyranny. And this descent from democracy into tyranny, Plato argues, begins at precisely that moment when "an excessive desire for liberty at the expense of everything else" becomes the prevailing cultural ethos; when pure negative liberty becomes the only standard of the Good.

Inventing Wheels

But the New Left radicals and Hippies—lacking any grounding in history and philosophy—did not understand that what they were saying, thinking, and doing had already been said, thought, or done before.[54] A long time ago, too. Instead, predictably, they declared that they were engaged "in an unprecedented undertaking."[55] The teenaged "student activists" claimed that their ideals and ideas for moral and social reform were their own "autonomous creations," which historian and classicist Allan Bloom more accurately calls an "outrageous pretension."[56] But of course the students felt that way. That is what young people do. They invent wheels. But the Hippies and activists were merely reviving old utopias.

Raymond Aron observed that "the student rebels have neither invented anything nor developed anything. Their themes of protest, their visions of the future, seem to be borrowed from writers long-since buried in obscurity."[57] And this was true even of their inspirational political guru Karl Marx. Philosopher Hannah Arendt observed that Marx's utopia itself—his vision of the future so beloved by the SocProg set—was scarcely little more than a reimagining of the Athenian *polis* from ancient Greece. Indeed, some of the most essential features of the Marxian project were cribbed, ripped off, or otherwise plundered from thinkers in antiquity.[58]

Canadian labour historian Bryan Palmer affirms but certainly does not agree with Aron's characterization that there was nothing new in what "youth" were doing. Instead, Palmer positively marvels at how the "youth" were able to incorporate ideas from Marx ("the rebel Hegelian, theorist of alienation, and beer downing author of a sheaf of love poems"), "Mao Tse Tung thought" and the "anarcho-surealist graffiti of a metaphorical Parisian Left Bank [?!]"[59] Marx *and* Mao now, together? Does anyone else *not* think it strange that we valorize a decade whose foundational ideas and ideologies led directly to the unnatural deaths—through terror-famines, massacre, imprisonment, and murder—of 100 million people?[60]

The End and the Beginning

The 1960s began with a bang but ended with a whimper.[61] Canadian journalist Peter Desbarats wandered through McGill University one summer night in 1969, after the energy of the decade had been spent, and the ruination and spoliation of young people complete. Desbarats espied a herd of Hippies "clustered on the grass like dark growths...hunkered down, arms trailing, hair obscuring their faces like apes." The enervated Hippies would occasionally make "a few guttural noises" but otherwise remained fairly silent.[62] Their age, the decade they had commandeered, was coming to an end and he saw this mingling, this silent herd, as the last gasp of a debauched generation. "Now that the whole youth thing is ending," he incorrectly prophesized, "it is up to us to assess the sham" (it was up to us, he said, because it will be an even longer time before the "youth" will be able to "evaluate their own mutilation" or what was elsewhere called their "self-dooming waste"). One of the most heinous crimes it set in train was its levelling and democratization of the arts and the creative life.

The young people marched under the slogan of "Do your own thing!" But what happened, he observed, was that "everybody did the same thing." Everyone became an artist, because their assumption was that everyone had creativity, and thus the real artist became like everybody else: "The mantle of the poet was available in every boutique and the real poet put on this sham garment, chirped a few lines for someone's cheap guitar and fell silent." What the Hippies failed to realize is that creativity—and, hence, originality—is not available to everyone. You cannot pursue "originality" because that element is, in the words of Stanislav Andreski, "a by-product" that is attained only as the result of a more specific desire.[63] It is the difference between an organic desire and a self-conscious one. When one is trying to *be* something, the results of those efforts will necessarily and by definition be shallow and derivative, and in so many ways that is exactly what the sixties were.

As Desbarats moved away from the herd of Hippies that summer night he observed, rightly, that "the silent, simian shapes squatting on the McGill campus seemed a parody" of the New World they tried to create or imagine. There have been many forgotten generations, he noted, but the generation of the sixties "may be the easiest to forget."[64] One wishes he were right. But he was wrong. The passing of the 1960s did not bring an end to that decade. Though these toxic ideas went into "remission" for a few years, generations of students throughout the 1980s and 1990s were weaned on subjects taught by the New Left crowd from the 1960s and now *they* write and teach in the Universities. The 1960s are not over, not by any stretch. The passions and polemics of that decade, the rehashed and regurgitated ideas, the Sophistry and the Cynicism and the sociology are all still very much with us. The attitudes, values, and beliefs of that decade have not been abandoned: they have been institutionalized.[65]

Endnotes

[1] It is sobering—nay, *humbling*—to submit to the necessity of admitting that one must be grateful to the 1960s for producing musicians like Jimi Hendrix, although it is gratifying to read that Hendrix was, apparently, in some areas, quite conservative. See Harry Shapiro and Caesar Glebbeek, *Jimi Hendrix: Electric Gypsy* (London: Mandarin, 1990), p. 387. Hendrix actually put in some time with the 101st Airborne Regiment. See, pp. 50-59. I heard somewhere that the opening of his beautiful song *May This Be Love* was designed to capture in music the feeling of freefalling out of a plane which, if you listen to the opening, makes sense.

[2] Peter Berger, "Sociology: a disinvitation? *Society*, Nov./Dec., 1992, p. 13. The entire article is an indictment of the sociological enterprise.

[3] Berger, "Sociology: a disinvitation?" p. 13.

[4] Karl Marx and Friedrich Engels, *The Communist Manifesto* (New York: Washington Square Press, 1964), p. 89.

[5] Berger, "Sociology: a disinvitation?" pp. 13-14.

[6] Berger, "Sociology: a disinvitation?" p. 18.

[7] James Henslin et al, *Sociology: a down to earth approach* (Toronto: Pearson, 2010), pp. 404-424.

[8] Berger, "Sociology: a disinvitation?" p. 18.

[9] Fervent: "*Ardent in feeling; burning, or very hot.*" From the Latin *ferveo* which means "to boil."

[10] Some advice here. Parents: if you have a child in university and you have any influence over them at all, please advise them to leave their sociology classes. Students: if you are in a sociology class, please leave. Sociologists: please stop.

[11] The life story of David Reimer is a chilling testament to the consequences of sociological untruths concerning gender. To make a long and tragic story short, young David had his sex "reassigned" after an "expert" recommended it and so was raised as a girl because, of course, gender is socially constructed. He later killed himself. See Henslin, *Sociology*, pp. 148-149. Too, the life story of porn actress Annabel Chong is similarly upsetting. Sociology argues that "you inherit your sex, but you learn your gender as you are socialized into behaviors and attitudes thought appropriate for your sex." Henslin, *Sociology*, p. 147. And so Chong, rejecting "society's" view of women who have lots of sex as "sluts," made it her mission to become a "female stud." The result here seems to have been the ruination and spoliation of a human being. One life ruined by a bad idea is bad enough and so one shudders at contemplating the enormity of the pain which an entire generation inflicted upon itself in the 1960s after similarly buying into sociological untruths about the transformative power of abundant promiscuous sex and the arbitrary and so suspect nature of morality and ethics.

[12] Marx had likely read Aristophanes for he was "scholar" of ancient Greece after all. Indeed, that is where he pillaged and plundered many of his ideas from.

[13] Raymond Aron, "Vision of the Future or Echo from the Past," *Political Science Quarterly*, vol. 84, no. 2, June 1969, pp. 289-310, p. 293. Of course this brings to mind the wonderful—and wonderfully philosophic—film *Fight Club* in which the principal character, Tyler Derden, rouses his troops, calling them "the middle children of history." They were the men who came of age in the 1990s—a kind of lost generation, without war, revolution, or economic depression to galvanize them, and thus a generation of men who had become wholly dependent upon random purchases of Ikea furnishings to keep them satisfied.

[14] Aron, "Vision of the Future," p. 294.

[15] Aron, "A Vision of the Future," p. 294. Italics added.

[16] Efraim Shmueli, "Modern Hippies and Ancient Cynics: a comparison of philosophical and historical developments and its lessons," *Cahier D'Histoire Mondiale* vol. 12, 1970, p. 491.

[17] Shmueli, "Modern Hippies," p. 491.

[18] Shmueli, "Modern Hippies," p. 490.

[19] *The Sixties: passion politics and style* edited by Dimitry Anastakis, pp. 7-9. (Montreal: McGill-Queens University Press, 2008), pp. 7-9. Many if not most universities across North America at that time operated on the principle of *in loco parentis*, a Latin phrase that means "in place of a parent." It essentially made universities the temporary guardians or parents of the students. The students felt aggrieved. They protested. And the concept was remaindered. And thank heaven they did, for now campuses across North America are, according to many news reports, shot through with and bedevilled by binge drinking, rape, assault, indecency, and any number of other moral calamities. But at least the tyranny of the universities was overthrown; at least Liberty and Freedom had their day.

[20] Shmueli, "Modern Hippies," p. 492.

[21] Shmueli, "Modern Hippies," p. 492.

[22] Thomas Carlyle, *The French Revolution: a history* (New York: The Modern Library, 2002), p. 179.

[23] "Impeccable Ideals; Stupid Means," in *Science News*, vol. 93, no. 22, June 1, 1968, pp. 518-519.

[24] Carlyle, *French Revolution*, p. 14.

[25] "Vagrancy Syndrome," *The British Medical Journal*, vol. 3, no. 5673, September 27, 1969, p. 732.

[26] Bryan D Palmer, "New Left Liberations: The Poetics, Praxis and Politics of Youth Radicalism," in *The Sixties in Canada: a turbulent and creative decade* edited by M. Athena Palaeologu (Montreal: Black Rose Books, 2009), p. 74.

[27] Aron, "Vision of the Future," p. 294; Palmer, "New Left Liberations," p. 73. I am reminded of the film *Walk Hard* in which the principal character, Dewey Cox, captures the spirit of the 1960s. Dewey opines: "It's hard for me to sit around at some birthday party when I know there's so much injustice goin' on in this world...I've got to think about other people." To which his wife Darlene sensibly replies: "You mean, like your family?" And to which an impassioned Dewey says: "No! I mean the people that's havin' injustices done to them, like women and midgets and such!"

[28] William A. Watts, and David Whittaker, "Profile of a Non-Conformist Youth Culture: a study of the Berkeley non-students," *Sociology of Education*, vol. 41, no. 2, Spring 1968, p. 178.

[29] "Impeccable Ideals, Stupid Means," p. 518.

[30] Aron, "A Vision of the Future," p. 302.

[31] "The Hippies," *Time Magazine*, vol. 90, no. 1, July 7, 1967, pp. 27-31.

[32] "The Hippies," *Time*, pp. 20-25.

[33] Karl Marx, *The Communist Manifesto* (New York: Washington Square Press, 1964), pp. 87-89. All subsequent quotations from Marx are taken from this section.

[34] James Henslin et al, *Sociology: a down to earth approach* (Toronto: Pearson, 2010), p. 383.

[35] Although economic oppression in the family does still exist: our sociology textbook assures us that "the recurring struggle over who does housework is actually an example of such a struggle over time, energy and the leisure to pursue interesting activities." Henslin, *Sociology*, pp. 284-285.

[36] Speaking of the sanctified, Marx's progeny Leon Trotsky would not even grant such status to human life. He famously referred to the sanctity of human life as "Quaker-papist babble."

[37] Henslin, *Sociology*, pp. 282-283.

[38] Martin Amis, *Koba the Dread: laughter and the twenty million* (Toronto: Vintage, 2003), p. 237.

[39] Palmer, "New Left Liberations," p. 71.

[40] Stanislav Andreski, *Social Science as Sorcery* (London: Andre Deutsch, 1972), p. 227.

[41] Aron, "A Vision for the Future," pp. 298, 304.

[42] Palmer, "New Left Liberations," p. 71.

[43] "Impeccable Ideals, Stupid Means," p. 519.

[44] Andreski, *Social Science*, p. 227.

[45] Peter Berger, *Invitation to Sociology: a humanistic perspective* (Woodstock NY: Overlook Press, 1973), p. 174.

[46] Berger, *Invitation*, p. 174.

[47] Alan Bloom, *The Closing,* p. 313.

[48] Aron "A Vision for the Future," p. 303. The vaunted Student Evaluation Process in which students evaluate their teachers (?!) derives from this period.

[49] Joseph S. Lobenthal Jr., "The Catabolism of Student Revolt," *Journal of Higher Education*, vol. 40, no. 9, December 1969, pp. 717-730, p. 719.

[50] Lobenthal, "The Catabolism," p. 719. Italics added. I am reminded here of a satirical *Onion News Network* skit in which the pundits decried testing based on what the teachers know, not what the students know. The scene was a portion of a skit asking whether or not "tests are biased against students who don't give a shit."

[51] Plato *The Republic* translated by Desmond Lee (London: Penguin, 1987), p. 383.

[52] Plato, *Republic*, p. 383.

[53] Plato, *Republic*, p. 384. Plato, like Oswald Spengler, does not get enough credit for his humour. In *The Republic*, for example, an increasingly frustrated and angry Thrasymachus asks Socrates: "Do you still have a wet nurse?" Socrates asks why, to which Thrasymachus stormily replies "Because she's letting you run around with a snotty nose and doesn't wipe it when she needs to!" See *The Republic* translated by G.M.A. Grube, revised by C.D.C. Reeve (Indianapolis: Hackett Publishing, 1992), p. 19.

[54] Speaking of historical and philosophical ignorance, I recall hearing a senior CBC news correspondent gushing over the 2015 election of Justin "The Shiny Pony" Trudeau (thanks Erza; my father, David, calls Trudeau "Peter Pan" which fits remarkably well; I personally prefer "Little Lord Fauntleroy;" "Zoolander" is good; I have heard him called "Little Miss Thang;" the most recent addition I am aware of is "The Tiny Dancer"). The reporter remarked with enthusiasm that a liberal Canada was back and that these changes "may even be permanent." Anybody who makes statements of any such kind should not be in a position where they are explaining anything to anyone. Confucius explains: "Learning

without thinking is labor lost; *thinking without learning is perilous.*" Italics added. See *Sources of Chinese Tradition* vol. 1 edited by Wm Theodore de Bary (New York: Columbia, 1960), p. 24.

[55] Palmer, "New Left Liberations," p. 71.

[56] Bloom, *The Closing*, p. 334.

[57] Aron, "A Vision for the Future," p. 308

[58] Hannah Arendt, "Tradition and the Modern Age," in *Between Past and Future: eight exercises in political thought* (London: Penguin, 1977), p. 19. The full idea from Arendt here is that Marx's descriptions of Utopia "reproduce the political and social conditions of the same Athenian city state which was the model of experience for Plato and Aristotle." The Marxian concept of "false consciousness" was an idea first developed by Plato who had a reprehensible character, Thrasymachus, argue that the values and beliefs of the citizens are actually the values and beliefs of the rulers and that they, the citizens, "are unaware of the influence their rulers have had in shaping their whole outlook on the world." See Plato's *Republic*, revised by Reeve, p. xiv. One strongly suspects with firm and unshakeable conviction that Marx did not credit Plato for that idea in the same way that Marx did not credit the Sophists and the Cynics for the idea of "free love" being more natural than marriage. We can also be sure that Marx did not credit the Cynics for pioneering the idea of the negative Liberty so central and essential to Marxism itself. Marxism would not exist without the idea of negative liberty: his entire system is dependent upon the idea. And even the "outrageous pretensions" of the students who claimed that their ideas were their own "autonomous creations" was *itself* a recrudescent manifestation of *Marx's* "outrageous pretensions" of claiming that *his* ideas were his own "autonomous creations." I must stop now, for I grow weary, and a mournful sadness descends.

[59] Palmer, "New Left Liberations," p.69. I simply have no idea what "anarcho- surrealist graffiti of a metaphorical Parisian Left bank" even means.

[60] Please see Mark Kramer ed., *The Black Book of Communism: crimes, terror and repression* (Cambridge, MA: Harvard University Press, 1999). It is a study which examines not the *intentions* of Marxist states, but their practical *results* which was, in rough numbers, about 100 million dead bodies in the twentieth century. Please see Martin Amis's *Koba the Dread* for an exploration of how and why the West seems to have excused Marx for initiating ideas that resulted in crimes that are roughly ten to fifteen times greater in scale than those of the Nazi's and Adolf Hitler. I call my cat Chairman Meow, yes, but with a healthy sense of irony. We in the West, though, seem to have a *huge* blind spot where Marx is concerned. Indeed we teach his subject in universities which is rather like teaching phrenology. And no I do not accept— in fact I "abolish" it—that tired and worn out old story that Marx later in life claimed he himself was no Marxist. The destruction wrought in his name was done so because he wrote a book in which he called for that very destruction. And then he signed his name to it.

[61] I recall the characterization of the end of the 1960s from Professor Martha Smith-Norris, my American History instructor at the U of S. A moderate, cautious, and highly sensible woman, she explained that the end of the sixties revolved around drug addiction, murder, suicide, illegitimate births, the collapse of families, crime, and confusion—but at least there had been Liberty and Freedom aplenty; Liberty and Freedom for all.

[62] Peter Desbarats, "The Most Forgettable Generation," in *Saturday Night*, vol. 84, September, 1969, p. 35. I thank Mr. Palmer for citing this article in *his* article on the 1960s. It is a wonderful, tart little piece. Palmer calls it "carping", but respectfully and probably obviously, I disagree. Anyway, thank you.

[63] Andreski, *Social Science*, p. 223.

[64] Desbarats, "The Most Forgettable," p. 36.

[65] Roger Kimball, *Tenured Radicals*, p xi.

CHAPTER FIVE

THE SOCPROGS

"And in the end the age was handed/the sort of shit that it demanded."
Ernest Hemingway, The Age Demanded, as cited
in Jacques Barzun's "The Artist" p. 20.

"It is just this lack of connection to a concern with the truth—this indifference to how things really are—that I regard as the essence of bullshit."
Harry G. Frankfurt, On Bullshit, pp. 33-34

"If you can't dazzle them with brilliance, baffle them with bullshit."
Ancient Western proverb.

"Pompous, abstruse, claustral, inflated, euphuistic, pleonastic, solecistic, sesquipedalian,
Heliogabaline, occluded, obscure, jargon-ridden, empty: resplendently dead."
David Foster Wallace on modern academic writing in, Consider the Lobster, p. 81.

"It is, then, in no cantankerous spirit against the present generation of academic
historians, but in all gratitude, admiration, and personal friendship towards
them that I launch this 'delicate investigation' into the character of history."
George Macaulay Trevelyan, Clio, a Muse, 1913

The Hippies and activists rolled into universities across the West in the
1970s after the desolation of the sixties, dragging with them their sordid
and bewildering intellectual heritage with its negations and its destructions; its
ideologies and its sociologies. They did, however, change their name for they
ceased calling themselves the New Left and, after a time, modestly labelled
themselves Progressives. Progressive is the adjective of the noun "progress"

which means "*a movement forward nearer a goal; advancement toward maturity or completion*." This claim, that they were advancing not just history but also society toward its goal, toward its maturity and completion, was complemented by their self-defined and super-excellent moral imperatives. According to historian Christopher Dummit, SocProgs aim at redressing historical wrongs, that they and they alone are going to give voice to the "oppressed and the marginalized," and this mission of Justice has given them a "feeling of righteousness."[1] Righteous: "*upright; virtuous; blameless; morally right; equitable; right-thinking*." But they shower themselves with still more and even greater laurels. Progressive historian Joan Wallach Scott once wrote that SocProg historians are actually more than just mere historians: they are "agents of renewal and change." And for good measure, she adds that those who would preserve the old ways "threaten the vitality of history."[2]

Let's hold up here for just a second and dwell—uncomfortably, yes, but only briefly—on this steaming pile of self-wonderment and self-congratulation. First, we should be seeing clearly by now that many of the cherished SocProg ideals and ideas which they feature as "new," "advanced," "modern," and cutting-edge are merely reheated, day-old oddities from ancient Greece that have been amplified, theoretized, and systematized. Historian R.G. Collingwood explains that a thing, in order to be called new (and hence actually deserving of the name "progressive"), must be a new "specific type" of thing and not merely a new action belonging to that specific type.[3] SocProgs are a type and so too are their theories and ideas—they may be more complicated, elaborate, and extravagant than when they first appeared in Athens, but the spirit and attitude that animates the ideas and even the ideas themselves (relativity, our inability to know and so grasp the truth, words as constructors of reality, the duplicity of language, epistemology and how we come to know things), are as old as the Western tradition.

Second, we have a group of historians who, according to their own definitions, are upright, virtuous, blameless, right-thinking, and who are remaking the discipline of history and indeed society, steering it upward toward an ever-finer and more perfect realm. Now, SocProgs get tetchy when they are not taken at their own self-valuations and self-estimations. That irritability arises out of the conceit that they are acting on behalf of Justice and Humanity and so if you quibble and spar with a SocProg then you are by definition quibbling and sparring with a Redeeming Agent of Mankind. But let's move beyond their self-definitions, their self-congratulation, and their self-wonderment. Let us instead carefully consider and examine the foundations of their thought and the expressions of same.

A SocProg Sampler

The trouble with ideas—especially bad ones—is that they move around quietly, invisibly; slowly saturating, barely attracting notice. The poisonous ideas of the sixties were plainly apparent because the Hippies were the physical manifestation of the ideas contained in *The Communist Manifesto* which itself is the physical manifestation of a bad idea. But those ideas are less easily apparent today in part because there is no gross and overt physical manifestation of them. Too, these ideas have escaped notice because we have somehow been able to contort ourselves into a position in which we frame this as a contest between the "regressive right" and the "progressive left." It isn't. But the ideas have worked their magic and have leaked out into the wider culture at large with the consequence that most people today speak or think like a SocProg without even knowing they are being SocProggy. One of the more interesting and comical manifestations of these bad ideas is air quotes.

It's a safe bet that you recently used air quotes in discussion. Men and women in the 1950s did not run around using air quotes. They faced the world head on. We use ironic air quotes for a couple of reasons. For one, it relieves us of the responsibility of facing a concept straight up and head on. Words (and therefore ideas) that make us uncomfortable—words like "man" for example—we will frequently ensconce in quotes, either with our digits or in the tone of our voices because the idea makes us uncomfortable. Being a man, or indeed merely saying the word, is evidently something with which we today have tremendous difficulty. Listen for it. That discomfort is very real and it is there.[4]

And second, air quotes allow us to come at something sideways, subtly undermining the idea, indicating not only our suspicion of it, but also—and this is most important—that we have *progressed beyond* such archaic and infantile concepts. And our quote fetish arises directly out of SocProg negations as we will see below. SocProgs are always and forever putting words in quotes.

The Joan Scott cited above actually puts the word "history" in quote marks.[5] And even Christopher Dummit and Michael Dawson, editors of the book *Contesting Clio's Craft*, couldn't make it out of the second paragraph of their introduction without putting the word "national" in quote marks.[6] So yes, we are all thoroughly "post-modern" and SocProggy in many ways. Their values have become our values, to greater or lesser degrees, whether we know it or not.

There are many several and bewildering entry points into the SocProg mind but we might begin our excursions there by considering their fixation with "the elites." You will find that most SocProgs hold a disturbing and complex obsession with "the elites." One can scarcely make it through *any* SocProg work without numerous times bumping into this thought cliché, this thought junk. These "elites" are so central to the SocProg worldview because "the elites" are responsible for much that is wrong in society, for creating and perpetuating ideologies which result in injustice and inequality.

The SocProgs have been educated by Karl Marx and sociology to believe that "the elites" occupy most positions of power and authority in our society and can manipulate it by implanting in it ideas, values, beliefs, and moralities which "the masses" would reject if given half the chance. Our introductory sociology textbook assures young and impressionable students that their distorted reality is actual reality. They write, to unintentionally comic effect, that "the elites in every society develop ideologies to justify their position at the top." Not only that, but "the ruling elites of democracies [maintain this position] by manipulating the media."[7] And just in case you get it in your head to resist "the elites" you had better first remember that "the elites also command the police and military and can give orders to crush a rebellion."[8] And "the elites" are not afraid to use this power because they are the state and as anyone knows, the state "claims the exclusive right to use violence and the right to punish anyone one" because, after all, "violence is the ultimate foundation of any political order."[9] From this sad, warped, and pathetic worldview, we are forced to conclude that a kind of delusional paranoia forms a not insubstantial portion of the sweaty and feverish SocProg mind. English scholar Christopher Butler affirms this when he writes that that "suspicion which can border on paranoia" is a key element of the post-modernist ideas from which the SocProgs develop their sociologies.[10]

The subject of what they call "cultural studies" is yet another of the tools used by the SocProgs to wreck history and negate settled values and standards.

This is an approach to the study of culture that is rooted in a Marxist conception of how the world works and which seeks to weaken cultural confidence.[11] Now, the Western cultural canon is, in Mathew Arnold's phrase, "the best that has been thought and said." And amongst the best in the Western tradition we count Homer, Plato, Aristotle, St Augustine, St. Thomas Aquinas, Shakespeare, Herman Melville, Thomas Carlyle. But for the Cultural Studies folks, Homer's *Iliad*, for example, is not a great book but merely "a marker of elite status" which contains no inherent value.[12] The idea that the *Iliad* and other great works are in fact "great" is, for the SocProgs, "a gigantic trans-generational lie concocted by the ruling classes ["the elites!"] as a means of inducing subordinate social groups to bow respectfully before the high culture of those who had benefitted from an elite education."[13] For the SocProgs, the Canon is representative not of beautiful thought embodied in sensuous form, but rather an expression, a *symptom*, of "a great overarching system of domination and exploitation" established by "the elites" in pursuit of their own self-interest.[14]

This idea of the elites using culture to oppress can be "debunked" in one of two ways. Historian Werner Jaeger suggests that it is a "fundamental fact" of human history that culture is developed by the nobility or "the elites."[15] But where the SocProgs go sideways is in thinking that it was developed *malevolently* with the aim of oppressing and stupefying the masses. Sociologist Stanislav Andreski also rejects Marxist claims that "the elites" developed high culture to serve their interests and oppress the masses mostly because he has never actually met anyone who has made this claim.[16] It is the Marxists who are making this claim on behalf of the people it purports to represent. The Marxists might reply that "the elites" are simply victims of their own "false consciousness," that they do not yet recognize that they are in fact embracing and perpetuating a cultural ideal that oppresses. And that is certainly an interesting idea and it does account for the fact that no one has ever actually admitted to their part in this conspiracy. But Andreski counters back that there is simply no evidence at all to support that idea.[17] And he is right. There is none. And here once again, we see that some of the foundational ideas of SocProg thought are upheld by nothing other than faith or, better stated, ideology.

By the way, if at this late stage you're still scratching your head here wondering why university professors are perpetuating the ideas of the biggest failure of the twentieth century, you're not alone. There persists to an astonishing degree, a kind of vague notion that even though the ideas of Marx failed (not just failed, but failed *spectacularly*; Marx is the poster boy for failure; if you look up the word "failure" in the dictionary, you should be able to see a photo of Karl Marx), there remains the notion that somewhere in that turgid, pretentious mess of Marxist theory—which few people have read because it's apparently unreadable—that "new historical perspectives" were opened up.[18] They weren't, but let's never mind that for right now.

The Spanish historian of philosophy Julian Marias offers two more realistic reasons why Marx matters. One, Marx created the ideas that formed the philosophical foundation of one of the twentieth century's "greatest" and also most violent mass movements. And two, Marx's ideas are "relatively useful" in appreciating and understanding at least a portion of the ugly realities of nineteenth century working life. But that is it. As Marias explains, Marxist ideas taken out of their exclusively nineteenth century European context are "absolutely inadequate" when applied to other eras or other countries. Once that theory is removed from its roots and used to explain twenty-first century reality, Marxian theory can only "violently distort reality" because the new reality that the theory is being asked to explain is a reality the theory was never meant to explain in the first place, and could never have imagined anyway.[19] The reason that the whole idea of our society being ruled by oppressive and menacing "elites" sounds so absurd and ridiculous is that the very idea of "the elites" comes from a theory which reflected nineteenth century Europe. And nineteenth century Europe is not twenty-first century North America. And so, when an antiquated theory written to explain a very periodic and temporary European reality is used as the lens through which we view modern North American reality, we necessarily get "violently distorted realities." We get sociological reality.

These then, though, are just a few of the ideas essential to the SocProg project and most if not all of them are aimed at one thing: to erode or make suspect through non-violent means, the traditions, values, customs, morality, and beliefs of a society they see as fundamentally flawed. Whilst the SocProgs may not masturbate in public, they, like the Cynics, are in fact engaged in a "thoroughgoing onslaught against custom and convention." Historian John Cairns was quoted in the *Canadian Historical Review* as saying that the SocProgs are "attempting to finish off what Marxism began [by] overturning conventional structures."[20] And they do this by teaching young and impressionable undergraduates in universities that the principles and values of Western culture (Liberty, Equality, Justice, Democracy) are mere talk and "hollow rhetoric" which "mask the self-interest of the wealthy and powerful" who exert control over the masses.[21] And that may have been true. Once. Centuries ago.

While rarely being explicit about what it is they are trying to do, the goal is in fact social and political change. For the SocProgs, it is a revolution, only a very quiet one, one without lachrymose Lenins and terrible Trotskies with their pitchforks and machine guns and soviets running amok in the streets. Indeed historian James Tracy observes of academics today that "one can be a revolutionary while sitting at one's word processor without having to rub elbows with sweaty and uncouth proletarians."[22] The really odd thing is that SocProgs will only rarely admit to:

a) being a SocProg;

b) the intentions or even the natural and obvious implications of their scholarship.

They may say they aim at nothing; that they're writing history as it really is. But that is just another untruth.

With their minds hobbled by theory and untruth, and their souls awash in the confusion which issues forth from their various negations and destructions, and lacking that all-important "settled external viewpoint" so crucial to creation, the SocProgs ply their grim hell-trade in seminar rooms across the West.[23] Since most SocProg historians partake of many of the same theoretical and ideological poisons, there is the happy yet very troubling result that the work of one of them in one country is almost totally indistinguishable from the work of another one in another country. That word "indistinguishable" is a synonym for "indistinctive" which means "*Having no distinguishing quality.*" (The elephant-in-the-room-question: can scholarship which contains no distinguishing qualities really be called scholarship?) And so our detailed examination of SocProg scholarship will focus on—indeed *need* only focus on—two articles which embody virtually all that is wrong and ruinous, and Sophistic and Cynical, with the SocProg approach.[24] Alexsandr Solzhenitsyn once said: "To taste the sea, all you need is one gulp."

The Historian as Marxist Gender Theoretician

Craig Heron's *The Boys and Their Booze: masculinities and public drinking in working class Hamilton, 1890-1946*, is a pretty standard example of the SocProg as Marxist and gender theorist.[25] Heron's article offers us a window into how a mind on theory thinks and how theory hobbles independent judgement and thought.[26] The article, not surprisingly, also contains a bewildering number of the thought clichés and fetish-phrases so beloved by the SocProg set. In no particular order, Heron's article deals in a rich and luxuriant smorgasbord of Marxian sociological thought: gender, social construction, elites, identity, public space, community, patriarchy, masculinity, femininity, authority, control, bourgeois values, hegemony, and more.

Heron sets out to examine "group identity" within "working-class communities."[27] Specifically, he has an almost anthropological interest in the "customs and rituals" of men going out and getting drunk after work or, in his sterile, theory-hobbled phrasing "drinking with other men in a public space." His basic idea is to trace how working-class men made their participation in these drinking sessions "an important part of their evolving expression of their masculinities." Masculinity is plural there because apparently there is a "multiplicity of masculinities" which theory designates as "hegemonic and subordinate." And Heron also wants to explore "how they interacted with the regulatory regimes that aimed at controlling them" and those two phrases "control" and "regulatory regimes" of course hint at "the elites" and "the ruling classes" over whom SocProgs darkly obsess.[28]

Before getting into the gender portion of his study, Heron first situates his working men in a late-stage capitalist tyranny. It was actually just Hamilton. Heron observes that "drinking with other men in a public space" was not fun but rather an "alternative to the harsh indignities of the capitalist workplace [and] the constraints of bourgeois moral and cultural codes."[29] More than that, drinking rooms were "a refuge from the increasing harshness of capitalist industry."[30] And since Heron situates his working-class men in a capitalist tyranny, all of their actions within this system necessarily become resistance and *therefore* Heron can argue that getting drunk was, again, not fun but rather "a collective defiance of bourgeois efforts to control them as well as the privilege to participate in a public life that was closed to most women in their communities."[31]

Despite the presence of this invisible tyranny, though, Heron assures us that his working men "made no direct challenges to the capitalist and patriarchal social order."[32] Perhaps this impotence came about because their minds were mired in "false consciousness," a condescending Marxist concept in which the workers don't resist the tyranny because they are ignorant and unaware of the overarching system of oppression in which they live. They will remain in ignorance until liberated by revolutionaries whose "revolutionary conscious-ness" will replace their own, in just the same way as Marx's consciousness has evidently replaced that of Mr. Heron.

With his theory-besotted mind drooping neath the weight of the ideas of a peculiar and long-dead German economist, Heron then imagines what work-ing-class men do, what they must be like when they get together. With that queer sense, that *unnatural feel* for all things human—the only true talent that the sociological mind seems to possess, and it is an *anti*-talent at best—Heron paints us a picture of what it was like at the bar when working men gathered to get drunk and escape from the brutal tyranny in which they lived. Heron says that, at the bar, these men would finally and at long last have the chance to talk about what was *really* on their minds:

> "Selling their labour for wages to their bosses [and] about the ways that the changing work world of capitalist management was eating away at their inde-pendence, creativity, and dignity on the job. In front of the bar, these men could plot a strike, or simply try to forget their long hours of paid labour and find other ways to build working-class masculine identities in their leisure time."

Heron's characterization of a working man's life here is rather like an abstract-impressionist painting someone did of something they had once heard about but never actually seen. Let's move slowly, thoughtfully, through this characterization.

First, it is Marxian theory, not Heron, that is painting the picture here. Marx held that a man's labour power is the only thing he has to sell and that if he does not sell it he will starve.[33] Thus, a working man is unnaturally forced by the capitalist tyranny to sell himself and his labour and in doing so the man abdi-cates his creative potential, his "life-being," and is for all intents and purposes enslaved in some way.[34] And it is this Marxian view of the working world that allows Heron to suggest that men getting drunk at a bar talk would actually talk about "selling their labour for wages to their bosses."

But working men do not do this. They complain about their bosses, they complain about their wages, they complain about their workload. Most men— it might even be safe to say *all* men—are actually quite happy to work and quite pleased to have the opportunity to "sell their labour for wages to their bosses."[35] But Marxian theory holds the opposite which apparently means that jobs themselves are unnatural somehow, merely further evidences proving the existence of an oppressive capitalist tyranny whose explicit goal is to deny men the chance to fully realize their potential. This view is, of course, absurd but it is the very thing which underwrites Heron's observation that after talking about selling their labour, men drinking at a bar will then turn to the related topic of "the ways that the changing work world of capitalist management was eating away at their independence, creativity and dignity." Real actual working men *do not do this.*[36]

For Marx, the dignity and creativity of man had been thwarted for millennia by capitalist oppressors. And that friction between oppressor and oppressed— those "internal contradictions" of which he famously spoke—would inevitably lead to the fall of capitalism. Marx was quite clear on that point: "Its fall and the victory of the proletariat are inevitable."[37]

We're still waiting.

At any rate, after this "inevitable collapse" for which Marx had "scientific proof," a world that has never existed would finally emerge. Marx's world was one in which there were no longer any capitalists and thus no longer any injustice but rather justice aplenty, for all and everyone. After the collapse, "society" would "regulate production" and the masses, liberated by the revolutionaries and emancipated from oppressive labour, would at last be able to unleash their fearsome creativity. Marx promised that in this new world which must inevitably appear, the worker would finally be free to "hunt in the morning, fish in the afternoon, rear cattle [?!] in the evening, and criticize after dinner just as I have a mind."[38] And it is precisely this delusion, this *anti*-reality that Heron embraces when he writes that work and jobs eat away at the independence, dignity, and creativity of the working man.

It helps to remember here that Marx dreamed of this kind of life because he himself hated work. Historian Paul Johnson researched the life of Marx and found that he apparently led a bohemian type of existence, "often idle and dissolute," characterized by irregular work habits and punctuated by dreary political sessions in which he could be found "sitting up all night talking, then lying half asleep on the sofa for most of the day."[39] And so of course he would construct dream worlds—all that leisure time, there, on the sofa, dreaming. But like Marcusian reality, Marxian reality (which is sociology's reality), reflects no *actual* reality that has ever existed at any time in 2,500 years of Western history, or even 5,000 years of recorded human history. Nothing like what Marx described has ever existed. Not ever. Nor will it.

Heron's understanding of a working man's life is derived almost totally from theoretical imaginings rather than any humanistic understanding of the real. The noted American classicist Allan Bloom reflected on the use of theory and drew certain important conclusions. Theory, he observed, provides a "simulacra of thought and experience, hardly better than slogans [and] which take the place of reflection."[40] Simulacra: *"An imaginary, visionary, or shadowy semblance; hence, a sham."* That is what is happening here with Heron. His characterizations are not human but theoretical; theory has taken the place of reflection and reflecting on a thing, which is to say, *"consideration of or meditation upon past knowledge or experience; thought"* is what historians are supposed to do, but which is plainly not happening in Heron's work. It is worth quoting at length what George Orwell had to say about verbal expressions inspired by political/theoretical abstractions:

> "When one watches some tired hack on the platform mechanically repeating the familiar phrases, one often has the curious feeling that one is not watching a live human being but some kind of dummy: a feeling which suddenly becomes stronger at moments when the light catches the speaker's spectacles and turns them into blank discs which seem to have no eyes behind them. And this is not altogether fanciful. A speaker who uses that kind of phraseology has gone some distance towards turning himself into a machine. The appropriate noises are coming out of his larynx, but his brain is not involved as it would be if he were choosing his words for himself...and this reduced state of consciousness, if not indispensible, is at any rate favourable to political conformity."[41]

Orwell hits on something important there: a reduced state of consciousness. This is the practical result of what happens when theory takes the place of reflection. Thomas Carlyle had this to say about men operating under theoretical consciousness (such as it is): "his vital intellectual force lies dormant or extinct; his whole force is mechanical conscious: of such a one it is foreseen that when once confronted with the infinite complexities of the real world, his little compact theorem of the world will be found wanting."[42] Heron's characterization of what working men do is ridiculous precisely because it is a simulacra, hence a sham. The sham grows directly out of his reduced consciousness, his mechanical consciousness, and the absence of reflection—and so, necessarily, the absence of thought.

And finally, the whole idea that men getting drunk will actually talk about "ways to build working-class masculine identities in their leisure time" is just, well, let's borrow here from American writer David Foster Wallace: "This is so stupid it practically drools."[43]

So, this is the environment in which Heron situates his working men: a late-stage capitalist tyranny in which they seek refuge in bars where they will apparently discuss how they can construct masculine identities. From here (and we're not even out of the introduction yet), Heron then proceeds with the larger task at hand. It is Heron's stated belief that the drinking rituals and customs of the working men were means by which they could construct masculinity. Masculinity derives from the word "masculine." Masculine: *Having the distinguishing qualities of the male sex; especially to the stronger, hardier, and more imperious qualities that distinguish the male sex.*" It is Herons intention to argue that these hardy and imperious qualities that have distinguished men for 2,500 years are actually "social constructions" which have "developed in specific contexts in constant interaction with those gendered as female and with other men (and boys) as a dynamic system of patriarchal power."[44] If you were still awake at the end of that sentence, please note Heron's phrasing of "those gendered as female." This phrasing suggests that women, too, had queer and unreal notions of "femininity" unwontedly thrust upon them by "the elites," and that we are only now breaking free of this lie; that we are now *beyond* that.

It is absolutely crucial here to understand where Heron is coming from. We have to explore this first because Heron does not explain it; indeed, there should warnings and disclaimers pasted all over SocProg scholarship. Heron and other "historians of masculinity" (Clio weeps!) are "feminist men" who, through rigorous re-education and Maoist sessions of self-criticism, have come to see masculinity not as the essence and core of being a man but rather (and this is troubling in oceanic, titanic ways) as a "deformation of their true self."[45] The entire premise of gender history, according to esteemed gender theoretician Joy Parr, rests on the conviction that "hierarchical social, economic, and political contexts rather than biology, history rather than nature, created woman," and thus man as well.[46] Parr roots her history and worldview in one single frivolous belief: "*refusing* assertions about universals in human nature."[47] Does no one else think it odd, certainly at the very least curious, that an entire sub-discipline of history is built upon a simple refusal of reality?

For the gender set, neither men nor women have inherent and intrinsic qualities. Man is not more aggressive or competitive than woman, but rather "the elites" created that fiction to exclude women from combat roles in the military, say. Women are not more nurturing than men; "the elites" created that idea to exclude women from the workplace. There are no inherent qualities to men or women. Our sturdy and reliable sociology textbook drearily explains: "You inherit your sex, but you learn your gender as you are socialized into behaviours and attitudes thought appropriate for your sex."[48] In other words, we humans are little more than Empty Vessels. This is a corrosive, toxic, and poisonous lie. And the lie has become a truth because politics made it so. Former feminist Carol Iannone once wrote of gender studies that it could "probably not persist in the absence of strong ideology. Once the special pleading disappeared and normative cultural, scholarly, and intellectual standards had asserted themselves, much of what is now being so assiduously studied would probably sink beneath notice."[49] In other words, once politics or ideology is removed from the equation, the whole enterprise will collapse. We await that development, with delight, and anticipation.

But still, and while it lasts, gender history and "historians of masculinity" are engaged in deeply moral project, a "reformation of masculine identity." For some men, says Parr, this reformation is "an intensely personal struggle to acknowledge guilt and complicity." Guilt and complicity in exactly what she does not indicate here, but one can assume it is male guilt for female oppression. Whatever it is, we can be assured that "historians of masculinity" are clearly demonstrating their intentions to "make a commitment to change" and to amend the sins of their constructed gender.[50]

This, then, is the intellectual swamp out of which Heron's article develops. He is using history as a tool to show how society has "deformed" men and, in doing so, validate a sociological theory. That this theory is rooted in mere "refusal" to accept reality evidently need not trouble anyone. Heron and Parr and the gender set are fired by conviction. Conviction: *a doctrine or proposition which one firmly believes; the forcing of acknowledgement of the truth.*[51] Heron is thus trying to force the acknowledgement of truth, (or, the other way about, establish the veracity of an untruth by breaking the truth) by arguing that drinking rituals were acts that created masculinity.

Heron observes that there is "a growing body of new literature" on masculinity. And "the best" of this "growing body" argues that "masculinity is not a cluster of timeless, universal, testosterone-induced behavioural traits but a process of social construction in a particular time and place." Heron argues, or perhaps gender theory tells him, that there were "four sites" (not five? how about six, say?) where "masculinities" were formed. The first site was the household, where tasks were assigned to young people and this division of labour included, ominously, "particular tasks for boys."[52] The second site where masculinity was inculcated was in Sunday school and elementary schools where young lads were given lessons in "moral probity." Now, all probity means is "decency" which in turns means goodness, honesty, and a sense of fair play—noble concepts to which all men should aspire. But in Heron's mind, moral probity is not only a construct, but also a part of something he calls "the hegemonic masculinity of empire."

We must be very careful here. Is Heron suggesting that decency and fair play were artificial constructs that served or buttressed British Imperialism or Imperialist goals in some shadowy way? The question must be asked because the phrasing "hegemonic masculinity of empire" raises red flags: what is he getting at *here*? It is frequently the case with SocProgs that their catchwords and fetish-phrases ("hegemony," "masculinity," "public space," "identities," "the elites," "the ruling classes," etc.) are always supported off stage by a whole web of sundry ideologies and political theories, but this fact frequently escapes notice because of the anodyne, almost casual way those words and ideas are presented.[53] SocProg fetish-phrases always represent larger ideas and ideologies and those words do in fact aim at something. The troubling thing is that the SocProgs never say so.

The third "site" where masculinity was "constructed" was in the streets where young men did what boys do but always with a careful emphasis (it has always ever been thus!) on steering clear and avoiding any "'feminine'" tendencies. Please note that Heron situates the word "feminine" in inverted commas. The inverted commas inform us that femininity as an idea, as a set of behaviours, is a "social construct" which does not reflect any actual reality, and that we are only now finally realizing this after 2,500 years of believing the opposite. And since we are now *beyond* archaic notions of intrinsic "femininity" we must nestle the word "feminine" in between inverted commas. And the fourth "arena of gender formation" was the workplace.[54] Thus interaction in these four "arenas" or "sites" would establish "the dominant forms and central dynamics of masculine norms and practices."

Ultimately, Heron concludes that "a working man's 'manhood'" (note the inverted commas around "manhood;" he puts them around the word "tough" too), took shape and were formed in these "arenas." Here they were taught by their parents, teachers, and "bosses" to be obedient but they also participated in "collective defiance" of the "bosses" through "homo-social activities" in and out of the workplace. For Heron, there were two "crucial features" to the development of working-class manhood. The first involved proving oneself "in semi-public spaces." And the other required him to "use his body to the fullest." And thus Heron argues that the truth of the ideas of someone named Robert Connell are validated here: "the social construction of gender and the material reality of an actual male body meet as masculinities are worked out through body action in 'reflexive body practices.'"[55]

We know that none of this is true. The conclusions he draws are wrong precisely because we know the premise itself is wrong. The whole thing is wrong (and I don't have the foggiest idea of what that last sentence even thinks it means). It is wrong because social roles do not construct gender, they *reflect* gender; they are a reflection of who we are as men and women, essentially. Now we can obviously move around and shift the roles that men and women adopt, but to parade gender around as a "social construct" is not an idea: it is an offensive assault on and, indeed, an insult to, human nature. But Heron's scholarship has one single and crucially important virtue: it panders directly to our dominant and established cultural ideas concerning gender identity which posit that gender is a social construct. And so Hemingway was right after all: in the end, the age will always be handed, the sort of shit that it demands.

Many idealists and utopians in the past have walked the road Heron is currently walking. The Bolsheviks provide us with the most perfect example.[56] And the most ghastly formulation of that Marxian idea of "social construction" can be found in Arthur Koestler's *Darkness at Noon*, in which the beastly prison Bolshevik, Ivanov, exclaims: "Has anything more wonderful happened in human history? We are tearing the old skin off mankind and giving it a new one."[57] And this project of "tearing off the skin of mankind" was rooted in the monstrously idiotic belief that "proper instruction and legislation" and better "social conditioning" can create a better human being.[58] This is just not so. It is simply a wrong idea, an untruth, a lie generated by abstract sociological theorizing animated by an ideology that rejects, refuses, and denies who we are, fundamentally, as human beings. Martin Amis once observed that "the militant utopian, the perfectibilizer, from the outset, is in a malevolent rage at the obvious fact of human *im*perfectability."[59] And, with his hi to Plato, philosopher-historian Karl Jaspers points out too that, yes, man has in him an ideal, a sense of what being complete would be, but he adds that achieving that finality will never happen, *can* never happen, because "man is not a finished and not a perfectible being."[60] Not ever will the opposite be true. The SocProgs seem to be arguing that the sky is green when it is clearly blue. But how does one *prove* the sky is blue?

The "historian-as-Marxist," though, is just one variant of SocProg intellectual expression. There is another type, too. We now turn to Canadian historian Marcel Martel who provides us with a textbook case—perfect beyond measure, actually—whose historical work on the Hippies reveals that so much of sophisticated SocProg thought is really just Athenian Sophistry by another name.

The Historian as Sophist

Martel's article examines the undercover operations of the Mounties against the Hippies in the 1960s. His aim is to demonstrate that the information the Mounties collected about drug use was used as a weapon to fight against drug law reform and the decriminalization of marijuana. This scholarly effort,

Martel assures us, will "contribute to the growing literature on state repression."[61] Because Canada, of course, was in the way of a fascist tyranny before the Hippies saved us.

The RCMP inserted themselves into various Hippie communities across Canada in the 1960s.[62] The reports filed by the Mounties detailed the dulling and enervating but pleasing minutiae of daily Hippie life, their appearance, general health, sanitation, living habits, and their "philosophy" or worldview. And in short, the Mounties were horrified by what they saw. There was rampant drug use, promiscuous sexual behaviour, a lack of cleanliness, laziness, and filth, all of which was the necessary and natural end-point of the sixties ethos of "Do your own thing!"[63] After all, when humans are left alone to "do their own thing,"—when they are set free and emancipated from all ethical and moral anchors and granted pure negative liberty—the results are rarely if ever good. The sixties provide us with all the proof we need on that point.

The Mounties may have been horrified by the Hippies but Martel is horrified instead at the Mounties (and the present writer is, in turn, horrified at Martel). Martel observes that "most officers could not restrain themselves from making value judgements" about the Hippies.[64] The Mounties wrote in their reports that most of them did not change clothes, only rarely showered, and were, in general, unkempt, unclean, and stank. The Hippie way of life *invites* judgement by even the loosest moral standards and that is what the Mounties did through the use of judgement-laden words like "dirty," "sloppy," and "unclean." But for Martel, these words do not reflect any kind of reality but instead they merely reflect "a strategy of dehumanizing these individuals."[65]

In Martel's SocProg mind, the world works like this: "civil servants often... comment on the lack of cleanliness as a way of justifying their policies of social control" and so by emphasizing the dirt, filth, and stink of the Hippies, the Mounties were not describing anything real but instead were actually trying to "undermine their social appeal." The Mounties were confronting reality but Martel, like Parr, refuses it and he does so because he has apparently disposed with traditional and transcendent ethics (the Seven Sins and the Seven Virtues) in pursuit of the idea that pure negative liberty is the only standard of the Good.

There was, in Hippie life, no daily routine, no regular schedule, and no work. This laziness displeased the Mounties for they remark on it unfavourably in their reports, but their observations on the Hippie layabouts were flawed.

Martel argues that these negative comments don't reflect any kind of reality but rather they "reflect what Tom Lutz calls a 'culture's repertoire of feelings about work.'" And so Martel flips laziness on its head: "since police officers valued work, the anti-work ethic was very disturbing for them and triggered emotional and negative reactions."[66]

Did you catch that?

The SocProgs call laziness an "anti-work ethic."

And Martel didn't even have the common decency to clothe that phrase in inverted commas.

Laziness is the very opposite of an ethic. The word "ethic" comes from a Greek word meaning "character" and which means "*an action in accordance with right standards*" [a SocProg: "Right standards?! Whose 'right standards'?!"]. Lazy means "*indisposed to exertion; indolent, slothful.*" Laziness is loaded as it should be (the consequences of laziness inform us that it is not desirable) with judgements of all kinds. But one can perhaps sniff out and detect where Martel is coming from here. Since the word "lazy" is related to the word "sloth," and is thus connected to the seven deadly sins of the Christian faith, and since sin is itself is an archaic notion which for millennia has thwarted the full realization of individual liberty—and which we binned anyway during the Enlightenment and which Marx further "abolished" in the nineteenth century—and since judgements today in the "as-you-like-it" twenty-first century are inherently fascistic, reflecting "socially constructed" values developed by "the elites," the SocProgs thus deploy "anti-work ethic," a sterile phrase that has been disinfected and cleansed of judgement, so everyone can have even more negative liberty.

Not only are the Hippies lazy and living in filth, they are enthusiastically promiscuous in their sexual behaviour. The sixties was a decade of sexual "liberation" during which people did what they wanted, with whom they wanted, when they wanted. The Mounties saw that, like the Cynics of 2,500 years ago, "some of the sexual acts were very perverted and on occasion involved their own children."[67] The Mounties observed men trading women for drugs and that, like the Cynics, "they were not ashamed to make love anywhere." [68]

But Martel observes that "sexual liberation" meant "sexual exploitation in the eyes of the RCMP."[69] Here, Martel is hauling out his relativism and instead of understanding the entirely unexceptional point that excessive promiscuity is potentially deadly and ruinous, spiritually, he frames the matter as a struggle between the liberty of the individual and the repression of the Mounties. Martel dismisses the concerns of the Mounties, suggesting that their flawed standards derive from something he calls "anglo-celtic masculinity," and thus any value or moral judgement from a group like that, *especially* on matters of sex, can be discarded.[70] We are here reminded: "It is as if purity should provoke a blush and corruption give ground for pride."[71] That comes from St. Augustine, on the rot and decay of Rome, 1,500 years ago.

As we might expect, Martel's relativism does in fact have a theoretical construct. A theory for something like this is almost always necessary because no one, left to their own devices, would think like this. Relativism is one of the outgrowths of Jacques Derrida's theory of deconstruction, itself merely a version of Protagoras' "two-sides-doctrine," and which holds that "truth itself is always relative to differing standpoints."[72] And more than that, for the de-constructor set, "the relationship of language to reality is not given, or even reliable, since all language systems are inherently unreliable cultural constructs."[73] The Mounties saw promiscuous sex and judged it. But since language does not reflect reality, and since the ideal of pure negative liberty appears to be the only moral and ethical standard being applied here, Martel is thus made free to argue that it is not the *act* that is wrong but rather it is the *perception* that is wrong. This is precisely what the Athenians did 2,500 years ago. After the Sophists had done their work, Athenian men began arguing in courts that it was not their behaviour that was wrong—it was the law itself that was wrong.

In addition to rejecting sexual morality, the Hippies also turned their noses up at house cleaning. The RCMP observed that Hippie homes were "filthy." Often they were called "slums," full of garbage, rodents, pets, and "pet excrement," sinks full of dishes, unmade beds, etc. But even when Martel is backed into a corner and forced to admit that something may be a little off here, he flips things the other way about. Rather than seeing the conditions of filth and slop as evidence of a kind of moral or character flaw, he instead blames the officers for failing to understand why Hippies "would choose to live in such abject conditions" in the first place.[74] Indeed, he says, the officers' reports were fundamentally flawed because "most had neither the skills nor the training to conduct sociological inquiries" and thus their judgements about the filth and stink in which the Hippies lived "revealed more about the values and judgements of RCMP officers, than inquisitive minds trying to understand these groups."[75] The SocProg mind operates like that and it is a perverse quirk: the idea that disapproval is somehow revelatory of a *lack* of understanding.[76]

Most Hippies had taken to heart the central message of the decade; tune in, turn on, and drop out, or some such nonsense. And since the Hippies abjured education, the Mounties responded to this negatively, too. Martel argues that the Mounties "disclosed their disdain" for the Hippie way of life because "they themselves had to complete at least eight years of education before joining the force."[77] So, the Mounties actually hated the Hippies because they themselves were forced to go through education while the Hippie did not, and thus there is the implicit suggestion lurking here somewhere that the Mounties actually *envied* the Hippies.

Welcome, then, to the spiritual and intellectual world of the SocProg Sophist. A world where there are no settled values or even basic moral standards. Every single criticism, reproof, and value judgement made by the Mounties is refuted or rejected as being nothing more than the by-product or backwash of their hyper middle-class values, their "anglo-celtic masculinity." Martel quotes historian Mary Louise Adams who argued that, during the Cold War—but especially in the sixties—there were concerted efforts on the part of the state to "construct normality."[78] And so our Mounties here were judging the Hippies and in doing so they were apparently "constructing normality" because evidently, not even normality exists outside our construction of it.

Martel's analysis of the Hippies is a valuable document not as a work of history, but rather as a kind of near-perfect case study of "the mental mechanisms that liberal intellectuals use to disguise the truth from themselves and others." Physician, writer, and essayist Theodore Dalrymple has provided a wonderful taxonomy of the type. First, when confronted with a reality which conflicts with their perception, the SocProg will deny the reality of the thing in question. If that does not work, they will then offer a "tendentious precedent" from history that purports to show how normal the thing in question is. And if that *still* doesn't work, if the problem is *so* bad that it cannot be explained away or rationalized, the thing itself in question is altered and "its moral significance is denied or perverted."[79] This is precisely and exactly the frightening pattern followed here by Martel, and we call it politicized Sophistry.

Dalrymple goes on: "the intellectual's struggle to deny the obvious is never more desperate than when reality is at variance with his preconceptions and when full acknowledgement of it would undermine the foundations of his worldview."[80] To protect their worldview, the SocProgs *must* deny reality—we saw them do this in their failed attempts to explain the sixties—or if not deny it then reshape it so that it conforms to their vision of it. The SocProg must break the truth. Again and for emphasis, it is not a coincidence that the rejection and negation of truth, reality, and objectivity comes from the SocProgs: their scholarship utterly depends on it. In Martel's relativist hands, the group he profiles—people who chose to live in filth, squalor, and sexual indecency, and thus not just inviting but *daring* judgement—come out the other end of Martel's examination not just unscathed: they come out virtuous.

In his defence, Martel is simply the product of his age. His discomfort with making judgements grows out of what philosopher Hannah Arendt calls the increasing "subjectivization" of our world.[81] Arendt explains that our increasing doubt about our capacity to know the truth of anything has had the practical effect of enshrining one's own opinion or belief as the only benchmark against which to measure actions. And thus all judgements, beliefs, and values have become simple matters of taste, and this is how Martel handles the Mounties: men who had not yet been properly "subjectified."

This "subjectivization" was one of the dynamics that ruined and spoiled Athens. Writing well before SocProg thought had even been developed in its modern form, the nineteenth century German philosopher-historian G.W.F. Hegel examined the corrosion of Athens in the fourth century BC and he concluded that it occurred as a result of "subjectivity obtaining emancipation for itself."[82] Sophistic subjectivity, Hegel observed, "menaced the beautiful religion of Greece, while the passions of individuals and their caprice menaced its political constitution." In short, Hegel explains that "subjectivity, comprehending and manifesting itself, threatened the existing state of things in every department." His conclusion here is disturbing because he writes that subjectivity in Athens "appears as the principle of decay."[83] We, today, so clearly divine the decay in Athens, but what do we say about that very same principle when it appeared in the 1960s? Or what do we call that principle today, as it permeates our consciousness in the twenty-first century? We call it Liberty.

But we forget that there are two types of Liberty, not just one.

Right about the time the Athenians were fouling themselves with Liberty, the ancient Chinese philosopher Mencius wrote that there are four intrinsic "senses" in human beings: sympathy, shame, modesty, and the ability to distinguish right from wrong. He goes on to say that "these four senses are so important that they are like a man's limbs. When a man possesses these four senses and yet does not wish to do anything with them, he is cutting his body with his own hands."[84] A man without a sense of shame, modesty, or a sense of right and wrong, Mencius concludes, "is not really a man." We know this to be true. It has always been true. Across cultures and across time, this has been and always will be an essential part of being human. But the SocProgs refuse even this most basic and essential reality because it interferes with their project of emancipating the individual, of freeing that "puppet" dangling at the end of so many strings ceaselessly jerked around by that strange and malevolent puppeteer of Peter Berger's imagination. And they tell us they are "making the world a better place to live" which is strange because their scholarship clearly reveals they have absolutely no idea of what it actually means to be a man or a woman, a human being.

A More General Consideration of the SocProg Abuse of Language and Thought

We can all take heart in the totally unsurprising fact that SocProg history doesn't sell. One smiles. Christopher Dummit notes that what is "abundantly clear" is that ordinary Canadians are "not with the professors."[85] The abstract working classes, the oppressed women, the beleaguered immigrants, the harassed and haggard homosexuals about whom the SocProgs write do not buy the books that are written on their behalf. And this disconnect between scholar and subject goes all the way back to the forefather of the SocProgs, Karl Marx, who viewed *real* actual working men with contempt, and they in turn loathed him.[86]

People are not buying or reading SocProg wares because the writing is as bad as writing can get, if we define good writing as understandable, readable, enjoyable, and satisfying. And here once again, this is nothing new. It is apparently characteristic of the Progressive mind of any age that their writing is an offense against good taste. George Trevelyan observed that the principal weakness of that "scientific" history in the 19th and early 20th century was the writing itself.

It was, he said, "a very serious weakness—spinal, in fact."[87] And this weakness grew directly out of the rejection of history as an art and the attempt to turn it into a science, as the SocProgs, too, have tried to do. Indeed, Hannah Arendt wrote of sociologists: "if their language is repulsive...it is only because they have decided to treat man as a natural being whose life process can be handled the same way as all other processes."[88] Treating Man as a "process" is, we recognize, wrong. Treating Man as human is the correct way. The former is what sociologists do; the latter, what historians do.

Trevelyan observed that "writing is not a secondary, but one of the *primary* tasks of the historian."[89] And he is right. History is one of the few academic disciplines with its very own muse and that fact is not inconsequential. Clio, the Muse of History, is one of the seven daughters of Memory, and her job is to inspire. The ancient Greek writer Hesiod wrote that one day the Muses descended and "from a laurel in full bloom they plucked a branch and gave it to me as a staff and then breathed into me divine song." The Muses, Hesiod explained, "with sweet voices speak of things that are and things that were and will be and with effortless smoothness the song flows from their mouths."[90] But the SocProgs have turned their back on and rejected the way of Clio, perhaps because she herself never underwent a bracing and rigorous program of ideological re-education.

Joy Parr, the historian who "refuses" truths about human nature, gives us a textbook example of why no one buys SocProg books. In the example below, Parr is reflecting (?) on how gender was "made by history," and how knowledge of that fact apparently caused "a cascade of temporality" (?!). When one is busy "refusing" reality, it helps to have language like this handy:

> "Identities [were] in fact severalties, multiple, evocable, scrutable, but settled in contingency rather than certainty. Knowing this meant not 'knowing what was' but knowing what was brought to the fore and forced into congruence both seeking the circumstances which made this precedence and symmetry plausible and reckoning the contradictions which could be its undoing. This knowing is less agnostic than pantheistic, seeking explanation by inclusion rather than excision. And like all historical knowledge, this knowing is interim, expectant, augmentable, recombinant."[91]

Are you still there?

Good.

We must profitably speculate here on why Parr specifically and sociologists generally would choose to write like this. In the first instance, Parr may be writing in this fashion deliberately. SocProgs as a general rule believe everything is political, and when they say everything, they mean it. Obfuscatory writing of this kind is apparently sometimes intended to "signify a defiance of Cartesian clarity which arose from a suspect reliance upon bourgeois certainties concerning the world order."[92] In so many words, SocProgs feel that writing clearly and directly would simply "reproduce a bourgeois view of the world."

It is more likely the case, though, that Parr's writing is actually a reflection or a manifestation of the fundamental intellectual confusion inherent in the sociological worldview. The philosopher Hannah Arendt compared philosophy and sociology, what they seek and what they do; their essential functions. She concluded that while philosophy inquires into "being" or "existence," sociology, confusingly, inquires into the ideologies that underpin the interpretations of our existence and thus "sociology focuses on the very thing that philosophy deems irrelevant."[93]

For Arendt, sociology is not engaged in a direct reckoning with "existence" or with "being," but is instead "taking a detour by way of a reality they consider more original [than reality itself]" and which, of course, is a path that leads nowhere.[94] And when one finally arrives at nowhere, as Parr apparently has, one must use incomprehensible language to hide from one's own self the fact that one is explaining a reality that does not exist. Marcuse wrote of a reality that did not exist; Marx envisioned a reality that will never exist; and here is Parr doing the same thing, explaining non-existent realities.

If Parr's bad writing is a little too dense and opaque (Opaque: *"unintelligible; obscure; dark, lying in shadow"*), we might consider the anti-thought and anti-art contained in this conclusion about gender written by Jane Nicholas. She argues that "masculinity and femininity were not fixed but rather a conglomeration of discourses, images, practices and representations that exist only in constant flux and in relation to other socially constructed ideas of age, race, class, and ethnicity."[95] Here we see a scholar who not only writes poorly, she thinks poorly. The proof is that no one, left alone with their own mind, thinks things like that. One must undergo some kind of education and training in political thought before one can write in that fashion. Writing of this sort simply does not occur naturally.

The example here from Nicholas provides us with support for Orwell's observation that writing driven by ideologies will always result in "prose [that] consists less and less of *words* chosen for the sake of their meaning and more of *phrases* tacked together like the sections of a pre-fabricated hen-house."[96] Writing is another word for thinking. Writing is thought expressed. Writing and thinking go hand in hand. Good clear writing means good clear thinking. The one cannot be separated from the other. And since SocProgs don't actually think (their theories and ideologies think for them), their writing, then, necessarily becomes "a series of phrases tacked together like a prefabricated hen-house."

SocProgs can take even the most promising history and turn it into its opposite. David S Churchill examined "Draft Resisters, Left Nationalism, and the Politics of anti-Imperialism" and the article certainly sounds appealing, but then he starts writing. Apparently, what he's really after is to "sceptically question the epistemological legitimacy and construction of who might in fact be constituted or interpolated as 'ourselves' within the dynamic historical context of the Canadian nation state."[97] Good God. All he wants to know here is who is Canadian and why they think so and thus Churchill provides us with wonderful proof of John Lukacs' observation that SocProg scholarship is characterized by "a large amount of words in the service of a small amount of thought."

Sometimes, though, SocProgs forego the large amount of words and head straight for the small amount of thought. In their book *Debating Dissent: Canada and the sixties*, Laura Campbell, Dominique Clement, and Greg Kealy indicate that the central and highly unexceptional purpose of their book is to "challenge readers to conceptualize the 1960s not as a decade in Canadian history, but as a social, political, cultural and economic *phenomenon*."[98] This idea has been out there for a pretty long time. Since the 1960s, actually.

Not only are the editors fiercely committed to exposing the obvious, but they also claim what they are doing is unique ("in many ways"). They "critically examine" the idea of the "decadal approach" to the 1960s and "challenge the stereotype" of the "quiescent 1950s" and "co-opted 1970s."[99] To establish the veracity of this modest and unassuming argument, they enlist the services of academic Catherine Carstairs who examined "health food stores." The editors observe that her study reveals "concerns about food supply began in the 1950s and peaked in the 1970s," evidently thus proving that radicalism (certainly at least at it relates to "health food stores") existed outside the conventional bounds of the 1960s.[100] Unblinking, the editors persist in their solemn proclamations of the plainly self-evident: "one common theme that emerges from these chapters" they argue, is that the 1960s can be "partially [?!] characterized by a questioning of established hierarchical authority."[101] The editors desperately need to be informed that "these chapters" were not needed for that "theme" to "emerge." Every middle school kid in Canada already knows that.

Just as the whole enterprise seems to be tumbling over the edge into oblivion and senselessness before we even make it out of the introduction, they haul out the anti-thought, the thought-clichés, and they set about constructing one of those "prefabricated hen-houses" so beloved of the SocProg mind. The questioning of this "established hierarchical authority" they explain, "occur[ed] along a political continuum, including liberal demands for dialogue and greater representation with existing bureaucratic, institutional structures, challenges to hierarchy within personal individual relationships and demands to restructure the entire social and political system."[102]

For more small thought, we might turn to historian Keith Walden who examined the rituals surrounding "tea" and its connection to the "emerging liberal order" in Toronto ("1880-1914").[103] He undertook this noble and undervalued topic, he writes, because "Calling and balls ["Calling and balling?" No. I suppose not.] have drawn at least some serious consideration" but there was evidently little information concerning the "lived experience" of taking "tea." [104] Now, taking tea "was linked fundamentally to an emerging liberal order." In order to demonstrate this, Walden deploys his fierce sociological jujitsu as he explains that "while the commercial culture undoubtedly pulled women downtown they were also pushed there by the mounting inconvenience of a primary social ritual..."

Enough.

Finally, enough. [105]

SocProgs and Beauty

It is not just precision, clarity, and active philosophic thought that is absent from SocProg scholarship. So too is beauty. Beauty: *"any one of those qualities... that gratify the aesthetic nature; the perfection of form resulting from the harmonious combination of diverse elements in unity; a special grace or charm."* [106] For the record (this is just too easy), beauty's antonyms are: "awkward, clumsy, deformed, frightful, ghastly, grim, grisly, grotesque, hideous, horrid odious, repulsive, shocking, ugly, unattractive, uncouth, ungainly, unlovely, unpleasant."

The SocProgs will simper and sniffle that it is not their intention to craft beauty for they are engaged in a project of Social Justice. The rejoinder: scholarship is supposed to be a creative act and beauty, surely, must be attendant in at least some form, in some small way, in all creative acts and expressions of the mind. Beauty is inherent in creativity or, the other way about, creation is meant to draw out the clarity, precision, and beauty of the mind. But since creativity and beauty are entirely absent in SocProg scholarship, we draw the same sad conclusion but from yet another direction that it is not creative but imitative and derivative. It is a simulacrum (*"hence, a sham"*) of creativity, and the reasons for that are simple: orthodoxy of any kind, as Orwell put it, "seems to demand a lifeless, imitative style."[107]

We have intermittently been examining the distinctive qualities of "bullshit artists" as explained by Princeton philosopher Harry Frankfurt. He argues that poorly built things—"shoddy goods"—are analogous to bullshit.[108] The word "shit" suggests a product which is never "finely crafted" but which is usually "messy" somehow, or in other ways "unrefined." Excrement is "emitted or dumped," and while it may have in some instances "a more or less coherent shape," it is, as Frankfurt goes on to observe, "in any case, not *wrought*" which is to say it does not result from a creative act and is thus void of beauty.[109]

This idea of beauty is not incidental but rather essential. The Greeks had a concept called *arête*, an archaic word which meant, in the old days of Achilles, something akin to the physical courage of the warrior, his strength and skills, his honour. But *arête* later came to mean excellence or virtue in a thing; an ideal. Greek men had in their mind an idea of what the Ideal man should do and thus no self-respecting man could ever pass up an opportunity to achieve the highest *arête*, the highest excellence, "the beautiful" as they called it. As

Aristotle explained it, "a man who loves himself will sacrifice himself to take possession of the beautiful," which is to say to take possession of excellence.[110] Beauty and excellence in the Greek mind were coeval.

The test of whether or not one had taken possession of the beautiful was in the success of the thing attempted, not in the intention.[111] The SocProgs have great intentions. But even by their own admission, they have not "taken possession of the beautiful," they have not achieved excellence, aesthetically, intellectually, or spiritually, and so they have not succeeded. The crucial test here is that no one buys their books and that fact alone suggests people feel that there is something repulsive about their work. Repulsive: *"Exciting such feelings, as of dislike, disgust, or horror, that one is repelled; grossly offensive; causing aversion."* In the same way as theory shuts off the mind to active, philosophic thought, beauty and excellence will never serve untruth. Not ever.

SocProgs and Humour

Not to pile on here, but in passing it must be noted that SocProgs are also humourless. Humour: *"The sportive exercise of the imagination that delights in the incongruous."* This is what their scholarship is not. One can read a year's worth of the *Canadian Historical Review* and never once crack a smile. But this is what happens when writing and thinking are politicized: humour (and wisdom, and truth, and beauty, and creativity, and all the rest of them), exit the room. Humour is actually more important than you might think. The English writer and essayist Christopher Hitchens called it a sign of intelligence.[112] But we won't go *there*.

If anything should invite humour, or at the very least certainly a sportive dash of whimsy (Whimsy: *"a whim; caprice; freak"*), then it should be the whole idea of the impulsive and impetuous female shopper.[113] But when this subject is handled by SocProg historian Donica Belisle, it comes out like this: "Holding up stereotypes of corrupt and spendthrift women, commentators asserted a virile and modern masculinity that fused intelligence and civic mindedness with financial privilege and responsibility."[114] And thus Belisle's "case study" here "confirms Strange's and McMaster's contentions" that critics "drew upon derogatory constructions of womanhood to express concerns about modernization."[115]

Now then. American novelist Henry James is distinguished by his remarkable facility for constructing elaborate, dizzying, heroic, high-tower sentences that last all day long. His structure will serve us well in our summary of Belisle's efforts. To wit: Quite aside from the anti-thought, anti-art, and anti-wisdom contained in the conclusion there, and leaving out the fact that this article is yet another example of intrinsically flawed anti-historical reasoning from the general to the particular, and in addition to being still one more illustration of a writer "gumming together long strips of words which have already been set in order by someone else," and saying nothing of the fact that this article has little to do with Canada's history occurring in, as it does, but not concerning, not as such, Canada itself, this example is, like most SocProg scholarship, humourless.[116] Remorselessly, relentlessly humourless.

The SocProgs and the Community

Christopher Dummit observed that SocProg thought has become "the new common sense" which is odd because SocProg scholarship seems to insist upon demonstrating its lack of it.[117] This lack of common sense is one of the reasons why there is a quite frayed and distant relationship between Canadian universities and the communities they are supposed to serve. According to Carl Berger—who was writing this in the 1980s when the problem was nowhere near as bad as it is now—universities have become "isolated from the society in which they live."[118] There is a profound disconnect between the academy and the rest of us. SocProg ideas have become dominant inside the academy, but as historian Robert Conquest notes, there is clearly a disinterest in what the SocProgs actually produce, and moreover, what they do produce actually *reinforces* this separation and isolation. And this is dangerous because it leads to the development of an academic class completely unaware of and oblivious to any attitudes but its own.[119]

This isolation is reinforced still further by ceaselessly political nature of academic scholarship. The *Canadian Historical Review* is bursting with articles written by average work-a-day professors and whose content is unashamedly, unabashedly political. According to American writer Roger Kimball, "the issue is not so much—or not only—the presence of bad politics as the absence of non-politics in the intellectual life of the university."[120] Politics, he is saying, is everywhere. It informs every word and colours every act. And Kimball doesn't mean politics in the traditional sense of having a general political sensibility, or even that whole archaic right-left thing, but rather politics in the sense of having a political project, an ideological conviction that the world is in need of a bloodless revolution of thought and mind.

This impulse for politics-everywhere-all-the-time is traceable to Marx and his progeny the Bolsheviks. Both cleaved to the idea that all of life is necessarily and by definition political. Writing of the Bolsheviks in Russia, Martin Amis observed that "they want politics to be going on everywhere all the time, politics permanent, and circumambient. They want the ubiquitization of politics."[121] It was said that the real Marxists and Bolsheviks feel revolutionary and political *all the time* and thus Amis concludes that in Bolshevik Russia, even something so simple as sleep was political. In the same way that drinking in Hamilton was not fun but rather resistance, sleep, Amis writes, was not an expression of the body's natural desire for rest: "Sleep was just another opportunity to feel like a Bolshevik."[122]

So where does one go, what does one do, and how can one think, if one is disinclined to believe SocProg (un)truths? This is where Traditionalists come in. It's funny that in this day and age, when SocProg ideals represent the new commons sense and they themselves have become the new "elites," Traditionalists, almost by definition, are neither "conservative" nor "reactionary." Traditionalists, in one of those strange quirks of fate in which Clio seems to delight, have become the new subversives.

Endnotes

[1] Christopher Dummit, "After Inclusiveness," in *Contesting Clio's Craft: new directions and debates in Canadian history* edited by Christopher Dummit, and Michael Dawson (London: Institute for the Study of the Americas, 2009), p. 109.

[2] Joan Wallach Scott, "History in Crisis: the others' side of the story," *The American Historical Review*, vol. 94, no. 3, June 1989, p. 692.

[3] R.G. Collingwood, *The Idea of History* (New York: Oxford University Press, 1956), p. 324.

[4] I had long been faintly aware of this unease but it became fully apparent in class one day. A young lad referred to one of my fellow teachers as a "dude." Curious, I asked why he did not call him a man. He blushed, and couldn't answer. By the end of the discussion (which lasted the entire class), it became apparent that every single young man in the room—there were about eight—felt a very pronounced discomfort with using the word "man." They preferred "dude," "guy," or "male." In what seemed like desperation, one young fellow, C. Kriegler, exclaimed "why can't we just be called people!" The young Western women looked on, more than a little amused. One young woman from the Philippines, though, listened to the discussion with what seemed an expression of confused shock.

[5] Please see Joan Scott's article "History in Crisis." No specific "page number" is needed. Just open up the "article" and on virtually every page you will see whole families of "words" ensconced in quote marks. Here are some examples which, of course, all trace back to the Traditional approach to history she is so keen on consigning to the junk heap: "history," "truth," "objectivity," "tradition," "our history," "history-as-it-has-always-been-written," "crisis," "traditional," "man's," "man," "the historian." There are probably more but I "digress."

[6] Christopher Dummit and Michael Dawson, "Introduction: Debating the Future of Canadian History: preliminary answers to uncommon questions," in *Contesting Clio's Craft: new directions and debates in Canadian history* edited by Dummit and Dawson (London: Institute for the Study of the Americas, 2009), p. x. The sentence reads, in part: "...debates over the truth of history or the importance of 'national' history invited interventions that were largely polemical." By the way, Dummit uses the plural "interventions" which suggests there were many interventions. But there was only one intervention, and so we might rephrase his sentence to read, in part "...invited an intervention that was largely polemical."

[7] James Henslin et al, *Sociology: a down to earth approach* (Toronto: Pearson, 2010), p. 126.

[8] Henslin, *Sociology*, 127. I laughed out loud when I read this stuff. It was like it was written by a Truther, some troglodytic cellar-dwelling member of the tin-foil-hat brigade. But no: it comes from people who actually teach at universities.

[9] Henslin et al, *Sociology*, p. 260. [10] Christopher Butler, *Postmodernism: a very short introduction* (London: Oxford, 2002), p. 3.

[11] Butler, *Postmodernism*, p. 2. If you pay a visit to the Queen's University Cultural Studies website, you will see that cultural studies differs from Traditional areas of study in three ways: first, it is "multidisciplinary" which is usually code-phrasing which means sociology is present somewhere; second, they seek to conduct research interactively with a "wide range of communities;" and third—and most important for our purposes here—the cultural studies folks "emphasize themes of power, justice, and social change," which is to say they emphasize the ideology of Karl Marx.

[12] James D. Tracy, "A Descent to Cultural Studies," *Academic Questions*, Fall 2000," p. 29.

13 Tracy, "A Descent," p. 25.

14 Windschuttle, *The Killing*, p. 27.

15 Werner Jaeger, *Paideia: the ideals of Greek culture*, translated by Gilbert Highet (New York: Oxford University Press, 1945), p. 4.

16 Stanislav Andreski, *Social Science as Sorcery* (London: Andre Deutsch, 1972), p. 12.

17 Andreski, *Social Science*, pp. 12-13.

18 Robert Conquest, *The Dragons of Expectation: reality and delusion in the course of history* (New York: W.W. Norton, 2005), p. 50. Arguing against Marxists and even your more militant SocProgs is a difficult enterprise as they are "argument-proof and fact-proof...as was the case with their grandparents in the USSR." Conquest, *Dragons*, p. 51. On the readability of *Das Capital*, please see Paul Johnson, *Intellectuals* (New York: Perennial, 1988), p. 63. The full idea reads: "The French Marxist philosopher Louis Althusser found its structure so confusing that he thought it 'imperative' that readers ignore Part One and begin with Part Two Chapter Four."

19 Julian Marias, *History of Philosophy* (New York: Dover, 1967), p. 338.

20 As cited in Marlene Shore, "Remember the Future: the Canadian Historical Review and the discipline of history, 1920-95," *Canadian Historical Review*, vol. 76, no. 3, September 1995, pp. 410-463, p. 444.

21 Windschuttle, *The Killing*, p. 5.

22 Tracy, "A Descent," p. 27. I am again reminded here of *Walk Hard* in which Dewey Cox (modeled on Johnny Cash), finds himself in prison on a drug charge and says, with what starts out as passion but which quickly turns into something close to a frantic fear: "I understand the common man in a way I never did before. I gotta get *outta* here, so I can bring *joy* to the men back in here. But I *don't* want to *live* with them!"

23 "Plying a grim hell-trade" is a Carlyle-ism.

24 With devout and sincere apologies to Messrs Heron and Martel as men, there was no malice or intention to harm associated with my decision to use your work as representative of SocProg thought. The selection was in every way random and accidental and without methodology because, as John Lukacs put it, "history has no methodology." Mr. Heron, in your case I merely typed "Masculinity" into the *Academic Search Complete* search engine and your article was the first one that popped up whose title sounded interesting. Mr. Martel, your book chapter was discovered entirely by accident and was selected because the relativism it seems to counsel was proof of my argument that SocProgs are re-embodied Athenian Sophists. As well, your chapter was also evidence of philosopher Alasdair MacIntyre's argument that we live in an age characterized by what he calls "emotivism," or the idea that personal preference merely has replaced traditional/transcendent ethics, standards, and morals. See Alasdair MacIntyre, *After Virtue* (Notre Dame Ind.: Notre Dame Press, 2007). And so here I extend an invitation to both of you to go for a beer sometime. And, of course, I'm buying.

25 Craig Heron, "The Boys and Their Booze: masculinities and public drinking in working class Hamilton, 1890-1946," *Canadian Historical Review*, vol. 86, no. 3, 2005. Even just in the title we see three SocProg fetishes: masculinity, public spaces, and the working classes.

26 One is here reminded of that commercial in the 1980s of an egg frying in a pan as the voice-over drily observes that this is a mind on drugs. Same kind of thing applies here.

27 Heron, "The Boys," p. 411

28 Heron, "The Boys," p. 412.

[29] Heron "The Boys," pp. 411-412

[30] Heron, "The Boys," p. 419

[31] Heron, "The Boys," p. 412. Please note how Heron senselessly but admirably tackles two fetish-themes in a single sentence: gender *and* "the elites."

[32] Heron, "The Boys," p. 420.

[33] Karl Marx, "The Manifesto of the Communist Party," as cited in John Louis Beatty and Oliver Johnson eds, *Heritage of Western Civilization: select readings*, vol. 2 (Englewood Cliffs NJ: Prentice Hall, 1971), p. 208.

[34] "Labourers...live only so long as they find work and [they] find work only so long as their labour increases capital. These labourers, who must sell themselves piecemeal, are a commodity like every other article of commerce." See Marx, "Manifesto," in *Heritage*, p. 212.

[35] Reflecting on that just now, I simply cannot think of a single man I have ever met who was not happy to have a job. They may *dislike* a particular job, but I know of no man who dislikes "selling his labor to his bosses for wages," except maybe for my old university mate M. Polachic.

[36] If you want to, go ahead and try a little Marxian Validation Experiment. Go and find a real actual working man and ask him if he and his mates ever once sat down in a bar to discuss how "capitalist management was eating away at their creativity." Try it up in Fort Mac.

[37] Mark, "Manifesto," p. 215.

[38] Pipes, *Communism*, p. 15.

[39] Paul Johnson, *Intellectuals* (New York: Perennial, 1990), p. 73.

[40] Alan Bloom, *The Closing of the American Mind*, p. 254.

[41] George Orwell, *Politics and the English Language* (London: Penguin, 2013), pp. 13-1.

[42] Thomas Carlyle, "Characteristics," in *Selected Essays by Thomas Carlyle* (T. Nelson and Sons ltd., no date), p. 315.

[43] David Foster Wallace, *Consider the Lobster, and other essays* (New York: Back Bay Books, 2007), p. 89.

[44] Heron, "The Boys," p. 412.

[45] Joy Parr, "Gender History and Historical Practice," *Canadian Historical Review*, vol. 76, no. 3, September 1995, pp. 355-376, p. 368. *I* weep.

[46] Parr, "Gender History," p. 362.

[47] Parr, "Gender History," pp. 356- 360. Italics added

[48] James Henslin et al, *Sociology: a down to earth approach* (Toronto: Pearson, 2010), p. 147.

[49] Carol Iannone, "The Barbarism of Feminist Scholarship," *The Intercollegiate Review*, Fall 1987, p. 39.

[50] Parr, "Gender History," p. 368.

[51] Interesting: during the Bolshevik "psychodrama" Joseph Stalin relied on torture "not to force you to reveal a fact, but to force you to collude in a fiction." Martin Amis observes that everyone in the Bolshevik experiment was forced in one way or another to participate in a lie, an untruth, an unreality. See Martin Amis, *Koba the Dread: laughter and the twenty millions* (Toronto: Vintage, 2003), p. 61.

[52] Heron, "The Boys," p. 416.

[53] Conquest, *Dragons*, p. 4.

[54] Heron, "The Boys," pp. 416-417.

[55] Heron, "The Boys," pp. 450-451. The phrasing there is from Martin Amis. It is an "Amisism."

[56] Think of Bolsheviks as SocProgs only with guns, jackboots, work camps, and rich leather coats. We might also mention Robespierre's republic of virtue here. Think of the Jacobins as SocProgs only with powdered wigs and guillotines.

[57] Arthur Koestler, *Darkness at Noon* (New York: Scribner, 1968), p. 163.

[58] Pipes, *Communism*, p. 7.

[59] Amis, *Koba the Dread*, p. 254.

[60] Hans Meyerhoff ed., *The Philosophy of History in Our Time* (Garden City New York: Double Day Anchor Books, 1956), p. 335.

[61] Marcel Martel, "They Smell Bad, Have Disease, and are Lazy: RCMP Officers reporting on hippies in the late sixties," in *The Sixties in Canada: a turbulent and creative decade*, M. Athena Palaeologu editor, (Montreal: Black Rose Books 2009), pp. 165-166.

[62] Martel, "They Smell Bad," p. 174.

[63] Only instead of "Doing their own thing!" everybody just "Did the same thing!"

[64] Martel, "They Smell Bad," p. 175.

[65] Martel, "They Smell Bad," p. 175.

[66] Martel, "They Smell Bad," p. 179.

[67] Martel, "They Smell Bad," p. 181.

[68] Martel, "The Smell Bad," p. 181.

[69] Martel, "They Smell Bad," p. 181

[70] Martel, "They Smell Bad," p. 181. This fetish-phrase apparently belongs to "Canadian Studies" academic Steve Hewitt.

[71] St. Augustine, *City of God* translated by Henry Bettenson (London: Penguin, 1972), p. 83.

[72] Butler, *Postmodernism*, p. 16.

[73] Butler, *Postmodernism*, p. 17.

[74] Martel, "They Smell Bad," p. 177.

[75] Martel, "They Smell Bad," p. 177-178.

[76] Dalrymple, *Life at the Bottom*, p. 251.

[77] Martel, "They Smell Bad," p. 182.

[78] Martel, "They Smell Bad," p. 183.

[79] Dalrymple, *Life at the Bottom*, p. 251. The replacement of the value-loaded word "laziness" with the sterile "anti-work ethic" is very nearly brilliant. I wonder how long it took to invent that phrase.

[80] Dalrymple, *Life at the Bottom*, p. 244.

[81] Hannah Arendt, "The Concept of History," in *Between Past and Future: eight exercises in political thought* (London: Penguin, 1968), p. 53.

[82] G.W.F. Hegel, *The Philosophy of History* (Mineola, New York: Dover Publications, 2004), p. 267. Italics in original.

[83] Hegel, *The Philosophy*, p. 267.

[84] Mencius, "On the Nature of Man," in *The Essence of Chinese Civilization*, translated by Dun J. Li (Princeton NJ: D. Van Nostrand, 1967), pp. 6-7.

[85] Dummit, "After Inclusiveness," p. 103.

[86] Paul Johnson, *Intellectuals* (New York: Perennial, 1990), p. 61. The full idea reads: "[The workers] did not share Marx's apocalyptic visions and, above all, they did not talk his academic jargon."

[87] George M. Trevelyan, *Clio, a muse and other essays literary and pedestrian* (London: Longmans, Green and Co., 1913), p. 14.

[88] Arendt, "The Concept," in *Between*, p. 59.

[89] Trevelyan, *Clio*, p. 14. Italics added.

[90] Hesiod, *Theogony, Works and Days, Shield* translated by Apostolos N. Athanassakis (Baltimore: Johns Hopkins Press, 2004), pp. 11-12, lines 25-40

[91] Parr, "Gender History," p. 375. Once again—and I am sure that I am not alone—I simply have no idea what this even means.

[92] Butler, *Postmodernism*, p. 9.

[93] Hannah Arendt, *Essays in Understanding, 1930-1954: Formation, Exile, Totalitarianism* (New York: Schoken, 1994), p. 29.

[94] Arendt, *Essays*, p. 31.

[95] Jane Nicholas, "Gendering the Jubilee: gender and modernity in the diamond jubilee of Confederation celebrations, 1927," *Canadian Historical Review*, vol. 90, no. 2, June 2009, p. 250. See footnote number 6.

[96] Orwell, *Politics and the English Language*, p. 4. Italics in the original.

[97] David S Churchill "Draft Resisters, Left Nationalism and the Politics of anti-Imperialism," *Canadian Historical Review*, vol. 93, no. 2, June 2012, p. 230. At least I *think* that is what he is trying to do, for he later writes: "My engagement with the myriad national narratives, representations and ideologies from this period is approached from a critical perspective, and not to presumptively explain who Canadians supposedly are in an ontological sense, or to undergird nationalist epistemologies of legitimacy." To get the full flavour of the writing here, try reading it out loud.

[98] Laura Campbell, Dominique Clement, Greg Kealey eds., *Debating Dissent: Canada and the 1960s* (Toronto: University of Toronto Press, 2012), p. 3.

[99] This is an old and tired argument that began with Marxist literary critic Fredric Jameson and was then subsequently taken up by many dozens of others. We have Arthur Marwick who proposed a "long 1960s" from 1958-1974; Elizabeth Martinez, who proposes an even *longer* 1960s from 1955 to 1975; Bernadine Dorn, who suggests the 1960s began in 1954 and "they're not over yet" (I personally favour this approach); an exasperated Newt Gingrich simply calls it "the longest decade of the twentieth century." Then there is the insurgent John Margolis, who instead embraces the "short 1960s" arguing that they didn't begin until 1964; Bruce Schulman and others who argue the sixties were merely "1968" and Canadian David Frum muddies already muddy waters by arguing that the sixties did not occur until the seventies. So you see, for the editors of *Debating* to say that they want to "challenge" the stereotypes of the 1950s and 1970s in relation to the 1960s, they are more than a day late and substantially more

than a dollar short. Please see M.J. Heale, "The Sixties as History: a review of the political historiography," in *Reviews in American History* vol. 33, no. 1, March 2005, pp. 135-136.

[100] Campbell, Clement, Kealey, *Debating*, pp. 16-18

[101] Campbell, Clement, Kealey, *Debating*, p. 21

[102] Campbell, Clement, Kealey, *Debating*, p. 21.

[103] Keith Walden, "Tea in Toronto and the Liberal Order, 1880-1914," *Canadian Historical Review*, vol. 93, issue 1, March 2012, p. 1.

[104] Walden, "Tea in Toronto," pp. 4-5

[105] Well okay, just one more. In the June 2013 issue of the *Canadian Historical Review*, there was an article titled "The Gateway to the Last Great West: spatial histories of the Athabasca Landing Trail," by Matt Byce. "Spatial histories?" I thought. Byce assures the reader that his intention was to examine "meaning" and "the dynamics of power." Still uncomprehending, I Googled spatial history and was led to Stanford University's *Spatial History Project* (it's a project?) website where I quickly found that these "spatial historians" (?) "Operate outside of normal historical practice in five ways." If a project that "operates outside of normal historical practice in five ways" can still call itself history then maybe we should just call *everything* history.

[106] Since concepts like beauty are difficult to define, the dictionary philosophers offer a further explanation in prose below the principal entry. To wit: "Beautiful implies softness of outline and delicacy of mould. It is opposed to all that is hard and rugged."

[107] Orwell, *Politics and the English Language*, p. 13.

[108] Frankfurt, *On Bullshit*, p. 21.

[109] Frankfurt, *On Bullshit*, pp. 22-23.

[110] Werner Jaeger, *Paideia: the ideals of Greek culture* vol 1 translated by Gilbert Highest (New York: Oxford University Press, 1945), pp. 8-13.

[111] Anthony Andrewes, *Greek Society* (London: Penguin, 1967), p. 216.

[112] Christopher Hitchens, "Why Women Aren't Funny," in *Arguably: essays* (Toronto: Signal, 2011), p. 391.

[113] Men too are saddled with stereotypes. We have the whole "hardware-store power-tools-we-don't know-how-to-use" thing, and if anything should invite humour and whimsy it is men and power tools. Comedian Tim Allen built a dreary, lifeless career on men and power tools.

[114] Donica Belisle, "Crazy for Bargains: inventing the irrational female shopper in modernizing English Canada," *Canadian Historical Review*, vol. 92, no. 4, December 2011, p. 605.

[115] "Strange" is Carolyn Strange and "McMaster" is Lindsay McMaster, both of whom wrote books on women and work.

[116] Orwell, *Politics and the English Language*, p. 11.

[117] Dummit "After Inclusiveness," p. 109.

[118] Carl Berger, *The Writing of Canadian History: aspects of English Canadian historical writing since 1900* (Toronto: University of Toronto Press, 1986), p. 269.

[119] Conquest, *Dragons*, p. 48

[120] Roger Kimball, *Tenured Radicals*, p xiv.

[121] Amis *Koba the Dread* p. 14. The typical male reluctance to hand over the remote control to a wife or girlfriend is a good example the whole "personal is political" thing because that small act reveals imbalanced power relations, arbitrary yet silent declarations of authority, who has something and who is being denied something etc & co.

[122] Amis *Koba*, p.14. The wonderful film Dr. Zhivago played up this theme. When the character played by Omar Shariff confronts a vile and creepy Bolshevik after the revolution, he is informed that (and I'm quoting from memory here) "In Russia, the personal is dead." For an elaboration of how grotesque it got in the USSR, please see Arthur Koestler's *Darkness at Noon* (New York: Scribner, 1968), p. 155. Ivanov: "My point is this...one may not regard the world as a sort of metaphysical brothel for the emotions. That is the first commandment for us. Sympathy, conscience, disgust, despair, repentance, and atonement are for us repellant debauchery." In other words, being human was "repellant debauchery."

CHAPTER SIX
THE TRADITIONALISTS

"We have sunk to a depth in which restatement of the
obvious is the first duty of intelligent men."

Theodore Dalrymple, Not with a Bang but a Whimper, p. 38.

"The function of philosophy is that of rightly disposing men toward the truth."

Robert E. Cushman, Therapeia, p. xviii

"Can we not think of the aim of life as being simply to see?"

John Gray, Straw Dogs, p. 199.

"Mencius said, 'When the Way prevails in the Empire, it goes where one's person
goes; when the Way is eclipsed, one's person goes where the Way has gone. I
have never heard of making the Way go where other people are going."

Mencius, a fourth century BC Confucian philosopher, in Mencius, p. 192.

"Our intellect, no matter how independent of the past it may be in science and technol-
ogy, is ever renewed and consecrated by the consciousness of its connection with the
mind of remotest times. Indeed, it gets to know itself and value its lofty nature only
through comparison with that which it, the eternally unchanging, has been in all times.

Jacob Burckhardt, On History and Historians, p. 15.

It is hard to think of Traditionalists as being subversive, but there it is.
Silenced in the academy and viewed askance in the wider culture as curious
intellectual perverts, Traditionalists have in fact become the new dissidents, the
rebels fighting against elite orthodoxies.[1] The problem is that those orthodoxies revolve around the greatest of human desires, the desire for Liberty, Justice,

and Equality. One can sensibly and comfortably argue that much if not all of Western history can be traced back, in one way or another, to these very principles. Traditionalists and SocProgs both share a devotion to these principles—Plato beat Marx to the idea of the beauty of Justice by about 2,400 years—and it is only the worst and cheapest sort of carping that would suggest otherwise. Where the two sides differ, though, are the extent and degree to which those ideals can be reached.

The SocProgs see the world in Marxian terms of endpoints, culminations, and the final realization of human perfection; that the principles of Justice, Liberty, and Equality can in fact be fully and perfectly realized through proper legislation, instruction, and training. This view is, of course, utopian and anti-human and so therefore absurd. Traditionalists on the other hand tend to see these principles as aspirational human ideals toward which we should all strive, while at the same time taking into account human frailty and human nature. Too, Traditionalists harbor precisely zero conceits about our ability as humans to achieve the full and perfect realization of those ideals. And where "social justice" is concerned, philosopher John Hallowell writes that the very idea is "the manifestation of an order which must first be achieved *within*" before it can ever be achieved without.[2] And we call that positive liberty. But maybe that is just it. Maybe the reason why the SocProgs try so hard to "make the world a better place" is simply because that task is so much easier than trying to rightly order one's own soul. But it is the SocProgs not the Traditionalists who have managed to frame the argument in the academy and in wider cultural discourse, and if you disagree with a SocProg then you must disagree with Justice, Liberty, and Equality. And if that be true, then it naturally follows that you must then be a beastly Traditionalist or, even worse, a reactionary conservative.

Conservatism and Tradition

But let's thoughtfully reflect on these two words before we react to them for they are not as unsettling as one might think. First, all tradition means is this: *"the transmission of knowledge, opinions, doctrines, customs, practices, etc, from generation to generation."*[3] A Traditionalist merely respects, embraces, and tries to pass along the accrued wisdom of our cultural traditions, whilst SocProgs of course see absolutely nothing of value in the 2,500 years that preceded the 1960s. The first great articulate and penetrating voice of modern traditionalism was the English philosopher Edmund Burke. Writing about the French Revolution before it went totally off the rails, Burke cautioned that, "when ancient opinions and rules of life are taken away, the loss cannot possibly be estimated. From that moment we have no compass to govern us; nor can we know distinctly to which port we should steer."[4] Thus tradition serves as a crucial and important beacon, and to abandon it means we march forward blindly, in the dark. So yes, tradition does matter. It matters a great deal. Perhaps more than we are willing to admit.

Plato made this astonishing observation about tradition and what it means: "the beginning is like a God which, as long as it dwells among men, saves all things."[5] Hannah Arendt picks up on this theme. Plato and Aristotle, she says, inaugurated Western political thought and philosophy. Their ideas guided us for millennia, forming as they did the foundations and traditions of Western thought. But that tradition was "abolished" by Karl Marx and his acolytes in sociology who replaced thought, reflection, and wisdom with activism, revolution, and change predicated on that ludicrous notion of "progress," and which has only resulted, ultimately, in what Arendt calls the confusion and helplessness of the modern age.[6]

Arendt chastely observes: "only the beginning and end are, so to speak, pure and unmodulated; and the fundamental chord, therefore, never strikes listeners more forcefully and more beautifully than when it first sends its harmonizing sound into the world" and never more "jarringly" than at the end.[7] Plato and Aristotle were that beginning. They were that "fundamental chord" whose pure and unmodulated soundings formed the foundation of our intellectual tradition. And Marx represents the "jarring" end of that tradition. We today exist in the wake of that end; a world where our traditions have been remaindered, abandoned, or simply forgotten. And we march forward blindly in the dark, now, in confusion and helplessness—hence the value of tradition.

Dealing with the word conservative is a little trickier, loaded as it is in this day and age with all kinds of creepy menace. Indeed, it is not overstating the case to suggest that the word "conservative" can be deployed as an insult.[8] But let's suspend our reactions for right now and investigate the word itself. Conservative: "*Adhering to the existing order of things; opposed to change or progress; moderate, cautious, within a safe margin.*" That is by and large a fair definition but again, we must sink down into it not remain on the surface of it. It is true that conservatives are moderate and cautious, tending to bestow their favours on the safe margin, but it is not true that conservatives are "opposed" to "progress." As we will see later in this chapter, progress as applied to history itself simply does not exist. The whole concept of progress is, in circumstances related to the human experience and the human condition, a fantasy, an illusion, an *un*reality. And so no, conservatives are not opposed to progress. Conservatives are, rather, opposed to illusions and fantasies and unrealities.

Nor are conservatives "opposed" to change, but rather decently and properly circumspect about it. Most social and political change comes about as the result of an idea. Conservatives tend to focus their attentions on the *effects* of an idea before weighing in on its virtues. Isaiah Berlin, taking a swipe at the Marxists of his day, wrote that "it is only a vulgar historical materialism that denies the power of ideas and says that ideals are mere material interests in disguise."[9] Berlin is identifying the point which we often either forget or simply refuse to acknowledge: that ideas actually do matter and they really do have consequences and that is where conservatives tend to focus their attentions, on the consequences.[10]

But the SocProgs, with their innate and pathological hostility to tradition allied with that queer and puzzling assumption about the end of history, tend to fixate on the inherent and intrinsic virtues of the idea itself. The SocProg project as outlined by Peter Berger, for example, consists in freeing the individual from restrictions thus conferring more and greater degrees of Liberty. Let's leave aside for right now that Berger's liberty is negative in that it develops out of the wrecking of a thing: it is Liberty in and of itself that matters, never mind the consequences. But for conservatives, they usually (perhaps unconsciously) channel Edmund Burke: "The effect of liberty to individuals is that they may do what they please. We ought to see what it will please them to do before we risk congratulations."[11] Indeed.

There are two epistemological terms which can aid us here in developing a deeper appreciation of conservatism. The Latin word *a postieriori* means knowledge gained through experience, and *a priori*, which means knowledge that is not derived through experience. Conservatives tend to favour action rooted in past experience; SocProgs obviously favor the opposite, and that should not surprise anyone at this point because their chief philosopher openly proclaimed that his mission was to "act in contradiction to all past historical experience!" And this tendency to favour abstract ideas over real experience is precisely what makes the SocProg project so very dangerous: there is, by definition, little or nothing in history which supports *a priori* projects.

Our destruction of traditional notions of gender, for example, was an action rooted not in any past experience but rather in wrong-headed abstract sociological theorizing—something to do with the alleged existence of what they call a "patriarchy"—about what it means to be a man or a woman. The sociologists framed the issue as one of Social Justice. But it is, rather, an act of *in*justice because it is an idea that moves *against* human nature, *against* both truth and being. Indeed, let's be clear: it is an idea that *defies* human nature. Hence injustice. And there will be consequences to that action but no one can say for sure yet exactly what those consequences will be.

Writing 200 years ago, French philosopher-historian Alexis de Tocqueville took a shot at imagining the fallout that would accompany such ideas. He argued that men and women are different. Not unequal, just different; that "nature has appointed wide differences between the physical and moral constitution of man and woman." This should be an unexceptional point to make but even in writing it today one is struck by a very strong and overpowering sense that somehow one is running seriously, almost criminally, afoul of a prevailing and orthodox truth. Tocqueville, however, free of Marxian ideological pressure, speculated that any attempt at making men and women "alike" will result in this: "both [sexes] are degraded, and from so preposterous a medley of the works of nature, nothing could ever result but weak men and disorderly women."[12]

But sociology sees this alteration of our understanding of gender as "progress" and the changes thus represent just one more step taken down that road toward the final end of history. Again and for emphasis (for it must not be forgotten), the liberal mind is characterized by a belief in ultimate goals and end points; by a determined faith in "a golden age of the future."[13] And so virtually everything they do is animated by this absurd belief that history has a destination. And this illusion is allied with still another intrinsic liberal conceit in which they have historically identified themselves as being the next step in man's moral and political evolution, and so everything they do is somehow justified. No, not just justified: it is sanctified.[14] But conservatives harbour no such illusions about humanity or history or any other such thing, hence their suspicion of liberal projects, of "progress," of "change." Indeed, we might clarify the matter further by suggesting that there are no conservatives or liberals. There are only those who accept the world the way it is; and then there those who wish it to be something other than what it is.[15]

By the way, the word conservative comes to us from the Latin *conservare* which means "to preserve."[16] Preserve: "*To keep in safety; guard or rescue from destruction.*" The definition here assumes the existence of an agent which seeks to throw out, discard, or destroy a thing and thus the word at the same time describes those who would prevent that. Perhaps Traditionalists or "conservatives" might be better termed Preservatives.

Preservative Agents, say.

PrAgs, even.[17]

Traditionalists, as a rule, are reluctant to build systems and theories (what Thomas Carlyle called "logical card castles"), and so in deference to tradition, an *idea* of the traditional approach to history—to seeing, knowing, and understanding—will be proposed in this chapter. In the original Greek sense, "idea" generally meant a form or an image in one's mind; to *see* something, to have a vision of a thing. And that is what is proposed here: a vision of thought. And that, of course, compels us to return, once again, to ancient Greece.

The wise and perceptive historian of ancient Greece, Werner Jaeger, once wrote that it is a natural human impulse for people to seek out or return to the origins of their civilization. And he added that this imperative becomes particularly acute at the end of historical periods or epochs when "thoughts have petrified into rigidity."[18] Greece is important because it is the "spiritual source" of our civilization and our intellectual tradition, and it is there that we can "reorient ourselves."[19] Reorient, by the way, derives from the word "orient" which means "*to find the proper bearing.*" Re-orient, then, suggests a state of affairs in which that proper bearing has been lost.

Returning to Greece is a humbling proposition, but only if one is disposed to be humbled. There abound today so many conceits and pretensions which hold that we in this "modern" age have a better understanding and appreciation of being human than anyone in the past has ever had. That is simply just not true. Indeed, if we be honest with ourselves, especially after having waded through the mind of sociology, we *must* concede that we today have *less* understanding of what it means to be a human being today than the Greeks. And yes, we identify sociology as the principal source of that increasing, crippling, debilitating ignorance. The 2,500 years that separates us and them have not been a period of ascension; it has not been a time in which our knowledge of the human condition has evolved and developed in steadily ascending stages aiming at perfection. Yet that remains the general cultural assumption and it is a deeply disturbing one because it rejects history. It moves against history. There is so much truth in what American classicist Alan Bloom observed about the Greeks and thus of Tradition: "[the Greeks] can lead us to experiences that are difficult or impossible to have without their help."[20] And we badly need help. We need *their* help.

Basic Thought

Greek thought, properly speaking, begins with the pre-Socratics, a group of wandering philosophers largely of Ionian descent who were prominent between roughly 600-400 BC. They simply asked questions of the world, desiring only to know it and understand it.[21] These men were not historians but rather what we might call early scientists or naturalists because they confined their studies to the physical, natural world. It was their approach to inquiry, however, and the intellectual "tools" they used that are remarkable, tools which later drifted into and became the foundation for history, philosophy, morals, and ethics.[22]

The pre-Socratics are profoundly meaningful to us Westerners, but they also mark also a watershed moment in world history, too. For thousands of years prior to the appearance of the Greeks, humans had experienced the world and yet science, philosophy, and history—or, in a word, thought—remained in an embryonic state until the pre-Socratics and the Greeks showed up. The charmingly antiquated historian H.D.F. Kitto explains that, though there were many civilizations that preceded the Greeks, civilizations that were impressive beyond measure, they never developed the potential of the human mind to its fullest degree. Somewhat unfairly, but still fairly accurately, Kitto observes that "for centuries, millions of people had had experience of life—and what did they do with it? Nothing."[23]

The Greeks did not have a bible and nor did they have a priestly class which explained the world to them. There were some sketchy myths ("in which they [the pre-Socratics] placed no confidence"), but there was no Book of Genesis; little baby Greeks did not attend church on Sunday and there have the world explained to them.[24] It was the pre-Christian pre-Socratics who simply took it upon themselves, each in their own way and independent of the other (and without grants, sabbaticals, salaries, and dental plans) to look at the world and ask for the first time: "how does this thing work?" These pre-Socratics were the first philosophers, from the Greek word *philosophia*, which means *"love of wisdom."*

The pre-Socratics used an entirely secular approach to their inquiries which, too, was in and of itself groundbreaking. They believed that there was a discernible and natural, not supernatural, order to things and that this order was intrinsic.[25] Intrinsic: *"pertaining to the nature of a thing or person; inherent; real; true."* For the pre-Socratics, as historian Jonathan Barnes explains, the world was "not a random collection of bits, its history, not an arbitrary series of events." The pre-Socratics discerned early on this first and fairly basic truth: that underneath the only apparent bewildering and chaotic multiplicity of things, there lay patterns. Men die, but Man remains; plants return annually; the moon has phases; spring, summer, fall, winter; growth, regeneration, decay; every March, tens of thousands of ornery, nosily honking geese return to Canada and commandeer public parks. And so they—the pre-Socratics, not the geese—sensibly reasoned that we do not live in an arbitrary and chaotic universe, but a patterned one.[26] Their goal was to understand those patterns and thus the nature of this world.

The pre-Socratics deployed four "thought tools" in their inquiries and it will repay us in full if we reflect on them here. The pre-Socratics created a word to describe the Universe: *kosmos.*[27] The word itself has a couple of meanings. In the first sense, it means *"to order, arrange, marshal; an orderly arrangement."* In philosophic discourse, the word suggested that the universe was not a chaotic mess but magnificently ordered and therefore explicable, knowable, understandable. *Kosmos* also had a secondary meaning that meant *"to adorn something"* (from whence our word "cosmetic"), a thing that beautifies, a thing that is "pleasant to contemplate."[28] Thus the order they discerned, the patterns themselves, hinted at something that was not just arranged, but arranged beautifully.

The second tool the pre-Socratics deployed in their inquiries—and by far the single most important tool in the study of history, or even just for thought itself—was *phusis*. It comes from a verb that means "to grow," but the word itself came to mean the "nature of a thing." And this latter meaning also came with distinctions. There is the nature of that which grows or lives (a cat, say) and that which is made, like a table or chair. But the word, fundamentally, denotes or suggests a characteristic thing or things within each natural object that lives, breathes, or grows. This nature is an "intrinsic feature" of it, an *essential* feature, not accidental.[29] And this nature was so very important to comprehend because not only was it essential for understanding the thing in question, it was also *explanatory*: the reason a thing behaves the way it does is *because* of its intrinsic nature.

This insistence upon understanding the nature of a thing was of such importance because it was the first real step toward true understanding; toward seeking the "ultimate substance that lies beyond appearance."[30] They sought to call a thing by its right name (an ability that is all but non-existent today). The Greeks believed that anything that can be the object of knowledge must have an element of permanence, else how could it be known? Historian R.G. Collingwood explains: "If it [a thing] is knowable, it must be determinate; if it is determinate, it must be so completely and exclusively what it is that no internal change and no external force can ever set about making it into something else."[31] The SocProg set is currently embarked on a ruinous mission to reform society by destroying our traditional understanding of gender. The roots of that project lay in a "refusal" of the idea that men and women have their own unique natures, their own *phusis*, and so sociologists fail even on this most simple and basic point of pre-Socratic understanding. And they don't just fail—they fail *violently*, because their ideas do violence to human nature, to who and what men and women are, essentially, as human beings.

The next concept is *arche* which means "to begin, to commence," which is to say the beginnings or the origins of a thing.[32] For the pre-Socratics, the word suggested the following types of questions: "If the thing observed is natural and not made, what then accounts for its growth? What are the origins of this phenomenon?" Identifying the origin of a thing is, again, one of the most frequently sought goals of a historian or thinker. The much misused and misquoted German historian Leopold von Ranke believed that, in investigating the origin of a particular thing, the historian is engaged in the noblest of tasks, "seeking to break through to the deepest and most secret motives of historical life."[33] And, perhaps anticipating the theories of Karl Marx and his later sociologies, Ranke notes that some presume to discover what is there but they are deceiving themselves, "embracing a cloud....securing only formulas and empty wind in place of truth."

In certain instances, though, accounting for the origins of a thing cannot always be achieved. In the case of Greek history itself, in trying to account for and explain what is often called the Greek Miracle, philosophers Hannah Arendt and her peer Karl Jaspers sought to break through to those deepest motives but had difficulty trying to actually account for it. For his part, Jaspers was quite comfortable "wondering at the mystery" of the Greek Miracle because wonder itself, he wrote, was "a fruitful act of understanding."[34] Too often, Jaspers argued, historians go straight to explanation blithely skipping over or skimping on understanding which results in this: "[a] comfortable and empty conception of history as a comprehensible and necessary movement of humanity" or, in a word, progress.[35] For Jaspers, the practice of history is rooted entirely in understanding. Everything else flows from this. Hannah Arendt likewise shared his distaste for rationalizing something away into a box. Like Jaspers, understanding was, for Arendt, the supreme task of the historian. From first to last, Arendt always and in all realms "valorized understanding at the expense of explanation."[36] For Arendt, mere explanation reduces events to simple cause and effect and in doing so "empties them of meaning."[37]

The final concept that informed the inquiries of the pre-Socratics was *logos*, a word that literally meant "to say, or to state," but which, when used in philosophic discourse, meant to explain or give an account for a thing. Not to describe it but to give the reason for it.[38] And that assumes the deployment of rationality, reason, argument, logic, and evidence.[39] Another secondary definition of *logos* is even more appealing than the first. The philosophizing psychiatrist Viktor Frankl used the word as *meaning* and thus *logos*, then, aims at discovering the meaning of a thing.[40]

These four tools (habits of mind, really) were the starting point for the Greek inquiries into the world. And this approach was adopted by medicine, natural science and, of course, history and philosophy.[41] It is easy to explain these "thought tools" but practicing them is extremely difficult to do in part because there is one troubling word which unites these four concepts and that word is "understanding." Understand: *"to perceive the nature of [a thing]; comprehend."* And so we see there that this simple word which we use every day has aspirational and deep-reaching philosophic roots, and it asks us to see this world rightly, as it is, and there is nothing more difficult than that.

Perhaps the best "modern" example of this Greek approach to history can be found in the brilliant works of Tocqueville. There are what we might call "peaks" in the history of Western thought, intellectual heights reached, but only occasionally and at very infrequent intervals. Plato, St. Augustine, Shakespeare, Thomas Carlyle, Herman Melville, Isaiah Berlin, George Orwell, Martin Amis, as well as Tocqueville—all of these thinkers represent an apex or summit of spiritual and intellectual excellence. Excellent: *"having good qualities in a high degree; superior in worth or value; that which is excellent excels the majority of persons or things."* And these writers and thinkers retain such a deep and profound hold on our affections precisely because of that excellence, their powers of perception, insight, and wisdom, their profound ability to see, understand, and then reckon rightly with what they are looking at. And that is the case with Tocqueville.

In his work, *The Ancien Regime and the French Revolution*, Tocqueville outlines his task. He seeks a deeper understanding of the revolution by trying to determine "its real meaning," "its actual character," "the spirit at its centre," "its characteristic features," and "its essential character."[42] And his understanding of the Revolution's explanatory nature still stands today:

> Since the French Revolution did not simply have the aim of changing the former government but of abolishing the old structure of society, it had to attack simultaneously every established power, destroy every recognized influence, blot out tradition, create fresh customs and habits, and somehow drain the human mind of all those ideas upon which respect and obedience had been founded up to that time. That was the source of its strangely anarchic character."[43]

Now, quite apart from the compressed and concentrated brilliance of the thing, the passage also reveals what happens when the SocProg type gets its hands on guns and guillotines. But the point is clearly there: Tocqueville, examining the particular and drawing a conclusion from it, is using the intellectual tools of the pre-Socratics. He is trying to understand and perceive clearly the nature of a thing, as it exists. And gaining an understanding of that nature also and at the same time helps him to explain the thing in question. And all of this is rooted entirely in the simple desire to understand, which is the whole point and purpose of history.

There is nothing more than that.

And yet that is more than enough.

Objectivity

In this "modern" age, though, the whole concept of understanding the nature of a thing and seeing the world as it is—what used to be called objectivity (excuse me) "objectivity"—has been given a rough ride. Objectivity these days is snickered at as little more than a quaint and archaic curiosity pursued and desired by naïve and credulous simpletons. Scholars from across disciplines, we are assured, have converged on the consensus today that objectivity is "an illusion" and that we have at long last progressed beyond such infantile preoccupations.[44] The man who wrote a book on the subject, American historian Peter Novick, called the idea of objectivity "dubious" and what is more, the very notion is suspect, seen as "psychologically and sociologically naive."[45] There is nothing new in this critique. The Sophists made exactly the same point 2,500 years ago, only today it has taken on a political dimension.

Not only do we reveal our general stupidity if we believe in objectivity, we also reveal our ominous political biases as well. The SocProgs want everything to be political and that includes objectivity, too. Australian historian Keith Windschuttle quoted two SocProgs who argued the following thought cliché: "historians can never fully detach their scholarly work from their educational attitudes, ideological disposition, and culture" and thus the very notion of an objective order "is not simply an uneducated [?!] view, it is also an ideological position of traditionalists and the political right."[46] And there you have it. The science is settled as they say these days: if you believe in truth then you are just a stupid right-winger.

For the SocProgs, there is nothing real outside of our subjective interpretation of it.[47] Historians do not discover anything so much as we "construct" the past; we promote "one story among many" because anything we write only reveals our own hidden biases, hidden because we remain mired in "false consciousness;" mired in that "more original reality" that sociologists claim to have discovered but which, oddly, no one else can see but them; trapped and entangled in ideological superstructure.[48] Not even science can make truth claims. Scientists do not discover but rather construct reality, and so for the SocProg set, the really interesting thing about science is the "political questions aroused by its institutional status" which itself is shaped by "the ideological agendas of powerful elites.[49] Ah, "the elites." There they are, in science, too.

Setting aside the paranoid SocProg suspicions about the objective world, there are a number of more sensible reasons to dispute objectivity.[50] Critics of objectivity will harp on the idea that the historian's selection of archival material is itself an act which distorts the real and thus distorted reality is not objective reality at all. This line is used all the time in universities to attack objectivity. That this straw-man historian is simply being sloppy and dishonest rather than rigorous and honest is rarely brought up.

In another vein, objectivity sometimes assumes a degree of non-interference on the part of the historian, and non-interference quickly races into non-discrimination, and from thence into non-judgement. This, critics claim, is impossible or, at any rate, certainly not desirable.[51] Undesirable because that would render us incapable of making judgements where judgements seem to be required. Interesting side note here: English historian George Trevelyan wrote 100 years ago that one of the results of history practiced in a democracy would be the idea that "all sides in quarrels of the past were equally right and wrong."[52] He was actually not very far off on that one.[53]

But let us be clear and simple. Objective: "*Having independent existence apart from experience or thought; self-existent.*" This idea merely posits a world that exists outside of our subjective perception of it. There is nothing exceptional here. If a tree falls in the forest then yes, it will make a noise.[54] Out of this comes Objectivity: "*The power that enables an author or artist to treat subjects objectively or apart from his own personality.*" And so the *goal* here is for the historian to try and sacrifice self—to "extinguish self," as Ranke put it—to degrees to which he is able, with the aim of seeing the world that does exist rightly, as it is, "[as it] exists apart from experience or thought." But the more important point here is that the definition for objectivity suggests a certain "power" necessary to be objective. And it is this part over which most people skip. We'll linger.

Lingering

No one talks much about this stuff anymore, but there are a few key concepts that are pre-conditions for objective thought. These tools necessary to see the world as it is are the noblest of all things, the best of all that is in us and amongst them we count wisdom, honesty, and fidelity. These and other such like spiritual ideals, collectively constitute a foundation for the development of that power which is necessary for objectivity and they are exclusive to Traditionalists because the one word that connects and intertwines all of them is truth. These ideals, then, are closed off to Sophisticated SocProgs like Joy Parr who demently claimed that gender history operates on the basic principle that it "refuses" truths about human nature. And if the truth is refused then it necessarily follows that so, too, is wisdom.

Wisdom is defined as *"the power of true and right discernment."* And discernment means to *"see distinctly."* Training and habituating the mind to see clearly and discern what is there moves us down the path toward understanding and wisdom. Wisdom and discernment go hand in hand with the power of perception. Perception: *"Any insight or intuitive judgement that implies unusual discernment of fact or truth."* Wisdom, discernment, and perception revolve around and indeed depend upon the existence of truth. But what is truth? Well, here we get into some muddy terrain. Truth: *"the state or character of being true; that which is true; the quality of being true."* Our tires spin. But the dictionary philosophers hit on something when they attach truth to another idea. Truth: *"In the arts, faithfulness to the facts of nature, history or life."* The pre-Socratics were faithful to these facts of nature, history, and life. But what exactly are they?

Determining what constitutes these "facts of nature," these "truths," is, of course, difficult, otherwise everybody would be doing it and it thrills the SocProgs to challenge: "Facts?! Whose 'facts'? Facts of what nature? Socially constructed facts, no doubt!" But let's ignore them. Determining these facts of nature, history, and life is heavily dependent on another and much more knotty and thorny faculty: honesty. Now the SocProgs have elsewhere claimed that "moral probity" (in a word, honesty) is little more than a mongrel portion of "the hegemonic masculinity of empire." We all know that is not true. Our honesty tells us so. Honesty: *"Free from fraud."*

But what is it then? Honesty, like truth, is a slippery concept. We all know what it means, yet it also means something much more than just not telling a lie. Not telling a lie is merely the most visible portion of the word. But honesty is like an iceberg: the greater part of it, the deepest shades of its meaning, lay unseen because it is so difficult to capture in propositional form. The eighteenth-century German philosopher Immanuel Kant wondered at this very problem. Frequently, he wrote, "a thoughtful mind is often at a loss for an expression that should square exactly with its concept."[55] At which point, the thoughtful mind has two options: invent a new word, which for the harrumphing Kant was definitely *not* an option—"to coin new words is to arrogate to oneself legislative power in matters of language"—or to "look about in dead and learned languages" for something that approximates the concept being sought. Option number two is the way to go, then, because "honesty" also means *"an ornamental garden plant of the mustard family,"* which obviously takes us further away from where we want to go.

Honest: *"Chaste, virtuous, free from fraud."* All of those words matter for active philosophic thought but the one that perhaps matters most for our purposes here is the word sandwiched there in the middle: Virtuous. That word comes from the Latin *virtus* which means "strength" or "bravery." And Virtue itself, strictly defined, means *"the disposition to conform to the law of right; moral excellence; rectitude"* (if you listen carefully, you may be able to hear a SocProg shrieking here). But Virtue also has synonyms and honesty is one of them. Honesty by itself means free from fraud, not telling a lie, etc. But as a synonym for virtue, honesty becomes radiant and magnificent as our vision, to borrow from Carlyle, breaks out onto "a whole inward Sea of Light and Love."[56] Honesty as a synonym for virtue becomes *"the highest truthfulness of the soul to and with itself."*[57] This is what objectivity requires. This is the power that animates it: the highest truthfulness of the soul to and with itself.

The dictionary philosophers may not have known this, but their definition of honesty is channelling elements of Platonic philosophy. Plato wrote that the point and purpose of education, of philosophy—and we must remember here that the word philosophy simply means loving and so seeking wisdom—is developing the ability to see with the eye of the soul. He assumed that the vision of the soul, unlike our bodily senses, is uncorrupted and free from distortion or, in a word, honest. Plato explains it this way: "every seeker after wisdom knows that up to the time when Philosophy takes it over, his soul is a helpless prisoner chained hand and foot in the body, compelled to view reality not directly but only through its prison bars and wallowing in utter ignorance."[58] But when Philosophy sees a soul in this condition, she takes it over and, "by gentle persuasion, tries to set it free." And then, having done that:

> "She points out that observation by means of the eyes and ears and all the other senses abound with deception and she urges the soul to refrain from using them unless it is necessary to do so and encourages it to collect and concentrate itself in isolation, trusting nothing but its own isolated judgement upon realities considered in isolation and attributing no truth to any other thing which it views through another medium in some other thing; such objects she knows are sensible and visible but what she herself sees is intelligible and invisible."[59]

This approach to understanding borders on mysticism and, like truth itself, it is difficult to explain and that is as it should be. Truth is difficult. It is Ideology that is simple. But in Plato's educational ideal there, we, being human, recognize something very true and very real about us, about the capacities of our souls to aid us in reaching a greater and deeper understanding of the nature of this world.

There are very appealing similarities between what Plato wrote there and what Viktor Frankl wrote 2,500 years later in the twentieth century. Frankl argued for the existence of what he called "the spiritual unconscious."[60] It is a type of consciousness or awareness that is itself unconscious; it operates on its own. Frankl likened this consciousness to a "guard," of sorts. It is the guard that alerts a sleeping mother, he writes, to any sort of irregular breathing in her child. It is the guard that automatically awakens a man from slumber. It is a consciousness that shapes and informs our awareness. And there is no locating or manipulating this "guard" because "that which decides whether an experience will become conscious or will remain unconscious is itself unconscious." It is a thing that dictates to us, not we to it.

Creative types are well aware of a thing that operates unbidden in them, a thing which is beyond self. Indeed, Socrates himself spoke often about being animated by a spirit, a *daimon*, that thing in him that drove him to seek truth. And we all of us have had experiences in which we somehow intuit something; we know, see, or perceive a thing and the acquisition of that knowledge is not the result of the powers of logic, not as such, but rather the result of something larger than logic and reason. Plato called it "the soul," while Frankl called it "the spiritual unconscious" and, elsewhere, referred to it as a "trans-human agent."[61] The writer Arthur Koestler (borrowing from Sigmund Freud), called it the "oceanic sense." Koestler explains: "As if a tuning-fork had been struck, there would be answering vibrations, and once this had started, a state would be produced which the mystics called 'ecstasy' and the saints 'contemplation.'"[62] Whatever you wish to call it, writers, thinkers, and philosophers separated by thousands of years agree that there is, or certainly can be, an unconscious tool of perception in us which, unbidden, aids in the acquisition and development of awareness, knowledge, and understanding.

For Plato though, learning to see with the eye of the soul also relied heavily on the development of character.[63] And character is another word for all of those ideas we have been examining so far: honesty, virtue, fidelity, and under-standing. The apprehension of our world, discerning its true and proper nature, cannot develop out of a soul that lacks character, a soul set at imbalance by Pride or Arrogance, say. We valorize reason and rationality as we should, but there is so much more to understanding than just that. Character is not irrel-evant to understanding but, rather, it is essential. Philosopher Robert Cushman calls it "determinative." The ability to see, perceive, and understand; the search for and attainment of wisdom or even portions thereof; this is not just a rational-logical process and it has *nothing* to do with politics or ideologies. Politics and ideology foreclose on truth. The pursuit and attainment of wisdom and understanding cannot be done or achieved without the development of both the mind and soul or, what Cushman calls "the total disposition of the knowing subject."[64] Wisdom and character go hand in hand, and when they are at last wed the conditions are thus created for the cultivation and develop-ment of a philosophical soul and that leads on to the path of the philosophical way, which itself is "a way to a moment of existence in which there is a direct confrontation with reality."[65]

But developing the powers of the soul and the virtues of character is difficult. There are no classes in how to do it and anyway no one even really talks about this stuff anymore. We used to have traditions that aimed at inculcating that character of which Cushman spoke. But we got rid of those. And so we drift. We are free to partake of character as we wish even though it is the most important part of life and inquiry. Character, soul-virtue, honesty: all of these things are, we know, the most important parts of being human and they take a lifetime to develop. But a life so spent would be a good life. And history, or even just plain and simple thought, thus practiced would be good also; good because it would be pure and unpolluted.

Attaining this level of contemplation, developing this capacity for reflection and understanding was likely much easier in Plato's day. There were many fewer distractions, spectacles, and impediments that could obtrude between the soul and its goal of seeking the understanding and wisdom it desires. Too, Plato and the other Athenian thinkers lived in what we might call a pre-ideological world, and there were very few if any orthodoxies or dogmas that they were not ready and willing to enthusiastically call into question. Indeed, they lived in a world where competing opinions and discussion habituated them to see a thing from all sides.[66] The same simply cannot be said of our age. We may in fact be *less* free in our inquiries than the Greeks. There are certain questions that cannot be asked, there are certain things that cannot be said, and there are certain lines of inquiry that cannot be pursued. The demands of politics and ideology bind and gag what our souls seem to apprehend. Perhaps this is why the Greeks had their Seven Wise Men and our "modern" age does not have any wise men: we have replaced wisdom with ideology and its distressing and sickly handmaiden, sociology.

Objectivity simply posits an actual world that we can see and which, with great effort, care and above all, honesty, we can understand and then relate or explain. Not all of it, no; but some of it, yes. When truth and objectivity are denounced as naive, illusory, and silly, we are by implication and by definition denouncing wisdom, honesty, insight, perception, virtue, and all the rest of them because the very existence of these words is predicated on the existence of a reality which does in fact exist outside our subjective perception of it. All of these concepts are stacked together like swords, and if we rid the stack of truth and objectivity then the whole thing collapses. The nihilism inherent in the SocProg assault on truth and objectivity is very real and its implications are disconcertingly far-reaching and very poorly considered: when we bin objectivity and truth, we are at the same time and without even being aware we are doing so, also binning the best that is in us.

One is reminded here of the psychotic world of George Orwell's Ministry of Truth and their project to change society through the eradication of words. Winston's Ministry friend Syme enthused about his task, explaining to Winston that "we're destroying words, scores of them, hundreds of them every day." It is, for Syme, "a beautiful thing, the destruction of words," because what it does is "narrow the range of thought" with the ultimate goal of creating a language without shades of meaning in which "every concept that can ever be needed will be expressed by exactly one word." And thus it will be, "every year, fewer and fewer words, and the range of consciousness always a little smaller."[67] By the way, what Orwell describes there is precisely what political correctness seeks: to eradicate certain words and thoughts with the aim of cleansing society of its imperfections, and it does so in the name of Justice and Equality.

In the end, we must remember that objectivity was never proven wrong. It is just an idea which, today, seems out of place. Surely it is of more than passing interest that our modern cultural discomfort with objectivity grew directly out of the 1960s, an age of "negativity, confusion, apathy, and uncertainty" and whose conditions "have persisted into the present."[68] It is not objectivity that is the problem; it is *we* that are the problem. Our rejection of objectivity is merely a manifestation of our intellectual and moral confusion, our "spiritual distemper."[69] Objectivity was just sitting there until the 1960s came along and it suited the purposes of that demented age to say it didn't exist and that has become our received wisdom. And we, in our impotent and destructive confusion, are too weak, too bewildered to say otherwise. We do not recognize this confusion because that would require being honest with who we are and what we have become. And, evidently, we are not there yet.

Human Nature

In addition to rejecting truth, reality, and objectivity, the SocProgs also, depressingly, "refuse" the existence of human nature. Our reductive and mechanistic sociology textbook is clear on this point: "We aren't born with instincts."[70] But we must pause at the outset here. Sociology is asking us to accept the rather strange proposition that every single living and breathing creature on the planet—*trees*, even—is born with an innate nature except us. This is just not so. The behaviour of a cat, say, is not a "social construction" of "the elites" (feline or otherwise). We understand that cats behave the way they do because of their intrinsic nature and understanding that essential-not-accidental nature also and at the same time explains feline behaviour. And precisely the same is true for men and women, for human beings.

The Greeks, in revolutionizing philosophy and history, discovered man as he was, with certain properties, characteristics, and drives.[71] And understanding this nature of ours is crucial and essential to understanding not just history but also our world. Cushman observed that, for Plato, human nature, the very real and intrinsic moral order in man, provides us with "the primary data" for understanding this world, its realities, and its history.[72] This is a simple but infinitely complicated idea. After all, reckoning with it requires and demands rigorous honesty but it just makes sense. We are human and so "the human" is simply the only reliable clue we have that will enable us to determine the nature of our reality or our history.[73] Being human is the only thing of which we have a thorough and immediate understanding. But that understanding is fast becoming increasingly muddled because sociology has instilled in *generations* of young people the destructive untruth that we are merely socially constructed animals, an idea that necessarily means there is nothing inside of us to understand. There is a very real and very compelling reason why post-modern thought is sometimes called *anti*-humanism: it is a body of thought whose primary instrument—sociology—rejects, refuses, and denies who we are, essentially, as human beings.

The Greek conception of history, however, was structured around the clear recognition that there are immutable and unchangeable truths about us. The exploration of those truths is one of the reasons why Thucydides still makes for such powerful reading today. Thucydides argued that human nature was unchanging and permanent; that the human animal will, in certain situations, behave in the same way because that animal's nature is unchanging and permanent—and to which we might also add, finite and limited. Hence, one of the values and virtues of history: a careful reading of the past will lead to an understanding of human nature and in those revelations, the historian or the reader of history will become aware that "similar antecedents will lead to similar consequents."[74] But at the same time as that is true, man is also, by nature, consistently and irredeemably *ir*rational and *un*predictable, and so history does not admit laws and theories. Man will always find a way to defy the law *and* the theory.

So what is our nature? It is both good and bad. The stern and relentless Thucydides, for example, tended to focus on the bad but that does not make it any less true.[75] His basic ideas about being human were reflected in the writings of other thinkers and philosophers for 2,500 years. From Plato through St. Augustine and on down to Joseph de Maistre in the nineteenth century and Sigmund Freud in the twentieth, there has been a clear recognition that Man is both "social and evil."[76] Both Freud and Maistre rejected the typical Enlightenment view of Man as essentially good. With withering sarcasm, Freud once wrote: "For 'little children do not like it' when there is talk of the inborn human inclination to badness...and to cruelty as well."[77] Indeed, both Maistre and Freud were awed in a way at the "striking social naïveté" of the Enlightenment thinkers and their belief that man is an essentially rational creature always operating in self-interest and only after careful deliberation. That's just silly. And the SocProgs, children of the French *philosophes*, have inherited that naïveté about being human.

Now, we certainly need not go as far as Maistre did in his *total* absorption in human badness ("from the maggot up to man, the universal law of violent destruction of living things is unceasingly fulfilled"), but it would be foolish to ignore, as SocProgs do, his essential ideas about being human.[78] Perhaps, though, it is not foolishness that SocProgs exhibit, but rather a wilful ignorance or blindness rooted in a fear of being human. Or maybe it is not even fear but rather a profound discomfort with the idea that we actually are what we appear to be, and are not much more. But there again, what we are is more than enough.

The "proof" for the existence of human nature, if proof is really needed, can be found in history which, if read rightly, clearly shows us who we are as humans. Thucydides examined the revolution that broke out at Corcyra during the Peloponnesian War in the fifth century BC. The democrats had begun murdering the aristocrats in that ghastly fashion which revolutionaries have followed throughout history. And Thucydides was the first to identify and then articulate this basic truth about being human in revolutionary times: "with the ordinary conventions of civilized life thrown into confusion, human nature, always ready to offend even where laws exist, showed itself proudly in its true colors as something incapable of controlling passion, *insubordinate to the idea of justice*."[79]

And if we move down the road 2,000 years, we see that nothing changed in the interim. In his study of the French Revolution, Thomas Carlyle lingered on the September Massacres which, like the Corcyran massacre, were carried out, in broad form, by democrats against aristocrats (although in the French case—reflecting the profound changes that had occurred in Western history since antiquity—about 200 priests were tossed into the blender for good measure[80]). All told, something north of 2,000 people were slaughtered by the revolutionaries who, also, were trying to make the world a better place to live. The *sans-culottes* "plied their grim hell-trade, there, through the not ambrosial night." They used axes, swords, knives and blunt instruments. There were kangaroo courts, death, and revolutionary justice aplenty. Carlyle writes: "Woe, woe on him! Of such stuff are we all made; on such powder mines of bottomless guilt and criminality—'if God restrained not', as is well said—does the purest of us walk. There are depths in man that go the length of the lowest hell."[81] Objections?

Even Canadian military historian Tim Cook incorporates some of this kind of thinking into his work. It seems that during the First World War, Canadian troopers had a penchant at times for killing German soldiers who were in the process of surrendering. These were men who no longer represented a threat for they had laid down their weapons and had their hands in the air, sometimes clutching white flags. And our soldiers killed them. The incidents were terrifying enough, but Cook was more disturbed by the strange and almost prudish reluctance of Canadian historians to embrace this simple reality of war and thus of human nature. Cook asserts that it is "time to acknowledge that the western front left soldiers with two choices: kill or be killed."[82] This is just the way of it with us.

Thucydides, and Carlyle, and Cook, separated by thousands of years, clearly establish the following idea that at certain times and under certain circumstances man will, with his finite and limited nature, enthusiastically and with very little trouble discard civilized behaviour, law, and restraint (by the way, many of those oppressive and arbitrary social conventions, customs, and moralities that sociology is busy trying wreck and replace with nothing, are actually recognitions of—and thus designed to act as checks on—human nature). This was true of the civil wars in Greece 2,500 years ago, it was true again in 1792, it was true once more in 1917, it is true today in the Middle East, and it will be true once more in the future because our nature appears not to change. In revolutionizing history, the Greeks discovered this basic fact about us: Man has a nature, something intrinsic and essential which also and at the same time explains why he behaves the way he does. And one of the principal goals of the historian or the reader of history is to understand this.

Understanding just this one simple basic fundamental truth about who we are necessarily changes the way we view our world.[83] For Tim Cook, this understanding resulted in a sensitive, balanced, and level-headed examination of Canadians killing Germans when he could have easily taken the other more simple-minded approach and castigated them for violating "Canadian values." Historian John Herd Thompson did this very thing when examining the internment of Japanese Canadians during the Second World War. The internment of Japanese-Canadians was clearly an injustice, but Thompson goes the Full Monty, calling the event "an embarrassing record inconsistent with the national values expressed in the Constitution Act of 1982" and "as such...must be judged severely."[84]

This castigatory judgement is not thought or reflection on the human condition but rather righteousness, merely. Righteousness we recall means "upright, virtuous, blameless and right-thinking." But being righteous is the easiest thing in the world to be. Righteousness simply directs a kind of unthinking reactionary hostility out toward its object. It creates a binary framework in which the sophisticated "we" today look at the ignorant "them" in the past and that lofty position then allows us to fling Thunderbolts of Judgement unleavened by wisdom or understanding or even an appreciation of the infinitely disturbing complexities of being human. And so that is the problem with righteousness: it clouds perception and vision and thus perverts proper judgement. It gets in the way of advancing history's goal of understanding who and what we are.

We might with profit push away from our verdant Tahitian shores even further.[85] The English writer Martin Amis has spent his life writing about being human in his novels, his histories, and his non-fiction essays. He has explored a great deal of historical terrain in his work, but with a particular emphasis on two of the twentieth century's greatest crimes: the Nazi and Marxist-Bolshevik experiments. Amis has developed a keen understanding of history as well as a heightened and finely tuned ability to reckon rightly with what he is looking at, an ability which in and of itself is also a kind of talent. His novel *The Zone of Interest* concerns life in a Nazi concentration camp. And in that novel he writes:

> "Once upon a time there was a king, and the king commissioned his favorite wizard to create a magic mirror. The mirror didn't show you your reflection. It showed you your soul—it showed you who you really were. The wizard couldn't look at it without turning away. The king couldn't look at it. The courtiers couldn't look at it. A chestful of treasure was offered to any citizen in this peaceful land who could look at it for sixty seconds without turning away. And no one could."[86]

There should be nothing shocking or surprising here in Amis's characterization of being human. But there is a definite tendency amongst SocProgs to take the opposite view, wrapped up as they are in a warm and inviting cocoon of unreality in which they see humanity advancing and progressing, evolving and becoming.

Embracing this fairly basic fact about us does not degrade us, nor does it consign us to a kind of moral perdition, but, rather, it should enhance our appreciation of who we are. Rather than finding it a frightening and terrifying prospect, accepting these truths about us should be tremendously liberating. The SocProgs seem to believe, or pretend, or perhaps they just naturally assume, that the more time we spend on this planet, the better we get; that the simple sweep of an hour hand across the face of a clock, merely, changes us in fundamental ways. It doesn't. The Greeks lived by this precept seeing in it, as they did, the foundation for all subsequent knowledge: Know Thyself. But here it is, 2,500 years on, and we still have trouble with that one.

The SocProg might respond that Western history itself is the story of increasing Justice, Liberty, and Equality which clearly demonstrates our evolving human natures. But again, that is an incorrect reading. The thing that enabled or allowed those increasing liberties and equalities has been in us all along because it is in our nature. Historian and philosopher Karl Jaspers suggests that "at any given moment, parts of [our] energies, gifts, and impulses are realized, whilst others slumber unawakened."[87] And Jaspers goes on to say that the "varying unfoldment of [these] parts does not mean a difference in nature but *a difference of manifestation.*"

Slavery, for example, was accepted in the Greek and Roman world by most, but not all, people. It is not accepted in the Western world today. Hence, progress. But this is not a change in our nature but rather a change in cultural values. After all, there were many people in antiquity who thought slavery an abomination. The Cynic Antisthenes was one. What is culturally acceptable in any one given age does not mean our fundamental natures have changed. It only means that what we consider acceptable has changed. And besides, slavery has not disappeared. It is only that the *types* of slavery have changed. Plantation slavery is gone, yes, but today sexual slavery is the issue. And even the benighted plight of immigrant labourers at various points around the world raises uncomfortable parallels with slavery. And that latter point raises a further point: once we expand our vision beyond the borders of the West, what then do we find? Is it just Westerners who are progressing, evolving, advancing, and becoming? If that be so, then ought not we help the rest of the world advance, evolve, and become? Don't we have a moral and ethical obligation to help raise the rest of the world to our very high and sophisticated standards? And didn't we call that imperialism and colonialism once?

The point is that everything that is potential in us has been potential in us from the beginning. Thus, any changes that have taken place—the abolition of slavery, the extension of the vote, civil rights, etc—can be understood not as a result of some fundamental progression or evolution in our nature, but, rather, a "selection of that which was already present."[88] And thus what history reveals is not Progress at all, but Change, merely.

Progress: "*a movement forward nearer a goal; advancement toward maturity or completion.*"

Change: "*to make or become different; alter; vary.*"

And once we accept the fact that history only reveals Change and not Progress, we will then have gone some great distance toward ridding ourselves of that fatuous Marxian idea that there is a goal waiting for us out there, a destination, an endpoint. There isn't.

Ultimately, the problem for the SocProg set is that if they admit to the existence of intrinsic natures, then they are brought face to face with certain ugly truths about the human condition and they have great difficulty in dealing with this. Truths require and demand an honest, responsible, and rigorous accounting. And if history shows us anything at all, it clearly shows that we, as human beings, do not handle truths very well. We are in full flight from them today so much do they frighten us. So rather than facing up to truths we instead deny their existence and "refuse" them because to reckon rightly with them would saddle us with complexities that history quite clearly demonstrates we are either totally ill-equipped to handle or simply too reluctant to face. But always the truth of us will forever be far more interesting than the lies we tell ourselves. It is a truth of human nature, for example, that we frequently lie to ourselves. Our honesty tells us that.

History as a Manifestation of Human Nature

Plato did not write much about history, but there is much that could be learned from the little that he did. For Plato, history concerned human actions; human actions derive directly from human nature; and that nature develops out of the human soul.[89] Technically defined, all soul means is this: "*the incorporeal [intangible] nature of man, or principle of mental and spiritual life; the thinking, willing nature.*" That last bit is key: our thinking and willing nature. For Plato, understanding the soul, our thinking and willing nature, is the first step toward understanding the past. As philosopher RG Bury put it, the Platonic vision of understanding history is one in which we posit "the driving force of the soul [as] the maker of history."[90]

This approach to the study of the past should be unexceptional. But in this day and age, we simply do not speak in these human terms anymore. We speak of "conditioning" and of "social construction" and, it seems, of anything but being human. Historian Francis Fukuyama wondered at this very thing.

He himself developed an idea in which he tried to explain history in terms of Pride and Dignity (what the Greeks called *Thymos*) and along the way in doing so, he offered the casual but very true observation that the only language we have to see, understand, and explain both the past and the present revolves around Marxian economics.[91] "We inhabitants of Western liberal democracies," Fukuyama wrote, "are by now so used to accounts of current events that reduce motivation to economic causes...that we are frequently surprised to discover how totally non-economic most political life is." And he continued with the sobering suggestion that "we do not even have a common vocabulary for talking about the prideful and assertive side of human nature that is responsible for driving most wars and political conflicts."[92] And so positing the soul—or just being human—as the drive wheel of history can indeed sound foreign or strange in this reductive, mechanistic-sociologistic era. But it's an idea that has been around for a pretty long time and, as Bury rightly points out, "the historian who ignores this loses much."[93]

So, in *The Republic*, Plato uses his understanding of the soul, of human nature, to arrive at some sort of understanding as to how Athens fouled itself,[94] how she underwent such a profound change in the "general intellectual and moral collapse of the brilliant fifth century."[95] And one of the really interesting elements of Plato's account here was not just his clear recognition that he was in fact witnessing the degradation of Athenian democracy, but also his keen understanding that it was unavoidable. American statesman John Adams once wrote that there has never yet been a democracy that did not kill itself, and by that he seemed to have meant that a democracy contains within it the seeds of its own destruction. And Plato recognized this as well, and he accounted for these political and social changes based on his understanding of human nature and the human soul. As Bury puts it, Plato attributed these changes to "the spirit of man whose soul-structure [was] changing" because that is what democracy does to a human soul: it changes it.[96]

Plato explained it like this. The democratic man existed within a political order that was "delightful, free, and heavenly" precisely because it accorded so much individual freedom. The democratic man, having been pardoned by the Sophists and the Cynics from customs and conventions, was then free to pursue desires; he satisfies instincts and lusts and does what he feels.[97] This Liberty gradually seeped deep into the soul of all the citizens and demands for more of it increased. That is the way that Liberty operates in a human soul because humans want more of what is good.[98]

And so pervasive and ubiquitous Liberty and Equality produced the effects we looked at in Chapter Four. Fathers befriended rather than instructed their sons; teachers pandered to their students; elders avoided being stern to evade the reputation of being too strict; and finally, Liberty moved to "infect even the domestic animals with anarchy" who walked around with a "grand freedom."[99] The extreme of popular liberty is reached, Plato writes, when slaves have status and there is "complete equality and liberty in relations between the sexes."[100] And in the end, Plato writes, democratic Liberty leads to this (which to us, should sound awfully familiar; indeed, not just familiar but the same): "you find that the minds of the citizens become so sensitive that the least vestige of restraint is resented as intolerable, till finally, as you know, in their determination to have no master, they disregard all laws written or unwritten." And all of this develops out of "the excessive desire for liberty at the expense of everything else."[101]

The social and political changes to which Plato was witness, then, grew directly out of what he felt was an imbalance in the human soul. Plato famously likened the human soul to a charioteer leading two horses.[102] The charioteer represents reason and rationality and his aim is to guide as best he can the two horses leading him. The first horse is "upright and clean limbed." This horse "holds his neck high...his color is white, his thirst for honour is tempered by restraint and modesty." This horse "needs no whip" because it represents "spiritedness" something like our sense of dignity and honour, the best that is in us, and it always takes the side of reason against the baser appetites and desires which are represented by the second horse.[103] That second horse is "crooked, lumbering, ill-made; his coat is black and his eyes a blood-shot grey; wantonness and boastfulness are his companions; he is hairy eared and deaf, hardly controllable even with a whip." This horse represents what is potentially worst in us, the desiring part of the soul. This is how Plato saw the human soul: a charioteer trying to navigate two horses, one or the other of which was constantly trying to drag the whole enterprise into disaster for the sake of Desire or Pride.

Plato believed that for a soul—and by direct extension a state—to function properly and harmoniously, all of the elements must be there in appropriate measure, neither one nor the other predominating. The Spirited must be there as well as the Desiring; the Aggressive must be there in proper proportion to the Calm. Plato likens a state to a woven garment in which the varying temperaments that are naturally opposed are all stitched together in proper proportion and which thus abets harmony. But, it is the "unequal distribution of soul-qualities" that creates disproportions and imbalances and thus drives change.[104] Pride or Desire or even Reason, out of balance and unchecked will always create or generate a consequence, and so for Plato, balance in both the soul and the state was everything. He referred to that balance as the Due Measure. For Plato, moderation and goodness were very nearly one and the same thing.[105] But in Athens, a Liberty and a Freedom rooted in Equality and predicated on Justice seemed to have produced a state in which Desire abounded entirely out of its right and proper proportions, hence the degradation and decay of Athenian democracy.

Liberty in Athens was the freedom to have a say, the freedom to participate, the freedom to vote, the freedom, above all, to speak your mind. Equality was the right of all citizens to do so. Liberty and Equality recognize and thus validate the importance of each citizen. But Liberty and Equality also contain inherent qualities of expectation: once in play, both desire more.[106] Liberty, as jurist Robert Bork observed, has "continuous change built into it, precisely because it is hostile to constraints."[107] Indeed, the previous 200 years of Western history clearly validate Bork's assertion that "when one [constraint] falls, men are brought against the next constraint which is now felt to be equally irksome."[108] Liberty seeks the removal of restrictions; that is what Liberty does. Liberty: "*the state of being exempt from the domination of others or from restricting circumstances; freedom.*" But nothing is an absolute good. Nothing is an unqualified good. We have all heard the phrase "too much of a good thing." Too much Freedom and too much Liberty appear to have resulted in the rot and degradation of Athenian democracy. We see ourselves in the pages of Plato. We recognize our nature.

Writing 2,500 years after Plato, cultural historian Jacques Barzun used this same kind of approach in his bracing history of the decline of Western cultural life.[109] He narrates the then present-day twentieth century in sobering past tense. Like Plato's Athenians, Barzun's "Demotic Man" was characterized by an urge to "act as if nothing stood in the way of every wish." The people were full of what Plato called the "neat spirit" and Barzun, with a sideways glance at Plato, observed that "such an attitude expects no rebuffs, and overlooks those it provokes."[110] Barzun goes on: "In a heedless uncivil world, the driven needed to look after their wants as soon as they arose, to pay themselves back as it were, by self-coddling. So many curbs and hindrances to desire had been removed; the legal and conventional by new laws and new conventions, the natural ones by *techne* with the aid of science." And Barzun concludes that we, like Plato's Athenians, had developed precisely the same attitudes: "criticism or reproof was felt to be intolerable."

Thus, both Barzun and Plato account for the profound—and profoundly similar—changes in their societies using a simple tool: a keen and honest understanding of the human soul and a reckoning with human nature. RG Bury concludes that when we are looking at history, we are actually confronting the physical manifestation of human nature and thus "every beam of light which is thrown on human nature helps to illumine history."[111] Both Barzun and Plato were able to discern and explain social and political change because they understood human nature. They understood that once Liberty is granted, we are, because of our intrinsic natures, naturally *dis*inclined to resist reaching for more and greater freedoms, more and greater Liberty. As the pre-Socratics would have it, a perceptive and honest understanding of the essential nature of a thing here also and at the same time explains change. A simple enough approach, true, but goodness how difficult it is to execute.

"Progress"

There is, then, a kind of determinism implicit in the Greek conception of history and that idea is disturbing to many people voiding, as it only seems to do, our will and our agency. Changeless realities and the permanence of our human condition naturally imply that history will repeat itself. If human nature remains the same, then so, too, will its expressions, the record of which we call history: Sophistry then, sociology now. As a comfort here, though, Viktor Frankl reminds us of a couple of pretty crucial ideas that we seem to have lost or misplaced in recent years. Frankl writes that "the freedom of will means the freedom of human will and human will is the will of a finite being."[112] But that does not necessarily mean that we do not have a will of our own or a will that is cancelled by a changeless human nature. Frankl argues that the will which we do possess is the will to freedom and choice, the will to "take a stand on whatever conditions might confront [us]."[113] And that is no small thing.

But this cyclical notion of history was an organic and eminently sensible notion to the Greeks. When they first began speculating on history, they simply and quite naturally assumed that it was cyclical and this idea grew out of their conception of the way the world itself seemed to work, its patterns. Both Thucydides and Herodotus explained the human world "by analogy with natural physical change."[114] The world is a natural, biological unit functioning according to a harmonious pattern based upon the intrinsic nature of its elements. And that includes us.

The Greek belief in cyclicality, then, forestalls notions of an upward ascension of humanity or, in a word, Progress. The whole idea of history "going somewhere" was just not on for the Greeks; it never occurred to them. Nor the Romans.[115] This did not mean that history did not move or happen. Obviously it did. But they relied on the idea that what happened once would likely happen again in the future, although in a slightly modified but still recognizable form.[116] The Greeks and the Romans were quite happy just being. It was the Christians who birthed the idea that history ought to have a goal; that it must mean something.

Writing right around the time that Imperial Rome was set to implode, the brilliant Catholic theologian-philosopher-historian St Augustine began picking apart the Greco-Roman view of history. He called those pagan writers "misled and misleading sages" for their belief that history is aimless and directionless.[117] St Augustine just couldn't get his head around the idea that history was little more than a "merry-go-round."[118] Surely history is more than that; it *must* be. If history is cyclical, St Augustine argued, then it is the grim lot of humanity to simply waffle between "false bliss and genuine misery." "False bliss" because any pleasing state of affairs is fleeting and temporary; and "genuine misery" because decline and decay are always looming, always there.[119] There can be no true bliss, no "progress," if all we are doing is being ceaselessly hurled back into what has already been.

But St Augustine's faith helped him to shape and form the Christian view of history. He reasoned that "if the soul goes from misery to happiness, nevermore to return" then surely it is not insensible to ask "why cannot the same be true of the world? And of man created in the world?" And so the Christian notion of history as ascension or progression was born. History in the Christian view became the coordinated movement of mankind forward to an endpoint and final goal which was "universal concord at the end of days" and the final redemption.[120] The parallels with Marx here are obvious, irresistible, and stunning. For the Christians, each event in history took on a definite and defined purpose and meaning as humanity moved toward a community of believers who live in and through Christ.[121] Having summarily executed the idea of cyclical history, St Augustine counseled the following plan of action: "keep to the straight path in the right direction under the guidance of sound teaching."[122] It was thus that "progress" was born.

But over time, over millennia, as the West lifted itself out of the Dark and Middle ages and pushed into the "modern" era, Western society secularized itself and there grew to be an increasing discomfort with the idea of history as a manifestation of God's plan. The Enlightenment historians of the eighteenth century and the Positivists of the nineteenth jettisoned the idea of history as advancement toward the Kingdom of God. These historians instead sought for the laws that governed history.[123] And this search for "scientific laws" was complemented by the desire to use those laws powered by our will to change the world and "make it a better place." It should not surprise anyone that sociology was birthed in this age.

If we can stamp the nineteenth century with any concept or word it would be Progress. That incredibly complex and busy age was stained by and shot through with the pervasive belief that human kind itself had finally reached the apex of moral, intellectual, and ethical development (we are suffering from the same hubris today). Not only did they believe that they had solved war, for example, they had proven that a general European war was no longer possible.[124] This new and now secular notion of progress abounding at that time had many sources, but chief amongst them were the findings of Charles Darwin and his ideas concerning evolution.

Darwin argued that species changed and evolved over time. These changes were taken to mean progress, advancement, and maturity or, in so many words, that species got better.[125] The early sociologists like Marx and Auguste Comte latched onto this notion and applied it to the human experience, which was unfortunate because we are the only consistently and irredeemably *ir*rational creature in this biological world (it would never occur to a baboon to fly a plane into the side of a building). But the point is that history itself was still a progression and an evolution, only no longer did it concern the Kingdom of God; it concerned the Kingdom of Liberty, Justice, and Equality as prophesized by Marx who became a kind of modern Redeemer of Mankind animated this time around not by religion but political ideology.[126] Marx, very much the Darwinian, claimed that he had found "scientific" proofs in his theories of history which revealed that the utopia he envisioned was not only desirable and feasible: it was inevitable.[127]

To greater or lesser degrees, Liberals of all stripes in the nineteenth century adopted this Marxian attitude of progress, evolution, and maturation. Indeed the SocProg conceits of the twenty-first century which we have been examining so far—pride, arrogance, condescension, and the belief that they and they alone stand for humanity—are, in Marx's age, already readily apparent, clearly developed, and fully manifest. Historian Carlton J Hayes writes that liberals in the nineteenth century:

> "[T]ook to anathematizing anyone who did not join their coterie and embrace their detailed and exacting creed. So seriously did they regard themselves that (*following a not unusual human inclination*) others accepted them at their own valuation and conceded to them the magical word 'Liberal.' In the long run, they were to discredit the name and with it much that was fine in the broad liberal tradition itself."[128]

Modern SocProgs have also discredited liberal ideals by embracing not the philosophical liberal ideal (which is good) but rather Marxian sociological theory (which is the opposite of good). But we see the point there: Liberal thinking people, beginning in the nineteenth century, grew to see themselves as the more evolved political species, and believed that anyone who did not agree with them was, by definition, wrong.

And so Darwinian ideas of evolution spilled over from science into society and they had, and regrettably continue to have, a profound and perverting effect on how we see our history, our world, and especially our place in it. Hannah Arendt observed that there is a definite and unambiguous Darwinian tendency in Marx and Comte—a tendency that is readily apparent in the SocProgs—which views history as "the consistent interpretation of everything as being only a stage of some further development."[129] All of a sudden and for no real good reason then, humanity in the nineteenth century went from being to becoming. The very names the SocProgs give themselves ("progressive," "new," "advanced") are reflections of this flawed evolutionary notion.

So it was science which helped to accidentally create a hybrid mongrel of the concept of progress. We started with St Augustine's deeply religious notion of historical progress in the fifth century and we end up in the nineteenth century with the "secularization of its eschatological pattern."[130] In other words, we binned the religious underpinnings of the concept of progress but kept the basic idea because Darwinian science and Marxian theories had apparently validated it. Thus, the SocProgs, generally secular liberals, cleave desperately and indeed name themselves in honour of a materialist version of a crucial and dynamic strand of the Christian faith which was birthed, for all intents and purposes, out of wishful thinking. Irony: "*A condition of affairs or events exactly the reverse of what was expected.*"

Progress does have its place. The history of science, for example, does in fact reveal progress, a movement upward, that which is at the foremost part. But apart from those very few and quite limited areas where progress does exist, progress as applied to history or human moral, spiritual, and ethical development is an empty and baseless vacuity. The twentieth century is more than enough to purchase that point. Indeed, the point can be purchased several times over and even then we would still have enough remaining to purchase the point one more time.[131]

But we need not be scared about the truth that neither history nor humanity progresses. Most people never believed that anyway, and they didn't believe it for a long, long time. For 1,000 years, from the sixth century BC to the fifth century AD, the people of the West got along quite well without the "illusion of progress" and, as philosopher John Gray notes, a great many of those people still managed to have "happy lives."[132] Even civilizations outside the West likewise eschewed "Progress" and they too managed to live happy lives. The Chinese, for example, saw history as an expression of yin and yang. Yin was negative and passive whilst yang was positive and active, "the one is now the expression of the other and both operate in cycles of rise and fall and in a universal pattern"[133] In this way, and like the Greeks, the Chinese viewed Man and nature as part of a single unit operating according to cyclical patterns.[134]

But we have been living with the untruth of progress now for some 200 years. It has become part of the air we breathe. Gray explains: "If the hope of progress is an illusion, how—it will be asked—are we to live? The question assumes the aim of life is action; but this is a modern heresy." And that heresy was birthed and given form by Karl Marx. There are oceans of untapped spiritual and intellectual liberation waiting for us in the aftermath of the destruction of the concept of progress. Historian William Dilthey observed that "when a man lives with the certainty and finality of the excellence of the world" he no longer needs to worry or fear that it is, in fact, *beyond* his capacity to "form a life according to the desires of his own will."[135] Once the excellence and perfection of the world are accepted, and the fear which prevents that acceptance assuaged, there appears in view another and better goal. The goal of history is not to change or save the world, for, as Gray notes, that we could never do and anyway it doesn't need saving.[136] The goal of history, once the pall of progress is removed, becomes understanding. The Greek conception of history and of inquiry itself is rooted in this very thing. Indeed, the idea of Greek history, its cyclicality, and hence its "meaninglessness" *presupposes* that the task of the historian, then, is to understand.[137] Again and again we come back to this idea of understanding. Leopold von Ranke explained in a lecture that history's aim "is not so much to gather facts and to arrange them as to understand them."[138] And Carlyle notes that "the end of Understanding is not to prove and find reasons but to *know*."[139] The goal of history, then, is not to change the world, which we can't do, but to see the world rightly, as it is, in its excellence. And that we can do.[140]

Back to the Basics

Perhaps the purest and most unpolluted explanation of the meaning of discipline of history comes to us from Leopold von Ranke. He tells us that the historian must delight and take "joy in the particular in and for itself." He wrote that if a historian "has a love for the vital manifestation of humanity at all, then he must rejoice in it without any reference to the progress of things."[141] The historian must "revel" in the "vices and virtues" of humanity and all this "he should do for no other purpose other than his joy in the life of the particular individual [or event]" that he is considering.[142] Please consider Ranke's words here: joy, vital love, rejoice, revel. When was the last time you heard a historian talk like that? One gets the sense that the SocProgs feel no real joy or love in what they do mostly because we see no evidence of that joy or love in their scholarship. Joy and Love sit uncomfortably next to sweaty, funky Ideology. And still less does Ideology foster and encourage rejoicing. When Ideology enters the room, Rejoicing ceases smiling, packs her things up, and leaves it.

In the end, we have to conclude with some very basic and unoriginal ideas. History is not a social science. If it was a social science then we would call it a social science, but it is not which is why we don't. Sociology is defined as "the *science* that treats of the origin and evolution of human society and social phenomenon...and the *laws* controlling human institutions and functions." History, on the other hand, "recounts events with careful attention to their importance, their mutual relations, their causes, and consequences."[143] The fundamental difference between the two is the presence or absence of two words: science and law. History deals in neither.

The SocProgs are big on methodology.[144] But, as American historian John Lukacs observed, history has no methodology. SocProgs, as Lukacs points out, will likely not enjoy hearing that because it seems to devalue their efforts and indeed their academic careers and expertise, but, as he sagely advises, "ignore them."[145] History is a liberal art and is thus by definition "non-professional in its ways, its speech, its purposes."[146] History is a study of people, not systems. History is a discipline in which a human is studying the actions of other humans, and man's knowledge of Man, as Lukacs observed, is essentially different from his knowledge of other organisms.[147] By that he meant, as Socrates and Plato first observed, that we have intimate, direct, and immediate knowledge of what it is to be human and nothing else.

The German-born historian Werner Jaeger spent much of his life studying ancient Greece and he, like many others, was deeply moved by its spirit, its substance, and its aspirational ideals. He explained that it is the job of the historian to "plunge deeply into the life, emotion, and color of another more vivid world, entirely forgetting himself and his own culture and society." The historian must "think himself into strange lives and unfamiliar ways of feeling as the poet fills his characters with the breath of life."[148] And the goal of this approach? The whole point, purpose, and function of the historian? Jaeger answers back: "His task is not to improve the world, but to understand it."

Traditionalists respect origins and first principles and so here we are, then, at the first definition of history. The word "history" itself is the English translation of the Greek word *histoire*, which means "to inquire."[149] The word *histoire* first appears in Homer's *Illiad* and there it meant: "one who sees or knows."[150]

See: *"to perceive with the mind; understand."*

Know: *"To have a clear and certain perception or apprehension of, as a truth or fact; be certain of as objectively true."*

In other words, history was born of the impulse to use one's mind to perceive, apprehend, and understand the nature and reality of our human world. The *Illiad* was written something like 2,800 years ago. And for many Traditionalists, that first definition of history still stands.

E n d n o t e s

1 Funny story: I was speaking once with a colleague who had poked her head into my office for a quick little chat and she said, "I don't know if you know this or not [and here she nervously looked up and down the hallways to make sure no one was around, and then she whispered] but I'm pretty conservative." I was always struck by the invisible but obvious pressure she felt there.

2 John Hallowell, "Plato and His Critics," *Journal of Politics* vol. 27, no. 2, May 1965, p. 280.

3 There is actually a surprising amount of religious meaning that needs to be scraped away from that word before its secular application becomes clear.

4 Edmund Burke, *Reflections on the Revolution in France* (London: Penguin, 1969), pp. 172-173.

5 Hannah Arendt, *Between Past and Present: eight exercises in political thought* (London: Penguin, 1977), p. 18.

6 Arendt, *Past and Present*, p. 18.

7 Arendt, *Past and Present*, p. 18.

8 The phrase "right-wing" is in even worse shape. To call someone "right-wing" is to imply that they are actually a fascist in disguise.

9 Isaiah Berlin, *Four Essays on Liberty* (London: Oxford University Press, 1969), p. 119.

10 I first heard the phrase "ideas have consequences" from former U of S professor Robert Grogin. At that time, I only dimly apprehended the enormity of what he meant. Since then, though, the meaning has become quite clear.

11 Burke, *Reflections*, p. 91.

12 Alexis de Tocqueville, *Democracy in America,* vol. 2, translated by Henry Reeve (New York: Vintage, 1945), p. 222. No, Tocqueville was not sexist; he takes great pains to make that clear in this particular passage. But why not let's have an honest discussion about the differences between men and women and then come to a reconciliation of some kind rather than throwing human nature into the garbage can. Too, one might mention the women who brought down Jian Ghomeshi as proof of de Tocqueville's observation.

13 J Salwyn Schapiro, *Liberalism, its meaning and history* (Princeton NJ: D. Van. Nostrand, 1958), p. 18.

14 Carlton J.H. Hayes, *A Generation of Materialism: 1871-1900* (New York: Harper Row, 1941), pp. 46-48..

15 Conservatism, such as it is, is often called an 'anti-ideology' because it creates no visions for the future. It has quite enough to do dealing with the world as it is.

16 Peter Vierick, *Conservatism: from John Adams to Churchill* (Princeton NJ: D. Van Nostrand, 1956), pp. 10-11.

17 Viewers and fans of the old HBO series *Oz* may be permitted a chuckle here. In the fictional prison of Oz, a "Prag" was, as I am sure you will be able to determine from the world itself, not a good thing to be.

18 Werner Jaeger, *Paideia: the ideals of Greek Culture* vol. 1, translated by Gilbert Highet (New York: Oxford University Press, 1945), pp. xv-xviii.

19 Jaeger *Paideia*, p. xv.

20 Alan Bloom, *The Closing of the American Mind: how higher education has failed democracy and impoverished the souls of today's students* (New York: Simon and Schuster, 2012), p. 255.

[21] Jonathan Barnes, *Early Greek Philosophy* (London: Penguin, 1987), pp. 9-17 They are called Pre-Socratics because in most cases they predated Socrates, the father of Greek moral and ethical philosophy.

[22] Barnes, *Early Greek Philosophy*, p. 14

[23] HDF Kitto, *The Greeks* (London: Penguin, 1991), p. 8.

[24] Thomas Cahill, *Sailing the Wine Dark Sea: why the Greeks matter* (New York: Nan Talese, 2003), p. 145.

[25] Barnes, *Early Greek Philosophy*, pp 16-17.

[26] Cahill, *Sailing*, p. 146.

[27] Barnes, *Early Greek Philosophy*, pp. 18-19.

[28] Barnes, *Early Greek Philosophy*, p. 19.

[29] Barnes, *Early Greek Philosophy*, pp. 19-20

[30] Cahill, *Sailing*, pp. 164-165.

[31] R.G. Collingwood, *The Idea of History* (New York: Oxford University Press, 1956), p. 20. No matter how much dog food I feed my cat, no matter how many times I strap a leash onto my cat, force her to chase Frisbees, or teach her to fetch, she will in fact remain a cat with her own peculiar feline nature.

[32] Barnes, *Early Greek Philosophy*, pp. 20-21

[33] Leopold von Ranke, *The Secret of World History* (New York: Fordham University Press, 1981), p. 110.

[34] Taran Kang, "Origins and Essence: the problem of History in Hannah Arendt," *Journal of the History of Ideas*, vol. 74, no. 1, January 2013 p. 149

[35] Karl Jaspers, *The Origin and Goal of History* (New Haven: Yale University Press, 1965), p. 18

[36] Kang, "Origins," p. 142.

[37] Kang, "Origins," p. 142.

[38] Barnes, *Early Greek Philosophy*, p. 21.

[39] Barnes, *Early Greek Philosophy*, p. 22

[40] Viktor Frankl, *Man's Search for Meaning* (New York: Touchstone, 1984), see especially, pp. 103-135.

[41] Barnes, *Early Greek Philosophy*, p. 14.

[42] Alexis de Tocqueville, *The Ancien Regime and the Revolution*, translated by Gerald Bevan (London: Penguin, 2008), pp. 20-22, 26, 33.

[43] De Tocqueville, *The Ancien Regime*, p. 24.

[44] James T Kloppenberg, "Objectivity and Historicism: a century of American historical writing," a review of Peter Novick's *That Noble Dream: the "objectivity question" and the American Historical Profession*, in the *American Historical Review*, vol. 94, no. 4, October 1989, p. 1025.

[45] Kloppenberg, "Objectivity," p. 1015.

[46] Keith Windschuttle, "National Identity and the Corruption of History," *The New Criterion*, January 2006, p. 33. Thought-clichés are more than just clichés; thought-clichés are *thought-junk*.

[47] John Gray, *Straw Dogs: thoughts on humans and other animals* (London: Granta Books, 2002), pp. 54-55.

[48] Christopher Butler, *Postmodernism: a very short introduction* (London: Oxford University Press, 2002), p. 38.

[49] Butler, *Postmodernism*, p. 38.

[50] I myself recall fondly and with great pleasure the thrilling debates and arguments in upper-level seminar classes where we disputed truth, and the objective existence of reality, and whether or not "existence precedes essence." (Amis)

[51] Arendt, "The Concept of History," in *Between Past and Future*, p. 51 Arendt quotes a historian as saying that objectivity is both "lifeless" and "eunichic" from Eunuch: "*an emasculated man, usually one castrated before puberty.*"

[52] George M. Trevelyan, *Clio, a muse and other essays literary and pedestrian* (London: Longmans, Green and Co., 1913), p. 49.

[53] I recall as a TA leading a discussion on Canada in the First World War. A student—quite unconscious of how SocProggy she was—responding to the question of war guilt, solemnly observed that "no one was to blame because both sides thought they were right." I thought about that some. And then my head began to hurt.

[54] "But how can you *know*?" the SocProg will whine. To which our Sturdy Historian, thankful and grateful for his task, will deploy the inductive logic historians are supposed to use and argue from the particular to the general that we have enough experience of *particular* falling trees to *safely generalize* that all trees make noise when they fall.

[55] Immanuel Kant, *Critique of Pure Reason* translated by F. Max Muller (New York: Dolphin, 1961), p. 200.

[56] Thomas Carlyle, *Sartor Resartus* (London: J.M. Dent & Co. 1909), p. 49.

[57] Poeticisms in dictionaries abound and I thank Martin Amis for alerting me to this.

[58] Plato *The Last Days of Socrates* translated by Hugh Tredennick and Harold Tarrant (London: Penguin, 1993), p. 142.

[59] Plato, *The Last Days*, p. 142. Italics added.

[60] Viktor Frankl, *Man's Search for Ultimate Meaning* (New York: Basic Books, 2000), pp. 36-38.

[61] Frankl, *Man's Search*, p. 60.

[62] Arthur Koestler, *Darkness at Noon* (New York: Scribner, 1968), p. 260. Koestler goes on: "It was a state in which thought lost its direction and started to circle, like the compass needle at the magnetic pole; until finally it cut loose from its axis and travelled freely in space, like a bunch of light in the night; and until it seemed that all thoughts and all sensations, even pain and joy itself, were only the spectrum lines of the same ray of light, disintegrating in the prism of consciousness;" of *awareness*.

[63] Robert E. Cushman, *Therapeia: Plato's Conception of Philosophy* (Chapel Hill NC: University of North Carolina, 1958), p. xix.

[64] Cushman, *Therapeia*, p. 247.

[65] Cushman, *Therapeia*, pp. xviii. John Hallowell explained it this way: "Philosophy seeks to bring men to a decision about reality. It involves the whole man, his affections as well as his reason, his will no less than his mind. It seeks his acknowledgement of the Good of what, in a sense, he already knows but only dimly perceives." John Hallowell, "Plato and His Critics," *Journal of Politics*, vol. 27, no. 2, May 1965, p. 286.

[66] Andrew Ede and Lesley B Cormack, *A History of Science in Society: from philosophy to utility* (Toronto: University of Toronto Press, 2009), pp. 11-17.

[67] George Orwell, *1984* (New York: Signet, 1950), pp. 51-52.

[68] Kloppenberg, "Objectivity," p. 1014.

[69] The phrase belongs to Herman Melville.

[70] James Henslin et al, *Sociology: a down to earth approach* (Toronto: Pearson, 2010), p. xvii.

[71] Jaeger, *Paideia,* vol 1, p xxiii. Read any work by Plato or Thucydides or Theophrastus or Aristotle or Aristophanes and you will very quickly and clearly understand who you are as a human being. And of course Marx rejected all of that in its entirety, but Plato especially.

[72] Cushman, *Therapeia,* p. 244.

[73] Cushman, *Therapeia,* p. xx.

[74] Collingwood, *The Idea of History,* p. 23.

[75] It must also be noted that there are beautiful truths to us, too, but since the SocProgs insist on "exposing the crimes of the past" in the belief that only the vile is true and the celebratory is dunderheaded, I shall meet them on their ground.

[76] Graeme Garrard, "Joseph de Maistre's 'Civilization and its Discontents,'" *Journal of the History of Ideas,* vol. 57, no. 3, July 1996, p. 430. For a "peeled eyeball close-up" (Amis) of human nature, please see John Colapinto's *Undone* (Toronto: HarperCollins, 2015). He writes: "When you stripped men to their primal essence, they were all the same, all equally prey to the ferocious, feral appetites that roiled secretly behind even the most saintly exterior." That is on page 12. The phrase "feral appetites" is both frightening and accurate. Civilization is the only thing that keeps those "feral appetites" at bay, something that Thucydides, Carlyle, and Freud all explicitly confronted and recognized in their respective works.

[77] Garrard, "Civilization and its Discontents," p. 431.

[78] Garrard, "Civilization and its Discontents," p. 442.

[79] Thucydides, *The History of the Peloponnesian War* translated by Rex Warner (London: Penguin, 1972), pp. 242-245. Italics added because his phrasing there is so brilliant.

[80] Please see William Doyle's *Oxford History of the French Revolution* (London: Oxford, 2002), pp. 191-192.

[81] Thomas Carlyle, *French Revolution: a history* (New York: The Modern Library, 2002), p. 527

[82] Tim Cook, "The Politics of Surrender: Canadian Soldiers and the Killing of Prisoners in the Great War," *The Journal of Military History,* vol. 70, no. 3, July 2006, pp. 663 and 665

[83] Perhaps one of the greatest recent examples of this approach comes from Christopher Browning's *Ordinary Men: reserve police battalion 101 and the final solution in Poland* (New York: Harper Perennial, 1998). The book explains how and why ordinary men could undertake mass murder. It is simply in all of us to be able to do so, given the right circumstances, the right time.

[84] John Herd Thompson writing in "Canada's Ethnic Groups Series," published by the *Canadian Historical Association*: "Ethnic Minorities during Two World Wars" 1991, p. 15.

[85] From Herman Melville: "Consider them both, the sea and the land; and do you not find a strange analogy to something in yourself? For as this appalling ocean surrounds the verdant land, so in the soul of man there lies one insular Tahiti, full of peace and joy, but encompassed by all the horrors of the half-known life. God keep thee! Push not off from that isle, thou canst never return!" See *Moby-Dick* (London: Penguin 2003), p. 299. A hearty "thank you" here to U of S American literature professor William Berkeley who introduced me to Herman Melville (and also to DH Lawrence but we'll let that one pass).

[86] Martin Amis, *The Zone of Interest* (Toronto: Alfred A Knopf, 2014), p. 34.

[87] Karl Jaspers, "The Unity of History," in Hans Meyerhoff ed. *The Philosophy of History in Our Time* (Garden City New York: Double Day Anchor Books, 1959), p. 333.

[88] Jaspers "The Unity of History," p. 333.

[89] R.G. Bury, "Plato and History," *Classical Quarterly*, vol. 44, 1951, p. 88

[90] Bury, "Plato and History," p. 87.

[91] Francis Fukuyama, *The End of History and the Last Man* (New York: Perennial, 1992), pp. 144-145.

[92] Fukuyama, *End of History*, p. 145.

[93] Bury, "Plato and History," p. 89.

[94] Plato, *The Republic* translated by Desmond Lee (London: Penguin, 1987). For Plato's examination of "Imperfect Societies" see pp. 356-418. For his brilliant description of democracy and the democratic type, please see pp. 377-390.

[95] Jaeger, *Paideia,* vol 2, p. 5.

[96] Jaeger, *Paideia,* vol 2, p. 323.

[97] Plato *Republic*, p. 381.

[98] Witness the Eternal Struggle over that last piece of pizza.

[99] Plato, *Republic*, p. 383.

[100] Plato, *Republic*, p. 383.

[101] Plato *Republic*, p. 382.

[102] The following description of the soul is from Plato's *Phaedrus* translated by Walter Hamilton (New York: Penguin, 1995), pp 40-42.

[103] Francis MacDonald Cornford, *The Republic of Plato* (London: Oxford, 1945), pp. 129-130

[104] Bury, "Plato and History," p. 89.

[105] Bury, "Plato and History," p. 88.

[106] Even those with only a nodding acquaintance of news in our world today will have no trouble recognizing this. Just this morning (February 27, 2015), on MSN news, there was a story concerning the crucial issue of including transgendered people in the military. Indeed, I recall from memory about a month ago a story which was headlined to this effect: "Transgender rights: the new frontier" or some such. Both stories—and there are *many* others—revolve around Equality and Liberty both of which principles are still moving, still advancing, still seeking *more*.

[107] Robert Bork, *Slouching towards Gomorrah: modern liberalism and American decline* (New York: Regan Books: 1996), p. 61.

[108] Bork, *Slouching*, p. 61. In 1800, say, only men with money and property, men with a vested stake in society, could vote. Here, 200 years later, we have removed *all* restrictions on voting. Convicted rapists, murderers, and child molesters in prison can vote.

[109] Jacques Barzun, *From Dawn to Decadence, 1500 to the Present: 500 years of western cultural life* (New York: Perennial, 2000), pp. 781-787.

[110] Barzun, *From Dawn to Decadence*, p. 781.

[111] Bury, "Plato and History," p. 89.

212

[112] Viktor Frankl, *The Will to Meaning* (New York: Plume, 2014), pp. 4-5. Italics added.

[113] Frankl, *The Will to Meaning*, p. 4.

[114] Donald Kelley, *Versions of History from Antiquity to the Enlightenment* (New Haven: Yale University Press, 1991), pp. 18-19.

[115] Gerald A Press, *The Development of the Idea of History in Antiquity* (Montreal: McGill-Queens University Press, 1982), p. 4.

[116] Thucydides, *History*, p. 48.

[117] St Augustine *City of God* translated by Henry Bettenson (London: Penguin, 1972), p. 487. Historian Karl Lowith calls Augustine's position here a "refutation of the classical view of the world." See his *Meaning in History* (Chicago: University of Chicago Press, 1949), p. 160.

[118] St. Augustine, *City of God*, p. 487. See also, Hajo Halborn, "Greek and Modern Concepts of History," *Journal of the History of Ideas*, vol. 10, no. 1, January 1949, p. 6.

[119] St Augustine, *City of God*, p. 487.

[120] Gerhard Masur, "Distinctive Traits of Western Civilization Through the Eyes of Western Historians," *American Historical Review*, vol. 67, no. 3, April 1962, p. 593.

[121] Karl Lowith, *Meaning in History* (Chicago: University of Chicago Press, 1949), p. 182.

[122] St Augustine, *City of God*, pp. 487-488. He was a man of astonishing erudition and insight. His book *Confessions* is brilliant beyond all reasonable and sensible measures.

[123] Halborn, "Greek and Modern," p. 10.

[124] For a short but solid exploration of how confident the Victorians were in Progress and Advancement, please see John Keegan, *The First World War* (Toronto: Vintage Books, 2000), pp. 10-14

[125] Sidney Fay, "The Idea of Progress," *American Historical Review*, vol. 52, no. 2, January 1947, p. 236.

[126] Richard Pipes, *Communism: a history*, p. 9.

[127] Pipes *Communism*, p. 9. See also Lowith, *Meaning in History*, p. 33.

[128] Carlton J. Hayes, *A Generation of Materialism 1871-1900* (New York: Harper and Row, 1941), p. 49. Italics added there to highlight yet another intrinsic element of our human nature. Too, that last sentence there was likely written with Marx in mind.

[129] As cited in Taran Kang's "Origin and Essence: the problem of history in Hannah Arendt," *Journal of the History of Ideas*, vol. 74, no. 1, January 2013, p. 147.

[130] Lowith, *Meaning in History*, p. 2.

[131] The fourteenth century was likely the only century worse than the twentieth, although the fifth century is certainly in the running for that honour ushering in as it did the Dark Ages although historians don't like to use that phrase anymore. It's just too judgmental. And so they go with something like post-antiquity, or pre-Middle Ages, or pre-early modern or some such. The seventeenth century was also pretty grim, with its mindless wars for the sake of war; its massacres, burnings, rapings, pillagings, mercenaries, and such.

[132] Gray, *Straw Dogs*, p. xiv

[133] Wang Tsit-Chan, *A Sourcebook in Chinese Philosophy* (Princeton: Princeton University Press, 1963), pp. 244-246. I thank my former teacher, Dr. Man-Kam Leung, for turning me on to Chinese philosophy.

[134] Tsit-Chan, "A Sourcebook," pp. 245-246. Interesting: the Chinese appreciation of the all-important concept of Harmony develops out of the yin-yang notion of the inter-relatedness of all things and thus of the need to keep a balance between passive and active. And we can there detect certain Platonic ideas about Harmony and Balance. See Tsit-Chan, p. 246.

[135] As cited in Press, *The Development*, p. 7.

[136] Gray, *Straw Dogs*, p. xiv.

[137] Press, *The Development*, pp. 4, and 9-10.

[138] Leopold Von Ranke, *The Secret of World History* translated by Roger Wine (New York: Fordham University Press, 1981), p. 109.

[139] Thomas Carlyle, "Characteristics," *Selected Essays by Thomas Carlyle* (London: T. Nelson and Sons Ltd., no date), p. 315.

[140] Gray, *Straw Dogs*, p xiv.

[141] von Ranke, *The Secret,* p. 103.

[142] Von Ranke, *The Secret*, p. 103.

[143] Italics added.

[144] The SocProgs are funny in many ways, but perhaps the most amusing element to them is their footnote fetish. Pluck any SocProg article from the shelves and carefully consider the footnotes. They are not citing to merely indicate where information came from; their footnotes are bloated and ostentatious ejaculations of intellectual self-wonderment. The absolutely best satirical example of this hubris can be seen in Alan D. Sokal's "Transgressing the Boundaries: towards a transformative hermeneutics of quantum gravity," published in *Social Text* no. 46/47, Spring/Summer 1996. It was published as a joke. I printed the thing: the actual article is eleven pages while the "works cited" list is thirteen.

[145] Lukacs, *Remembered Past*, p. 7. I wrote a thesis for my graduate work. When the thing was complete my supervisor W.A. "Prairie Bill" Waiser told me I needed to write a few pages on methodology. I asked him what he meant. He said the committee needs to know my research methodology. I was confused, for I had deployed no methodology. But I thought "I *must* have a methodology." So I elaborated in excruciating and needless detail my "methodology" in place of what I actually did: I chased the idea through books, archives, and primary source material.

[146] Jacques Barzun, "History as Liberal Art," *Journal of the History of Ideas*, vol. 6, no. 1, January 1945, pp-81-88, p. 88.

[147] Lukacs, *Remembered Past*, p. 91.

[148] Jaeger, *Paideia*, vol. 2, p. xiii.

[149] I recall hearing in the 1990s that some academics, obviously oblivious to the history of history, claimed that the word was an oppressive patriarchal construct because what it really meant was "His Story" and thus for a brief time the empty and puerile "Her Story" was all the rage. That, like other untruths, did not last very long.

[150] Kelley, *Versions*, p. 19. See also Press, *The Development*, p. 121. History and thus a historian was "Someone who was known for the capacity to see clearly which of two conflicting accounts of an emotionally charged matter was correct." That capacity, as we have seen, revolves around wisdom, judgement, perception, seeing, all of which rely on honesty, or, the highest truthfulness of the soul to and with itself.

THE CONCLUSION

"It is time to explain myself—let us stand up."
Walt Whitman, Leaves of Grass, p. 67.

"Listen to me, if your minds allow you to think sensibly after they
have been drunk so long on the liquor of nonsense."
St Augustine, City of God, p. 43.

"I had fierce thoughts against the Liberals. It was the success of the Liberal cause which
fretted me inwardly. I became fierce against its instruments and its manifestations."
Cardinal John Henry Newman, as cited in Peter Viereck's Conservatism, p. 161.

"I think that when the lies are all told and forgot, the truth will be there
yet. It don't move about from place to place and it don't change from
time to time. You can't corrupt it anymore than you can salt salt."
Cormac McCarthy, No Country for Old Men, p. 123.

"But all lies have sentence of death written down against them, in Heaven's
Chancery itself; and slowly or fast, advance incessantly towards their hour."
Thomas Carlyle, The French Revolution: a history, p. 192.

Past Tense...[1]

"The tensions between Traditionalists and the Sociological Progressivists revolved fundamentally around their perceptions of the world and our place in it. For the Traditionalists, the world they lived in was perfect, a beautiful thing as it was, needing and deserving to be understood on its own terms, and so they strived to accommodate themselves to it, not it to them. For the SocProgs, the world was an *im*perfect thing, an ugly thing in need of renovation and redemption. The SocProgs altered and re-shaped the discipline of history in an effort to do the same to their world and in doing this they were merely taking their cue from the now largely forgotten subject of sociology. One of its practitioners had once observed that 'things' in society were not as they seemed, and that contained the implication that these 'things' needed to be made better. That was an untruth accepted by the people of that age mostly because they desired to be told such things. The SocProgs had busied themselves bustling about in search of what Hannah Arendt once called 'a reality more original than reality itself,' whilst the Traditionalists contented themselves with the one that already existed. The poverty of the SocProg position was always strikingly apparent and was really only ever the re-expression of the Sophistry and Cynicism that ruined and fouled ancient Athens. The confusion and corrosion the SocProgs set in motion simply grew out of a blind and thoughtless ideological pursuit of trying to create a new and better world because they were simply unwilling to accept the proposition that the world and its nature was stronger than them; that the world dictates to us, not we to it."

.....*Present Tense*

The philosopher Hannah Arendt suggested once that Plato and Karl Marx represent the two principal poles of perception in our culture, that they represent the beginning and ending of political thought. This thought began with the "teachings" of Plato and ended with the "theories" of Marx.[2] For Plato, if we want to discover true being, the Good, the Truth, we must turn away from the world and ascend to what Arendt affectionately calls "the clear sky of eternal ideas," which is simply the realm of thought, contemplation, and reflection. It is also the realm in which we locate true understanding, knowledge, and wisdom.[3] But thought and reflection ended when Marx, who "abjured philosophy," argued that true being and the realities of existence are not beyond men, in reflection, but in them, immediately, and thus it was in fact in our power to change the world. This was the end. And that is where we are living today.

Over the course of a lifetime, Plato counselled thought and reflection with the aim of accruing some measure of wisdom about the nature of our world through an understanding of it. The fiery Marx, by contrast, went straight *at* the world and tried to change it, seeming to skimp a little on understanding it first. For him the goal was a renovation, a revolution, a *fundamental reordering* of Western society, and on that point he was always quite clear: "Communists everywhere support every revolutionary movement against the existing social and political order of things!" This is un-Platonic. It is *anti*-Platonic. But to what will be our everlasting shame, it is Marxian ideas of upending the existing order of things that have taken root in our collective cultural consciousness via sociology and the SocProgs. Plato has simply been forgotten about, remaindered, just another one of the many traditions we unblinkingly and unthinkingly discarded in the mistaken belief that tradition does not matter. The classicist Allan Bloom lamented this development, observing that philosophy maintains only what he called "a fugitive existence" in universities.[4] Fugitive: "*Not fixed or lasting; transient; fading or liable to fade; evanescent.*"

Perhaps we can attribute the rejection and abandonment of philosophy, reflection, and contemplation to the uncertain ends that accompany that path. There is no activism in Plato. Platonic philosophy revolves around thought and reflection and has as its aim the development of our capacities to see, perceive, and understand. But those who partake of the Marxian-sociological vision have the much more attractive prospect of actually having something to do, a goal to reach, a desirable endpoint. That such an endpoint does not exist evades the SocProgs because the very idea of the absence of a goal is, for them, confusing. If there is no goal, then what? Then Plato.

One reflects here as to the type of world we could potentially have if simply trying to understand it and ourselves became the chief and most important goal, if we sought to appreciate this world in both its beauty and its ugliness, for there must be ugliness. That is a part of who we are. Marx missed this point. Plato got it. We still have trouble with it. Plato once wrote what a remarkable thing pleasure was because it is always accompanied by pain: "They will never come to a man both at once," he mused, "but if you pursue one of them and catch it you are virtually compelled, always, to have the other one as well."[5] And the same holds true for the other elements of our world. If you pursue Love, you will at one time or another run into its opposite Hate; if you pursue Liberty, you will bump into Restriction.

The point is that none of these elements of our world can exist separate from its opposite. Indeed, we come to know and appreciate a thing more deeply by knowledge and understanding of its antithesis. This is a truth. There is Love in the world and so there must be Hate. There is Beauty and so there must be Ugliness. And so why would one want to even think about breaking this truth?[6] Because politics, not philosophy, demands it and that, ultimately, is the core difference between the Traditionalists and the SocProgs: philosophy and politics.

Philosophy: it means "*a love of wisdom*."

Politics: it means "*to speak or act for political reasons;*
hence, to scheme for advantage."

The one is transcendent and sublime, while the other is shallow and cheap.

"Internal Contradictions"

Sociology seeks to make society a better place and so it is confounding that this lofty goal is achieved by ruining and despoiling the human beings in it. The plague of "political correctness," for example, has become an elemental part of our daily existence in the West. This intellectual and spiritual perversity is part of sociology's cleansing effort to purge "society" of its imperfections by eliminating or even criminalizing the thoughts and ideas which it finds offensive; thoughts and ideas which impede "progress." That "progress" does not even exist makes the whole effort even more absurd, for it then becomes an intellectual movement predicated on a falsity, chasing an unreality. That such absurdities develop out of the sociological mind, however, should not really surprise anyone, not at this point. Indeed, we *expect* sociology to come up with such things.

Now, all of this purging and cleansing is done in the name of Justice, but what kind of Justice is it that tells us there are only certain things that human beings can say, think, and feel? It is the Justice of a dogmatic and inflexible political ideology which seeks to make the world resemble what it thinks it should be. And the agents of that ideology—sociologists and SocProgs—are not just committing intellectual crimes by insisting that their view of the world is the only right one; they are committing violence against being human. Philosopher Isaiah Berlin explains:

> "To manipulate men, to propel them towards goals which you—the social reformer—see, but they may not is to *deny their human essence, to treat them as objects without wills of their own and therefore to degrade them*. That is why to lie to men, or to deceive them, that is, to use them as means for my, not their own, independently conceived ends, even if it is for their own benefit, is, in effect, *to treat them as sub-human*."[7]

Treating people as subhuman; denying that they have any right to a will of their own; degrading them: these are the starting points for tyranny. The repulsive Bolshevik experiment in Russia was directly rooted in this kind of antihumanism, and so too is politically correct thought and Marxian sociology. We have seen throughout this book not just how easily but how *comfortably* the words and ideas of Bolsheviks sit next to the words and ideas of sociologists and SocProgs, for they all partake of the same ideas, worldview, philosophy, and language. And such intellectual sameness should not just be disturbing: it should be *alarming*. But instead we have grown accustomed to it. Indeed, we continue sickening ourselves by teaching these ideas in our universities.

It is of more than passing interest here to consider the life and writings of 1970s Czech dissident Vaclav Havel. He actually lived in a state constructed on Marxist principles: its laws, its beliefs about society, its ways of relating to, understanding, and explaining the world all refracted through a Marxist prism, which is the same prism through which the vision of the SocProgs refracts (and it is important to remember that the state Havel describes here was a *mild* Marxist state, not one of the blood-soaked ones, and, more, his essay was written long after those early murderous disasters, terror-famines, and bloody holocausts of the revolutionary period). Havel paints a distressing picture of an intellectually rotten and corroded society, a society in which the people had been made weak, stupid, and ineffectual by ideology. Havel observed that the key element of getting along in that state was to believe in the lies and forsake one's own conscience for the approved way to think.[8] He wrote that "individuals need not believe all these mystifications, but they must behave as though they did or they must at least tolerate them in silence."[9] For the people, the equation was simple: "they need not accept the lie. It is enough for them to have accepted their life with it and in it."

Any systematized set of ideas or bodies of thought that generate or result in RightThink are, by definition, vulgar intellectual obscenities. But this is precisely what happens with SocProg thought: it creates, generates, and perpetuates RightThink because it has found The Answer. Indeed, it seems that whenever Marxist ideas constitute the inspiration for a social or political order, or even the foundation for intellectual thought, RightThink is never far behind. Like Plato's pleasure and pain and his theory of opposites, we cannot have Marxist ideas of Justice without the unjust obscenity of RightThink.

Havel goes on to tell us the story of the Greengrocer. The grocer places in his shop window daily a sign with the slogan "workers of the world unite." But Havel says the grocer does not do this out of any personal desire to see workers uniting; he does this because he does not wish to exhibit any tendencies that fall outside the bounds of the approved ways of thinking; he wants to assure the community he adheres to the correct thoughts. And so while the sign says "workers of the world unite" what it actually means, says Havel, is this: "I, the greengrocer, live here and I know what I must do. I behave in the manner expected of me. I am obedient and therefore I have the right to be left in peace."[10] RightThink in our society operates in much the same way. Our culture's equivalents to Havel's greengrocer signs are rainbow flags, multiculturalism, diversity, and tolerance. And we must speak approvingly of these things or not at all.

In the end though, Havel's Marxist state collapsed and so too will the subject which Marx birthed in the nineteenth century. Unlike oceanic philosophy and history, the puddle of sociology is finite. Sociology's chief task is to unmask and debunk. But there are only a limited amount of "shams" in society that sociologists can unmask and debunk to show, like some queer carnival barker, "that it is evil in disguise."[11] Now, the sociologist Peter Berger earlier suggested that sociology can go on debunking and unmasking *ad infinitum*. But, since that is a logical absurdity as well as being intellectually ridiculous, we must conclude that sociology, not history, has a terminal point, an end point, a point at which there is, finally, nothing left to debunk and unmask, nothing left to expose. To borrow a phrase from its founder—and using it with a much higher degree of certainty than he—sociology will inevitably collapse because of its own internal contradictions.

Toward the end of his life, the sociologist Peter Berger changed his mind about sociology. He came to realize that the subject which he had helped to develop and create was shot through with substantial and perverse intellectual inconsistencies, with "contradictions" as it were. We recall from Chapter Two the Athenian Sophist Protagoras who came to counsel the opposite of the Sophistry he had been teaching because of the intellectual, spiritual and moral ruin that lay strewn in its wake. Well, in 1992, Peter Berger does the same thing: he renounces the sociology to which he had "invited" people in 1963. Writing as he was set to retire, Berger, according to Peter Baehr, "gave notice that the party, as he knew it, was probably over." The riches of sociology—if ever there were any—had been wasted and spent, "squandered by 'parochialism, triviality, rationalism and ideology.'"[12] "Should I," Berger asked, "issue a solemn disinivitation so as not to be responsible for yet more innocent students being seduced into what may well be a bankrupt enterprise?"[13] He answers with "a less than hearty no." Not a "hearty no" but a "less than hearty" one because to answer with the "hearty yes" that is so obviously lurking there in the very question would be to undermine his *entire* life's work and statements such as that do not come easy. So he soft-peddles it.

Berger calls for a reformation of sorts, a return to what he calls the "classic" period of sociology which seems to include just two people (Durkheim and Weber), and which stretches across just forty years—1890-1930.[14] Berger outlines a general program of "reversal" and "revival," a sociology that is "cosmopolitan and methodologically flexible and is emphatically and militantly anti-ideological."[15] But then he asks the necessary rhetorical question: "Is any of this possible?" To which he is forced to provide the implacable answer: "Probably not." Although he does say people can always surprise. But, where sociology is concerned, they didn't, they haven't, and they won't. Berger was writing at precisely that moment when political correctness was just beginning its long and toxic rampage through Western society. It is still rampaging. So no, they didn't. Sociology, it would appear, doubled down on ideology.

Berger was forced to admit in 1992 what Stanislav Andreski had known by that point for twenty years: that sociology was a "sloppy pseudo science." But it really never was anything more than that, not essentially. The most famous work of the man who created the subject—*Das Capital* by Karl Marx—was stained by and shot through with error, omission, distortion, dishonesty, and careless use of facts which, to Marx, were only ever "ancillary, buttressing conclusions already reached independently of them." Thus the founder of sociology itself was himself a "sloppy pseudo scientist." Ought it surprise anyone, then, that his progeny shares in his personal oddities and quirks?

Marx left his mark, his personality, all over sociology. Historian Karl Jaspers wrote that Marx's approach to research "is one of vindication, not investigation, but it is a vindication of something proclaimed as the perfect truth with the conviction not of the scientist but of the believer."[16] And that ideological conviction of Marx's is the very same conviction that creates the RightThink so prevalent in sociology and which has tumbled out of that subject and is running amok in the Western world today. All of the attitudes of sociology—its hostility to questions, its intolerance of opposition, its *grievous* condescension—these are all qualities that the man himself possessed.

Marx, you may be surprised to realize, was not a kind and generous man. He was angry, he hated actual working-class men (they didn't like him much either), he did not tolerate opposition, he was frequently described as a "dictator" and he was not interested, as we saw in Chapter Two, in finding the truth: he was more interested in proclaiming it.[17] And that is precisely what sociology does. The sociological project of "making the world a better place to live" assumes from the first that it, like Marx, has already found the truth. And if that is the case, then those who question The Truth can, should, and will be treated with hostility, disdain, and contempt—precisely the way Marx dealt with those who disagreed with him.

And so Marx's poisoned soul is the soil out of which sociology grows and it clearly shares with the man many of his flaws, inconsistencies, and perturbations. That this subject is taught at universities is a not testament to the value of his ideas—"Marx was an academic; or rather, and worse, he was a failed academic"—it is, rather, a testament to the need of humans to believe in something. Anything, it would seem. And anyway, sociology is not a subject; it is an unintended consequence of the Marxian project of negative liberty. Saving the world gives people something to do when there is nothing left of that world but self.

Berger had asked that very telling and revealing question in 1963: "By what right does the sociologist peddle such dangerous intellectual merchandise amongst young minds?" It took him thirty years but, forced by the internal and infernal logic of sociological thought itself, he finally answered his own question. He disowned that intellectual merchandise and, in doing so, admitted that sociologists have no right to "dispense" that sociological "poison." And in 2013, Peter Baehr, in his warm and overly generous critique of Berger's incompatible idea of "sociological humanism," arrives at the same conclusion: "How could one, in good faith, aspire to induct young minds into a subject that had managed, institutionally, to become authoritarian in its political correctness and, in its formulaic mantra of class-race-gender, a crashing bore?"[18] Neither history nor philosophy indicts itself in this way. Neither history nor philosophy asks of itself these types of self-implicating, self-hating, self-damning existential questions. Only sociology does that, but for good reason. And soon, one day, it will hear the answer.

Socrates once spoke about something he called "the involuntary lie of the soul." This is a kind of innocent yet ultimately harmful self-deception in which false knowledge has been gained and, once gained, it then has to be defended. And there is no task more difficult than eradicating false knowledge because, as philosopher Robert Cushman explains, "the self has become identified with and committed to its own error." And it is thus that "ignorance takes on a moral dimension because it now involves pride."[19] And when Logic and Reason face off against Pride, Pride will always win. Logic and Reason are the most powerful rational tools we possess, but they are simply not strong enough to defeat Pride because it is not a rational tool. Pride can only ever be self-defeated. And that is what appears to have happened with Peter Berger. It took him a lifetime, but he grew so increasingly uncomfortable with what sociology was doing to young minds that he, at the end and like Protagoras before him, was compelled to renounce it. And so Berger provides us with a perfect example of what Plato described in his famous cave allegory 2,500 years ago. Berger ascended to the light whilst those he left behind remain chained in the cave, mistaking all of those flickering and transient shadows on the wall for something real.[20]

The Wisdom of the Ancients

Most of the greatest historians and philosophers in the Western tradition did not have university degrees nor were they seeking jobs, status, tenure, and preferment. Thucydides, Plato, Aristotle, Socrates, St Augustine, St Thomas Aquinas, and later thinkers like Thomas Carlyle, Alexis de Toqueville, and Herman Melville: most of them never had what we might call formalized higher education.[21] Yet our souls remain wedded to these thinkers precisely because they were able to ascertain truths about the human condition and realities about the human experience that each generation must, of necessity, learn again. And there is the key point: we do not come into this "modern" world in full possession of the knowledge which the ancients struggled to learn about being human. We must make a conscious effort to *re*learn, to catch up on, those 2,500 years of accrued wisdom about the human condition. Each generation is born blank, intellectually. And so each generation must make a conscious effort to stock their minds with the wisdom of those who have preceded us. But we forget or indeed we simply just decline to do so because we are still taught to see history as a political or providential ascent—"ancient-medieval-modern"—and thus the past is a place of wretchedness and ignorance that is in every way totally incomparable to the Glorious Present with its beguiling illusions of even more and better "progress." Historian Donald Kelley observed that the discipline of history "does not seek an ever more perfect model of the world and proceed to discard old visions."[22] The very same thing holds true for history itself.

The great thinkers of the past all shared many attributes. They all partake of those virtues which are scarcely if ever talked about anymore, virtues like wisdom, understanding, honesty, perception, and fidelity to the truth. Fidelity. It means having "faithfulness" whilst discharging a particular duty. But fidelity also has a secondary meaning (related to radio frequencies): "freedom from distortion." Thus the good historian and the good philosopher, which is to say the good lover of wisdom or the good *seeker* of Wisdom, for they are all the same, will be true and trustworthy and free from distortion such as Plato counselled. The great thinkers of the past possessed fidelity; they were all shorn of what Allan Bloom called ideological "doctrinarism" and they all represent the basic embodiment of what universities are supposed to foster and encourage.[23]

Indeed, Bloom says that even after 2,500 years, Socrates remains the representative essence of what inquiry should be. Socrates fearlessly sought the truth; he sought what Werner Jaeger brilliantly called "the divine center."[24]

Seeking truth is everything. But if that word "truth" still makes you uncomfortable because you have been taught by a SocProg that it does not exist, perhaps we can come at it another way. Historian John Lukacs, in pleasing Platonic ways (my goodness, how deep that river runs!), observed that the purpose of medicine is not perfect health but the struggle against illness; the purpose of law is not perfect justice but the pursuit of it through vigilance against injustice; "and so the purpose of the historian is not the *establishment* of truth, but the *pursuit* of truth through a reduction of ignorance, including untruths."[25] And maybe then at that point, when we have reduced the number of untruths that abound, then maybe we can look up and see where we're at.

Lukacs argued that people today who read or study history in the academy are "weary of puerile inventions" such as the type we examined in Chapter Five, and he adds that that they are "famishing for the truth."[26] Famishing is an interesting choice of word. Famish: *"to cause to suffer or die from lack of nourishment."* SocProg scholarship does not nourish because it is concerned with the destruction and negation of the truth, of reality, and of objectivity. And all of this destruction occurs alongside their denials and rejections, their *refusals* of who we are, fundamentally, as human beings. The SocProgs have defiantly cancelled not just the truth but also the Western world's accumulated knowledge and understanding of what it means to be a human being and, in doing so, they are boldly striking out against Wisdom itself. Hence, famishing.

We cannot apprehend right now how badly SocProg thought is disfiguring our collective souls. But therein lay the beauty of history. Future historians will be able to see clearly the amount of the bill that we ultimately had to pay for the destruction and defacing of the truth. We simply cannot see it right now. The SocProg assault on our senses is so "unrelenting" that we have finally grown numb to an environment that is "increasingly polluted," and we just can't see through that pollution.[27]

History matters so very much to us that its widespread abuse and mis-use, in *universities* no less, should be painful and grievous to us all. We are born with an instinct toward history. Carlyle calls history "the first distinct product of man's spiritual nature; his earliest expression of what might be called "thought."[28]

And he goes on to write that a "talent for history may be said to be born with us" because "there is no tribe so rude that it has not attempted history." History is a crucial part of our kit, our makeup, our *nature* and our insistence on abusing it in the pursuit of nebulous and absurd political aims is, in every way, a tragedy. Tragedy: *"a very terrible or sorrowful fate or end."*

Twilight

The SocProgs write history and at the same time they are history and their appearance does in fact tell us something about the movement of Western history itself. For the Greeks, history was cyclical and that was an idea that developed out of their understanding of the world operating according to patterns. The sun rises and falls, the seasons come and go, day follows night, and it seems everything, including anything created by human hands, is subject to this basic pattern of birth, growth, maturation, and decay. The philosopher R.G. Bury paraphrases Plato on this point: "Everywhere, the general law prevails which condemns all that is mundane, all that is phenomenal, however seemingly perfect, however temporarily stable, to ultimate decay and transformation, if not actual destruction."[29] And that includes democracies.

This idea is not necessarily apocalyptic and need not relate to biblical notions of the end of time. It merely posits that every social and political order, every civilization, has its periods of youth, maturity, vigour, decrepitude, and then dissolution.[30] The truth of this is to be found in the fact that there has never been a civilization that has *not* been subject to this pattern, and so let's take it as a given that we are not exceptional. Let's assume that it is folly, a kind of Hubris, say, to believe that we in the West can side-step not the "iron laws of history" of which Marx ignorantly spoke, but rather the patterns that govern our world.

But knowing—or, better yet, *divining*—when an age or epoch ends and another begins is not an easy task. Carlyle wondered at this very thing writing that our standard household clocks strike when the hour is past but he observed that "no hammer in the Horologue of Time peals through the Universe when there is a change from Era to Era."[31] We often fail to see the shift from age to age or even identify that an age is winding down mostly because—and this is especially true in our case—we are so fixated on what we have wrongly inter-preted as the impressiveness of the present. It is a part of our nature, Carlyle wrote, that "men understand not what is among their hands."[32] But maybe history itself can point out to us where we are in the continuum of that change.

The first experiment in democracy in Athens lasted for about 250 years.[33] It began with the social and political reforms of Solon in 594 BC, and ended with the subjugation of Greece in 338.[34] During the intervening years, of course, Athens ruined herself with Sophistry and Cynicism and they did so to such a degree that the Athenians were totally unable to recognize, face, and confront the threat of the aggressive and covetous Macedonians who finally took Greece in 338 BC. The Athenian orator Demosthenes railed against this apathy in the assembly, saying that his fellow citizens were treating the looming threat "as if [Macedonian King] Phillip were a hailstorm, praying that he would not come their way but not trying to do anything to head him off."[35]

This inability to reckon rightly with the approaching threat, Demosthenes argued, had many sources but chief amongst them were bad, Sophistic politi-cians who had muddied the issue, those who "aim[ed] to please their hearers rather than tell them what is best for them to hear."[36] He makes a pointed refer-ence to the Athenians in the early days of their democracy, those Athenians who vanquished the Persians at the stunning and brilliant battle of Marathon. These men, Demosthenes said, recognized the Persian threat and fought willingly for their freedom, whilst the Athenians of his own age seemed to have been "resolved to servitude." He goes on: "Men of Athens, there was something then in the spirit of the people which is not there now...something which admitted defeat on neither land nor sea." And the loss of that spirit, he concluded, "has ruined everything and made chaos of our affairs."

To make his point of "moral deterioration" clear, Demosthenes enlisted the poetry of Solon, one of the most revered men of ancient Greece. Solon was the law maker who set Athens on her path toward democracy, and he wrote a poem about his mission to bring justice and harmony to Athens:

"This is the message my heart bids tell to Athens, that great are the ills that lawlessness brings. But lawfulness is order and right everywhere, and often sets chains about the wicked, makes the rough smooth, checks the selfish, dims pride, withers the sprouting flowers of doom, makes crooked judgements straight, makes gentle unbridled acts, curbing the words of discord, curbing the wrath and pain of strife, and all under her reign is order and wisdom.[37]

That ideal of Solon's, however, the ideal of order, right, and wisdom had evanesced by the time of Demosthenes, mostly because the peddlers of Sophistry and Cynicism had so thoroughly confused, corrupted, and sickened the Athenian mind. On the eve of Athenian subjugation, there was precious little wisdom; there was little to no order and certainly not any right; there were crooked judgements aplenty and contentious words of discord. Indeed, it would appear that no one in Athens was allowed or even encouraged to speak the truth, whatever that word had come to mean by that time. Demosthenes corners the Athenians on this issue: "Free speech is an essential privilege of all in Athens. You have even allowed foreigners and slaves to share in that privilege and servants may often be seen saying what they please with greater licence than citizens, yet you have banished it completely when it is a question of offering you advice."[38] In other words, there seemed to have been right and wrong things to say in Athens, too, and those right and wrong things were not reflective of Truth but rather reflective of the perverse and corrupt "wisdom" of that time. Demosthenes suggested that the Athenians had been "spoiled, flattered, and every word spoken has been aimed to please you." The Athenians had arrived to a point at which they desired to hear only what they *wanted* to hear rather than what they *needed* to hear. And it was in that sickened condition that they entered into a period of subjugation which would last for centuries. Greece never became again what it once had been. The Western world's second experiment in democracy is, today, about 240 years old, or roughly the same age as Athenian democracy at the time of conquest. And today as then, and as Solon wrote, there is precious little wisdom at hand; we seem to have lost all sense of order and right; crooked judgements don't just abound—they are taught in our universities. There is much discord and very much confusion. And we in the West today are facing a threat which (once again) bad, Sophistic politicians and (this time) their partisans in the media seem to be suggesting is not really a threat at all. We too have been so corrupted, confused, and sickened by Sophistry and Cynicism that we take excruciating and ridiculous pains to suggest that the religious fanatics who say they want to kill us in the name of their religion don't actually mean what they say. Instead, the Western mind—but especially the Canadian mind—attributes terrorism to either "mental illness" or, more commonly, "marginalization," an idea which Marxian sociology tells us is the "result" of "systemic" problems "inherent" in Western civilization.[39] Demosthenes had to finally shame his Athenians to action because they seemed unwilling or unable to do so. He lamented: "It is disgraceful to say after the event: 'who could have imagined this would happen?'" And so one wonders here who or what will finally shame *us* to action.

Historian Johann Huizinga, in his study of the European Middle Ages, arrived at a general conclusion about historical epochs: "It occasionally happens" he wrote, "that a period in which one had hitherto been looking for the coming to birth of new things, suddenly reveals itself as an epoch of fading and decay."[40] And that is how we come to our own age. Blinded by our wondrous technological progress and our machines and computers and our fetish-phones, our self-wonderment is flattered still further by our pursuit of what we wrongly see as ever more perfect degrees of Liberty and Equality and Freedom. We presume, or rather we prefer in our Vanity to believe that our age is one of ascension. But we base that assumption on little more than shoddy conceits and a sense of history that is so very badly out of tune if not outright nonexistent. And it is thus that we are made doubly blind.

We come to our world expecting to see light and so we see light. But it is not light at all. It is, rather, twilight. If we look closer, we see that the shadows have already begun growing longer.

And there, off in the distance,

we dimly apprehend a darkness, gathering,

and it is coming this way.

Endnotes

[1] I borrow the idea for narrating the present in the past tense from historian Jacques Barzun who did it to stunning effect in his *From Dawn to Decadence 1500 to the present: 500 years of western cultural life* (New York: HarperCollins, 2001), see esp. pp. 781-785. I make no claim to achieving his stunning effect here. I merely thought it was an interesting approach.

[2] Hannah Arendt, "Tradition and the Modern Age," in *Between Past and Future: eight exercises in political thought* (London Penguin, 1977), pp. 17-18. In reflection here, one gets the sense that, in a certain light, the entire Marxian project can be seen as nothing more than a gigantic and enormous trans-generational "F[expletive deleted] You!" to Plato. Marx always said that the point of philosophy is to change the world, and that statement is little more than a petulant and defiant repudiation of the Platonic Way. We can almost hear Marx say to Plato: "Get outta my way old man!" And of course Diogenes had called the Platonic way "useless" 2,400 years before Marx did.

[3] The brilliant Catholic theologian St Augustine—a Platonist himself, 1,000 years after Plato existed—also argued this point, though with religious colourings. He counselled: "Do not go outside; return within yourself. Truth dwells in the interior of man." See Julian Marias, *History of Philosophy* (New York: Dover, 1967), p. 117.

[4] Allan Bloom, *The Closing of the American Mind: how higher education has failed democracy and impoverished the souls of today's students* (New York: Simon and Schuster, 2012), p. 271.

[5] Plato, *The Last Days of Socrates* translated by Hugh Tredennick and Harold Tarrant (London: Penguin), p. 112.

[6] We see daily evidence in our culture of the desire to have only the Good without the Bad. We have zero tolerance policies against bullying, racism, poverty, discrimination, and even causing offence in a general way. These policies do not seek to mitigate—they seek to *eradicate*. By its very name, a Zero tolerance policy assumes that there can or indeed should be a world of Love without Hate. This is absurd. Nonetheless, anyone who runs afoul of these proscriptions is usually punished in some way, which is odd.

[7] Isaiah Berlin, *Four Essays on Liberty* (New York: Oxford, 1969), p. 137.

[8] Vaclav Havel, *The Power of the Powerless*, https://s3.amazonaws.com/Random_Public_Files/powwerless.pdf p. 9.

[9] Havel, *The Power*, p. 9.

[10] Havel, *The Power*, pp. 5-6

[11] Baehr, "The Undoing," p. 386

[12] Baehr, "The Undoing," p. 389.

[13] Peter Berger, "Sociology: a disinvitation?" *Society*, Nov/Dec 1992, p. 12.

[14] What of the sociology that comes after 1930, then? The vaunted "Frankfurt School" of Marxists of which Marcuse was a part? Is it, as Berger seems to imply, *all* junk? Likely, yes.

[15] Berger, "Sociology: a disinvitation?" p. 18.

[16] Paul Johnson, *Intellectuals* (New York: Perennial, 1988), p. 62.

[17] One of Marx's close associates wrote that he, Marx, had an outstanding personality and a very rare intelligence and that "if his heart had matched his intellect and he possessed as much love as hate I would

have gone through fire for him." But as it was: "he is lacking in nobility of soul. I am convinced that a most dangerous personal ambition has eaten away all the good in him." Even the revolutionary, Michael Bakunin, felt compelled to write: "his heart is not full of love but of bitterness and he has very little sympathy for the human race." See Johnson, *Intellectuals*, pp. 72-73. This, then, is the man whom sociology celebrates as its founder; this is the spiritual and intellectual source of their project to "make the world a better place to live."

[18] Baehr, "The Undoing," p. 389. "Sociological humanism" is like "a black white," or "a cold hot," or "a light dark."

[19] Robert Cushman, *Therapeia: Plato's Conception of Philosophy* (Chapel Hill NC: University of North Carolina Press, 1958), p. 46.

[20] The ancient Chinese philosopher Confucius explained the Cave this way: "Those who are born wise are the highest type of people; those who become wise through learning come next; those who learn by overcoming dullness come after that. Those who are dull but still won't learn are the lowest type of people." See *Sources of Chinese Tradition* vol 1, edited by Wm. Theodore de Bary (New York: Columbia, 1960), p. 24.

[21] Whenever I read anything by Plato, I always reflect on the fact that he never had a university education. He came from a wealthy family, he was a citizen soldier and a wrestler; occasionally, he wrote poetry. But he didn't have a PhD—didn't even have a lowly three-year BA—just an utterly astonishing intellectual and spiritual capacity, combined with a clear, unpolluted vision.

[22] Donald Kelley *Versions of History from Antiquity to the Enlightenment* (New Haven: Yale University Press, 1991), p. 1.

[23] Bloom, *The Closing*, p. 268.

[24] Werner Jaeger, *Paideia: the ideals of Greek culture,* vol. 2, translated by Gilbert Highet (New York: Oxford, 1945), p. 23.

[25] John Lukacs, *Remembered Past: John Lukacs on History, Historians, and Historical knowledge* edited y Mark Malvesi and Jeffrey Nelson (Wilmington Del.: ISI Books, 2005), p. 18. Italics added.

[26] Lukacs, *Remembered Past*, p. 101. By the way, anecdotal evidence supports Lukacs' contention that people are famishing for the truth. I heard from one of my old professors in 2014 that undergraduates in his classes are angered, frustrated, and irritated at having to read the type of stuff we examined in Chapter Five.

[27] Robert Bork, *Slouching towards Gomorrah: modern liberalism and American decline* (New York: Regan Books, 1996), p, 3. I would literally surrender my life to be able to read a history of the early twenty-first century written 100 years hence. I would give my life for that knowledge.

[28] Thomas Carlyle, "On History," in *Selected Essays by Thomas Carlyle* (London: T. Nelson and Sons, 1867), p. 231.

[29] R.G. Bury, "Plato and History," in *Classical Quarterly*, vol.4, 1951, p. 88.

[30] Carlyle, "Characteristics," in *Selected Essays*, p. 32.

[31] Carlyle, "On History," in *Selected Essays*, p. 235

[32] Carlyle, "On History," in *Selected Essays*, p. 235.

[33] The Roman Republic lasted a similar amount of time. It was established in 509 BC and about three hundred years later, Rome was well along the path to decadence and exhaustion. The final century or two

of the Republic was a horror-show of murders, assassinations, violence, war, rebellion, and slave revolts. Even Senators murdered people (and of course, here, I am thinking about Tiberius and Gaius Gracchus). By the time Octavian assumed the role of Emperor in 27 BC, the Republic had been dead in spirit for about 150 years.

[34] True, the machinery of democracy continued to function after conquest but can the democracy of a subjugated state really be called democracy? Too, the machinery of the Roman Republic remained in place for a time after the ascension of Octavian. But was it really the Republic anymore?

[35] Thomas Martin, *Ancient Greece: from pre-Historic to Hellenistic times* (New Haven: Yale, 1996), p. 190.

[36] *Classics in Translation vol. 1: Greek literature*, edited by Paul MacKendrick and Herbert Howe (Madison: University of Wisconsin Press, 1952), p. 287.

[37] *Demosthenes and Aeschines* translated by A.N.W. Saunders, (London: Penguin, 1974), p. 118.

[38] *Classics in Translation*, p. 287.

[39] The man who has absolutely no business at all being my Prime Minister—Him, of course; Little Lord Fauntleroy—blamed the 2013 Boston Bombings on "society." Idle questions: why can't Muslim societies have "systemic" problems? And why can't one of those problems be terrorism? By the way—and for the record—Islam is a "religion of peace," but only it seems (and scarcely at that), within the confines of Western liberal democracies. Outside of those confines, we can see Islam at its finest in Saudi Arabia, Yemen, Pakistan, Egypt, Libya, Syria, Iran, Iraq, all of which are failed or failing states. To gain an unpolluted appreciation of the nature of Islam, the reader must absolutely attend the brief but penetrating analysis of that religion written by Swiss historian Jacob Burckhardt in *On History and Historians* (New York: Harper-Torch: 1958), pp. 46-52. It is a realistic and tough-minded assessment of what he calls "a low religion of slight inwardness" which conquered through force and "invalidated...the entire history (custom, religion, previous ways of looking at things, earlier imagination) of the peoples converted to it." So I guess Islam is a religion of peace, but only after conquering, taking what it wants, and forcing conversion upon the people it subjugates.

[40] Johann Huizinga *The Waning of the Middle Ages* (Garden City NY: Doubleday Anchor, 1954), preface.

BIBLIOGRAPHY

Primary Sources

Acheson, T.W. "Presidential Address: Doctoral Theses and the Discipline of History in Canada, 1967 and 1985." *Historical Papers, Journal of the Canadian Historical Association,* vol.21, no. 1, 1986. pp. 1-10.

Belisle, Donica. "Crazy for Bargains: inventing the irrational female shopper in modernizing English Canada", *Canadian Historical Review.* vol. 92, no. 4, December 2011, pp. 581-606.

Churchill, David S. "Draft Resisters, Left Nationalism and the Politics of anti-Imperialism" *Canadian Historical Review.* vol. 93, no. 2, June 2012, pp. 227-260.

Cuthbert-Grant, Gail. Presidential Address: "National Unity and the Politics of Political History" in the *Journal of the Canadian Historical Association*, vol. 3, 1992. pp. 3-11.

Dummit, Christopher. History 5118, Trent University, Department of History: http://www.trentu.ca/historyma/documents/HIST-5118H-GW2013.pdf

Fingard, Judith. Presidential Address: The Personal and the Historical, *Journal of the Canadian Historical Association*, vol. 9, no. 1, pp. 3-13.

Henslin, James M. et al. *Sociology: a down to earth approach.* Toronto: Pearson, 2010.

Heron, Craig. "The Boys and Their Booze: masculinities and public drinking in working class Hamilton, 1890-1946", *Canadian Historical Review,* vol. 86, no. 3, 2005, pp. 411-452.

Leith, James A. Presidential Address: The Future of the Past in Canada on the eve of the Twenty-First Century, *Journal of the Canadian Historical Association*, vol. 6, no. 1, 1995.

Martel, Marcel. "'They Smell Bad, Have Diseases and are Lazy': RCMP Officers' reporting on Hippies in the late Sixties", in M. Athena Palaeologu ed. *The Sixties in Canada: a turbulent and creatyive decade.* Montreal: Black Rose Books, 2009.

Nicholas, Jane. "Gendering the Jubilee: gender and modernity in the diamond jubilee of Confederations celebrations, 1927", *Canadian Historical Review*, vol. 90, no. 2, June 2009, pp. 247-274.

Stewart, Mary Lynn. 2011 Presidential Address of the Canadian Historical Association, *Journal of the Canadian Historical Association*, vol. 22, no. 1, 2011, pp. 1-34.

Strong-Boag, Veronica. Presidential Address: Contested Space: The Politics of Canadian Memory, *Journal of the Canadian Historical Association*, vol. 5, no. 1, 1994, pp. 3-17.

Walden, Keith. "Tea in Toronto and the Liberal Order, 1880-1914" *Canadian Historical Review*, vol. 93, issue 1, March 2012, pp. 1-24.

Secondary Sources

Books

Amis, Martin. *The War against Cliché: essays and reviews, 1971-2000*. Toronto: Vintage, 2001.

Amis, Martin. *Koba the Dread: laughter and the twenty million*. Toronto: Vintage, 2003.

Amis Martin. The *Second Plane: September 11: Terror and Boredom*. New York: Alfred A. Knopf, 2008.

Amis, Martin. *The Zone of Interest*. New York: Alfred A. Knopf, 2014.

Anastakis Dimitry ed. *The Sixties: passion politics and style*. Montreal: McGill-Queens University Press, 2008.

Andrews, Anthony. *Greek Society*. London: Penguin, 1967.

Arendt, Hannah. *Essays in Understanding, 1930-1954: formation, exile, and totalitarianism*. New York: Schoken, 1994.

Arendt, Hannah. *Past and Present: eight exercises in political thought*. London: Penguin, 1977.

Aristophanes. *The Clouds* translated by Alan Sommerstein. London: Penguin, 1973.

Aurelius, Marcus. *Meditations* translated by Martin Hammond. London: Penguin, 2006.

Barnes, Jonathan. *Early Greek Philosophy*. London: Penguin, 1987.

Barzun, Jacques. *From Dawn to Decadence, 1500 to the Present: 500 years of western cultural life*. New York: Perennial, 2000.

de Bary, William Theodore, Wing-tsit Chan, and Burton Watson. *Sources of Chinese Tradition vol 1*. New York: Columbia, 1964.

Beatty, John Louis, and Oliver Johnson. *Heritage of Western Civilization: select readings, vol. 2*. Englewood Cliffs NJ: Prentice Hall Inc., 1971.

Berger, Carl. *The Writing of Canadian History: aspects of English-Canadian historical writing since 1900*. Toronto: University of Toronto Press, 1986.

Peter Berger. *Invitation to Sociology: a humanistic perspective*. Woodstock New York: The Overlook Press, 1973.

Berlin, Isaiah. *Four Essays on Liberty*. London: Oxford, 1969.

Bloom, Allan. *The Closing of the American Mind: how higher education has failed democracy and impoverished the souls of today's students*. New York: Simon and Schuster, 2012.

Bork, Robert. *Slouching Towards Gomorrah: modern liberalism and American decline*. New York: Regan Books, 1996.

Bothwell, Robert. *The Penguin History of Canada*. Toronto: Penguin, 2006.

Branham, R. Bracht and Marie-Odile Goulet-Caze, eds. *The Cynics: the cynic movement in antiquity and its legacy*. Berkeley: University of California Press, 1997.

Burckhardt, Jacob. *The Greeks and Greek Civilization*. New York: St Martin's, 1998.

Burke, Edmund. *Reflections of the Revolution in France*. London: Penguin, 1969 [1790].

Butler, Christopher. *Postmodernism: a very short introduction*. London: Oxford University Press, 2002.

Butterfield, Herbert. *The Whig Interpretation of History*. New York: Norton, 1965.

Cahill, Thomas. *Sailing the Wine Dark Sea: why the Greeks matter*. New York: Nan Talese, 2004.

Careless, JMS. *Careless at Work: selected Canadian Historical Studies by JMS Careless*. Toronto: Dundurn Press, 1990.

Carlyle, Thomas. *Selected Essays by Thomas Carlyle*. London: T. Nelson and Sons Ltd., no date.

Carlyle, Thomas. *The French Revolution: a history*. New York: The Modern Library, 2002.

Chan, Wang Tsit. *A Sourcebook in Chinese Philosophy*. Princeton: Princeton University Press, 1963.

Conquest, Robert. *The Dragons of Expectation: reality and delusion in the course of history*. New York: W.W. Norton, 2005.

De Tocqueville, Alexis. *The Ancien Regime and the Revolution* translated by Gerald Bevan. London: Penguin, 2008.

Dillon, John and Tania Gergel eds. *The Greek Sophists*. London: Penguin, 2003.

Doyle, William. *Oxford History of the French Revolution*. London: Oxford, 2002.

Dudley, Donald R. *A History of Cynicism: from Diogenes to the 6th century AD*. Hildesheim, Germany: Georg Olms Verlagsbuchhandlung, 1967.

Dummit, Christopher and Michael Dawson eds. *Contesting Clio's Craft: new directions and debates in Canadian history*. London: Institute for the Study of the Americas, 2009.

Durant, Will. *The Story of Philosophy*. New York: Washington Square Press, 1966.

Ede, Andrew and Lesley B Cormack. *A History of Science in Society: from philosophy to utility*. Toronto: University of Toronto Press, 2009.

Finley, Moses. *The Ancient Greeks*. London: Penguin, 1963.

Fornara, Charles William. *The Nature of History in Ancient Greece and Rome*. Los Angeles: University of California Press, 1983.

Frankfurt, Harry G. *On Bullshit*. Princeton: Princeton University Press, 2004.

Frankl, Viktor. *Mean's Search for Meaning*. New York: Touchstone, 1984.

Frankl, Viktor. *The Will to Meaning*. New York: Plume, 1998.

Frankl, Viktor. *Man's Search for Ultimate Meaning*. New York: Basic Books, 2000.

Freud, Sigmund. *Civilization and its Discontents* translated by David McClintock. London: Penguin, 2014.

Fukuyama, Francis. *The End of History and the Last Man*. New York: Perennial, 1992.

Granatstein, Jack. *Who Killed Canadian History?* Toronto: HaperPerennial, 2007.

Gray, John. *Straw Dogs: thoughts on humans and other animals*, London: Granta Books, 2002

Keillor, Garrison. *WLT: a radio romance*. New York: Penguin, 1991.

Hamerow, Theodore. *Reflections on History and Historians*. Madison: University of Wisconsin Press, 1987.

Hamilton, Edith. *The Greek Way*. Alexandria, Virginia: Time-Life, 1981.

Hard, Robin. *Diogenes the Cynic: sayings and anecdotes with other popular moralists*. London: Oxford, 2012.

Hayes, Carlton J.H. *A Generation of Materialism: 1871-1900*. New York: Harper Row. 1941.

Hegel, G.W.F. *The Philosophy of History* translated by J. Sibree. Mineola, New York: Dover Publications, 2004.

Hesiod. *Theogony, Works and Days, Shield* translated by Apostolos N. Athanassakis. Baltimore: Johns Hopkins University Press, 2004.

Hitchens, Christopher. *Arguably: essays*. Toronto: Signal, 2011.

James, Clive. *Cultural Amnesia: notes in the margin of my time*. London: Picador, 2007.

Jaspers, Karl. *The Origin and Goal of History*. New Haven: Yale University Press, 1965.

Jaeger, Werner. *Paideia: the ideals of Greek culture* translated by Gilbert Highet. New York: Oxford University Press, 1945.

Johnson, Paul. *Intellectuals*. New York: Perennial, 1990.

Kagan, Don. *Thucydides: the reinvention of history*. New York: Viking, 2009.

Kant, Immanuel. *Critique of Pure Reason* translated by F. Max Muller. New York: Dolphin, 1961.

Keegan, John. *The First World War*. Toronto: Vintage Books, 2000.

Kelley, Donald Kelley. *Versions of History from Antiquity to the Enlightenment*. New Haven: Yale University Press, 1991.

Kimball, Roger. *Tenured Radicals: how politics has corrupted our higher education*. New York: Ivan R Dee, 2008.

Kitto, HDF. *The Greeks*. London: Penguin, 1991.

Li, Dun J. *The Essence of Chinese Civilization*. Princeton: D. Van Nostrand, 1967.

Lower, Arthur, R.M. *From Colony to Nation: a history of Canada*. Don Mills Ontario: Longman's, 1946.

Lowith, Karl. *Meaning in History*. Chicago: University of Chicago Press, 1949.

John Lukacs, *Remembered Past: John Lukacs on History, Historians, and Historical Knowledge* edited by Mark Malvasi and Jeffrey Nelson. Wilmington Del.: ISI Books, 2005.

MacKendrick, Paul and Herbert Howe eds. *Classics in Translation volume one: Greek Literature*. Madison: University of Wisconsin Press, 1952.

Marias, Julian. *History of Philosophy* translated by Stanley Applebaum and Clarence C. Strowbridge. New York: Dover, 1967.

Martin, Thomas R. *Ancient Greece from prehistoric to Hellenistic times*. New Haven: Yale University Press, 2000.

Marx, Karl and Friedrich Engels. *The Communist Manifesto* translated by Samuel Moore. New York: Washington Square Press, 1964.

Melville, Herman. *Moby-Dick, or the whale*. New York: Penguin, 1992.

Mencius. *Mencius* translated by D.C. Lau. London: Penguin, 1970.

Navia, Luis E. *Diogenes the Cynic: the war against the world*. Amherst New York: Humanity Books, 2005.

Orwell, George. *Politics and the English Language*. London: Penguin, 2013.

Orwell, George. *1984*. New York: Signet, 1950.

Pipes, Richard. *Communism: a history*. New York: The Modern Library, 2003.

Plato. *Gorgias* translated by Walter Hamilton. London: Penguin, 1960.

Plato. *Phaedrus* translated by Walter Hamilton. New York: Penguin, 1995.

Plato. *Protagoras and Meno* translated by WKC Guthrie. London: Penguin, 1956.

Plato. *The Republic* translated by Desmond Lee. London: Penguin, 1987.

Plato. *The Republic of Plato* translated by Francis MacDonald Cornford. London: Oxford, 1945.

Plato. *The Republic* translated by G.M.A. Grube. Revised by C.D.C. Reeve. Indianapolis: Hackett Publishing, 1992.

Plato. *The Symposium* translated by Walter Hamilton. London: Penguin, 1951.

Porch, Douglas. *The French Foreign Legion: a complete history of the legendary fighting force*. New York: HarperPerennial, 1991.

Press, Gerald A. *The Development of the Idea of History in Antiquity*. Montreal: McGill-Queens University Press, 1982.

Ranke, Leopold von. *The Secret of World History: selected writings on the art and science of history* translated by Roger Wines. New York: Fordham University Press, 1981.

Rankin, H.D. *Sophists, Socratics and Cynics*. London: Croom Helm, 1983.

Russell, Bertrand. *History of Western Philosophy*. New York: Routledge, 1996.

Sayre, Farrand. *Diogenes of Sinope: a study of Greek cynicism*. Baltimore: John Furst Co., 1938.

Schapiro, J. Salwyn. *Liberalism: its meaning and history*. Princeton: D Van Nostrand. 1958.

Shapiro, Harry and Caesar Glebbeek. *Jimi Hendrix: Electric Gypsy*. London: Mandarin, 1990.

Spengler, Oswald. *The Decline of the West* translated by Charles Francis Atkinson. New York: Vintage, 2006.

St. Augustine. *City of God* translated by Henry Bettenson. London: Penguin, 1972.

Thucydides. *History of the Peloponnesian War* translated by Rex Warner. London: Penguin,1972.

Trevelyan, George M. *Clio a Muse and other essays literary and pedestrian.* London: Longman's Green and Co. 1913.

Tocqueville, Alexis de. *Democracy in America*: *vol 2* translated by Phillips Bradley., New York: Vintage, 1945.

Peter Viereck, *Conservatism from John Adams to Churchill.* Toronto: D. Van Nostrand, 1956.

Journal Articles and Essays

Aron, Raymond. "Vision of the Future or Echo from the Past." *Political Science Quarterly*, vol. 84, no. 2, June 1969, pp. 289-310.

Baehr, Peter. "The Undoing of Humanism: Peter L. Berger's sociology of unmasking." *Soc* (2013): 50 pp. 379-390.

Barzun, Jacques. "The Artist as Prophet and Jester." in *American Scholar* vol. 69, no. 1, Winter 2000, pp. 15-33.

Barzun, Jacques. "History as a Liberal Art." *Journal of History of Ideas*, vol. 6, no. 1, January 1945, pp. 81-88.

Barzun, Jacques. "The Paradoxes of Creativity." *American Scholar*, vol. 58, no. 3, Summer 1989, pp. 337-351.

Berger, Peter. "Sociology: a disinvitation?" *Society*, Nov/Dec, 1992, pp. 12-18.

Bliss, Michael. "Privatizing the Mind: the sundering of Canadian history, the sundering of Canada." *Journal of Canadian Studies*, 26 (1991), pp. 5-17.

Bury, R.G. "Plato and History", *Classical Quarterly*, vol. 44, 1951, pp. 86-93.

Cook, Tim. "The Politics of Surrender: Canadian Soldiers and the Killing of Prisoners in the Great War." *The Journal of Military History*, vol. 70, no. 3, July 2006, pp. 637-665.

Desbarats, Peter. "The Most Forgettable Generation." *Saturday Night*, vol. 84, September, 1969, pp. 35-36.

Fay, Sidney. "The Idea of Progress." *The American Historical Review*, vol. 52, no. 2, January 1947, pp. 231-246.

Garrard, Graeme. "Joseph de Maistre's Civilization and its Discontents." *Journal of the History of Ideas.* Vol.57, no. 3, July 1996, pp. 429-446.

Genovese, Eugene. "Heresy yes- sensitivity no" in *The New Republic* April, 1991, pp. 30-34.

Halborn, Hajo. "Greek and Modern Concepts of History." *Journal of the History of Ideas*, vol. 10, no. 1, January 1949, pp. 3-13.

Harlan, Louis. "Broadening the Concept of History." *Journal of Southern History*, vol. 57, no. 1, February 1991, pp-3-14.

Havel, Vaclav. *The Power of the Powerless* http://s3.amazonaws.com/random_public_ files/powerless.pdf

Heale, M.J. "The Sixties as History: a review of the political historiography." *Reviews in American History* vol. 33, no. 1, March 2005, pp. 133-152.

Iannone, Carol. "The Barbarism of Feminist Scholarship." *The Intercollegiate Review*, Fall 1987.

"Impeccable Ideals; Stupid Means" in *Science News*, vol. 93, no. 22, June 1, 1968, pp. 518-519.

Kang, Taran. "Origins and Essence: the problem of history in Hannah Arendt." *Journal of the History of Ideas*, vol. 74, no. 1, January 2013, pp. 139-160.

Kloppenberg, James T. "Objectivity and Historicism: a century of American historical writing." *American Historical Review*, vol. 94, no. 4, October 1989, pp. 1011-1030.

Lobenthal, Joeseph S. Jr. "The Catabolism of Student Revolt." *Journal of Higher Education*, vol. 40, no. 9, December 1969, pp. 717-730.

MacCunn, John. "The Cynics." *International Journal of Ethics*, vol. 14, no. 2, January 1904, pp. 185-200.

McDougall, Walter. "Mais ce n'est pas l'historie: some thoughts on Toynbee, McNeill and the rest of us." *Journal of Modern History*, vol. 58, no. 1, March 1986, pp. 19-42.

Marcus, John T. "The Consciousness of History," *Ethics*, vol. 73, no. 1, October 1962, pp. 28-41

Masur, Gerhard. "Distinctive Traits of Western Civilization Through the Eyes of Western Historians." *American Historical Review*, vol. 67, no. 3, April 1962, pp. 591-608

Pfitzer, Gregory. "History Cracked Open: 'New' History's Renunciation of the past" in *Reviews in American History*, vol. 31, 2003, pp. 143-151.

Palmer, Bryan D. "New Left Liberations: the poetics, praxis, and politics of youth radicalism." *The Sixties in Canada: a turbulent and creative decade* M. Athena Palaeologu, ed. (Montreal: Black Rose Books, 2009),

Parietti, Guido. "Tear Your Mask and Have it Too: a reply to Peter Baehr." *Soc* (2013) 50 pp. 391-394

Parr, Joy. "Gender History and Historical Practice." *Canadian Historical Review*, vol. 76, no. 3, September 1995, pp. 354-376.

Sayre, Farrand. "Greek Cynicism." *Journal of the History of Ideas*, vol. 6, no. 1, Jan 1945, pp. 113-118.

Scott, Joan Wallach. "History in Crisis: the others' side of the story." *The American Historical Review*, vol. 94, no. 3, June 1989, pp. 680-692

Schulman, Bruce J. "Out of the streets and into the classroom? The new left and counterculture in United States History textbooks." *The Journal of American History*, vol. 85, no. 4, March 1999, pp. 1527-1534.

Shmueli, Efraim. "Modern Hippies and Ancient Cynics: a comparison of philosophical and historical developments and its lessons." *Cahiers D'Histoire Mondiale* vol. 12, 1970 pp. 490-514.

Shore, Marlene. "Remember the Future: The Canadian Historical Review and the Discipline of History, 1920-1995." *Canadian Historical Review*, vol. 76, no. 3, September, 1995 pp. 410-463.

Tracy, James D. "A Descent to Cultural Studies." in *Academic Questions*, Fall 2000, pp. 24-31.

Thompson, John Herd. "Ethnic Minorities during Two World Wars." *Canadian Historical Association*, 1991.

"The Hippies." *Time Magazine*, July 7, 1967, vol. 90, no. 1, pp. 22-31.

Vagrancy Syndrome." *The British Medical Journal*, vol. 3, no. 5673, September 27, 1969, p. 732

Watts, William A. and David Whittaker, "Profile of a Non Conformist Youth Culture: a study of the Berkely non-students." Sociology of Education, vol. 41, no. 2, Spring 1968, pp. 178-200,

Windschuttle, Keith. "National Identify and the Corruption of History." in *The New Criterion* January 2006, pp. 29-34.

p . s .

In a final reflection here (and to end on a positive note) why not let's give positive Liberty a go. There are only a handful of decades remaining in the West's second experiment in democracy, so it certainly couldn't hurt anything to give it a whirl, not at this late stage of the game. Let's have the first revolution in Western history in which the revolutionaries are seeking not to overthrow "society," but to overthrow themselves. We'll call it the "Revolution of Inner Freedom." Our placards shall cry out "Down With Anti-Human Sociology!" and "Up With Bourgeois Middle Class Values!" and "We Want Our Eternal Truths Back!"

We shall not march in the streets but rather we shall march on our own souls. We shall actively resist sociological seductions, but that resistance will occur in our minds which we will train to recognize, fall upon, and dismember Marxian lies and untruths.

Just imagine it. Plato tried to. A society composed of citizens whose minds and souls are well and decently ordered, and that order—nay, that *harmony*—has been brought about not through external force but rather self-compulsion; an act of choice not of coercion.

Imagine a society rooted not in cheap and scheming politics, but in the transcendent.

A society based not in rancid ideology, but in beautiful philosophy.

Imagine